The First Buber

The Martin Buber Library

Martin Buber as a young man.

The First Buber

Youthful Zionist Writings
of Martin Buber

Edited and Translated from the German by
Gilya G. Schmidt

Syracuse University Press

Gilya G. Schmidt is associate professor of religious studies and chair of the Fern and Manfred Steinfeld Program in Judaic Studies at the University of Tennessee in Knoxville. She is author of *Martin Buber's Formative Years: From German Culture to Jewish Renewal, 1898–1909* (University of Alabama Press) and editor and translator of *National Socialism and Gypsies in Austria* by Erika Thurner (University of Alabama Press).

Contents _____

Introduction _____

When the first Zionist Congress was convened in Basel, Switzerland, one century ago in August 1897, the platform hammered out by the delegates concerned primarily the establishment of a Jewish homeland in Palestine. Although Zionism is a twentieth-century political movement to gain a land charter, the idea goes back to the fall of the First Temple in 587 B.C.E. if not before. At no time was Zionism a passive undertaking. While in Babylonian captivity, the Israelites mourned the loss of Jerusalem "by the waters of Babylon" and yearned for a return to the city, a wish granted to a remnant under Cyrus of Persia in 535 B.C.E. In the Middle Ages, during the Golden Age of Spain, Yehuda Halevi (?1075–1141) left his comfortable life among the Jewish elite to fulfill a lifelong dream of beholding the glory of God in Zion.* In "Zwischen Ost und West" (Between east and west) he wrote,

> My heart is in the East, and I myself am on the western edge.
> How could I enjoy drink and food! How could I ever enjoy it?

* Buber was not the first to attempt to reform fellow Jews regarding Zion. Yehuda Halevi, too, chided his fellow Jews for not wanting to go to Zion. As in Buber's time, most of Halevi's contemporaries were satisfied with their lives among the nations and did not wish to take on the unpleasant task of rehabilitating the ancient homeland. Only a small fraction heeded the call of the herald in either time. [G. S.]

Alas, how do I fulfill my promise? My sacred vow? since
Zion is still in Roman bondage, and I in Arabic bonds.
All goods of Spain are chaff to my eye, but
The dust on which once stood the tabernacle is gold to my eye!*

Not until the mid-nineteenth century did the Hibbat Zion
(Lovers of Zion) regularly send small groups to Ottoman Palestine
to settle and live off the land. When the Zionist movement was
founded by Theodor Herzl in 1897, it did not take long for the Turkish sultan to become alarmed at the prospect of large numbers of
Jews in his empire.

To be sure, a safe haven for Jews was the goal of the Zionist organization and the need of the Jewish people. Yet as a delegate, at the
second Zionist Congress in 1898, Martin Buber saw a much greater
need than the guarantee of land to prepare for the task ahead—to return the Jewish people to Judaism. By that phrase Buber did not
mean to Jewish religion; that was the province of the rabbis, but to
return to Jewish culture.

In Buber's view, after nearly two thousand years in exile, it would
take more than to load "a people onto ships like dead freight, send
them across to the land, and then expect the soil to perform a miracle."† It would take spiritual preparation. Buber felt that the Jews of
nineteenth century Europe exhibited a *galut* [Diaspora] mentality
that needed to be transformed. Whether in the emancipated West or
the Czarist East, Jews were slaves to the conditions of life in a given
majority culture. Jewish values, customs, and practices took second
place to those of the host nation whether as a result of assimilation or
oppression. It was Buber's contention that this attitude needed to
change before Jews emigrated to the land. A transformation of the
spirit was needed to a Jewish soul that felt free to feel, think, and act
Jewish. The process would be deliberate, arduous, slow, and, for
those who now look back and try to understand it, fascinating. Mar-

* Translation is mine. Franz Rosenzweig, *Ninety-two Poems and Hymns of Yehuda
Halevi*, ed. Richard A. Cohen, (Albany: SUNY Press, in press). Text, "Zwischen Ost
und West," in Franz Rosenzweig, *Jehuda Halevi: Zweiundneunzig Hymnen und Gedichte*
(Berlin: Verlag Lambert Schneider, 1927), 129. [G. S.]

† See the essay "The Jewish Cultural Problem and Zionism" (sec. 39).

tin Buber was courageous, brilliant, outrageous, and a challenge to the existing way of thinking.

In 1898 Buber was twenty, a university student in Leipzig and then Berlin with a need to find an anchor, to reconnect to his Jewish roots.* But he had no intention of returning to the *maskilim* (enlightened) among whom his grandfather lived in Lvov (Lemberg), Galicia, or of adopting traditional Judaism or even Hasidism. Although Buber had strong ties to ethical Judaism as early as his bar mitzvah, he did not wish to connect to Reform Judaism, also strongly based on ethics. Rather, Buber's revolutionary and rebellious mood sought a way to modernize Jewish culture so it would serve the Jewish people in the twentieth century. He chose the new minority Zionist movement as the vehicle and platform for his activism. From the beginning his activities spanned a wide range. While organizing a Zionist chapter in 1898, he also wrote his first Zionist poems with a strong pronationalist message and followed them with many short articles meant to jolt people into some form of action. Buber's attitude in these articles is confrontational, outrageous, irreverent. He is clearly seeking to challenge those who encounter his words to activate some sort of response although he had no idea what the correct response would be. He did not always feel comfortable enough to give his own name; he occasionally published under the pen name Baruch or even just the initial *B*, especially in early works.

This book contains a collection of Buber's early Zionist writings mostly in poem or short article form. Most were written from 1898 to 1902; a few especially appropriate ones are from later years. Nahum Glatzer's acclaimed translation of Buber's famous "Three Speeches on Judaism" (along with later speeches), which Buber delivered to the Prague Zionist student organization Bar Kochba between 1909 and 1911 has been the earliest of Buber's comprehensive works available in English. These first three speeches are a direct result of Buber's efforts to incorporate Zionism and Hasidism into a new kind

---

* See Buber's essay, "Mein Weg zum Chassidismus," in *Martin Buber Werke,* vol. 3, *Schriften zum Chassidismus* (Munich: Verlag Lambert Schneider, 1963); also Gilya G. Schmidt, *Martin Buber's Formative Years: From German Culture to Jewish Renewal 1897–1909,* Tuscaloosa: Univ. of Alabama Press, 1995). [G. S.]

of Judaism. From this time forward (1909) he became an authority figure and a spokesperson to whom people listened with respect. It is the activist writings preceding these early years that are included in this volume and have so far not been available in English, with the exception of poems "The Disciple," "Elijahu," "The Magi,"* and a selection from the essay "Jewish Science."† Yet, without a doubt, these writings contain Buber's most prescriptive efforts for a Jewish cultural renaissance.

In 1916 Buber collected many of the pieces included in this book in a volume that he called *Die jüdische Bewegung*. It became volume 1 to be followed by a second volume with the same title in 1920 that included his later essays (1915–19). In 1920 a second edition of volume 1 appeared with some changes. These collections, which have been republished in German many times, but were never translated into English, ended Buber's direct efforts for Zionism.

The materials in this book are organized mostly chronologically in testimony to Buber's own creative involvement and organic development. Where I felt it would be helpful for a better understanding of the content, I added notes of explanation marked with the initials G. S. All other notes are Buber's.

Buber did not accept that Jews had achieved all they could accomplish. Life, even emancipated life, among the nations was gradually unmasked as an unsatisfactory, even impossible, task. Full integration could not be assumed as it had been in 1871. But did the Jewish people know it? Did they even know that they were a people?

Widely read and well informed on contemporary literary and cultural as well as national movements, Buber courageously hammered away at his fellow Jews, forcing them to consider Zion in their ideas, in their lives, in their activities, to the ultimate step of living in the land, a step that he himself did not take until 1938 because he felt he

---

* See Maurice Friedman, *Martin Buber's Life and Work: The Early Years 1878–1923* (London: Search Press, 1982) 18; and Martin Buber, *A Believing Humanism; Gleanings*, translated and with an introduction and explanatory comments by Maurice Friedman (New York: Simon and Schuster, 1969/1967), 37, 41, 43. [G. S.]

† See Paul Mendes-Flohr and Jehuda Reinharz, eds., *The Jew in the Modern World*, 2d ed. (New York: Oxford Univ. Press, 1995), 241–43. [G. S.]

was needed more in Germany and Western Europe than in Eretz Israel. After awakening others to the notion of Zion, he needed to sustain their interest. In what way is Hanukkah not only a Jewish but a Zionist festival? What is the relevance of Purim to the Zionist? What does it mean to be a Zionist? How does one become a Zionist? What motivates a person to become a Zionist? All of these questions deal with the ideological foundation of Zionism beyond the attainment of the land—with the quality of life in the Jewish homeland. What language should the people speak? Yiddish? or French? or German? or all of these as in Herzl's *Altneuland* (1902)? Not in Buber's view. The only language fully suited to Jewish renewal was Hebrew, the very language that Ben Yehuda was just fashioning from biblical Hebrew.

Buber cleverly appropriated biblical slogans for his own purpose, portraying European Jews as in a stupor, exhausted, wounded, nearly beyond help. In "The Awakening of Our People," (sec. 1) Buber, the herald, commands Israel to "Get up, my people! Your redeemer approaches!" The redeemer, however, was not the Messiah—Buber's messages had no messianic pretensions—but the Zionist organization whose members, in a down-to-earth way, intended to rehabilitate Europe's Jewry to full humanity. How better could they achieve this than through Israel's youth who existed parallel to Germany's *Wandervögel,* a romantic, idealistic group of guitar-strumming men and women who joined in song around weekend campfires to celebrate their nationalism and love for nature. When Buber looked at his young Jewish compatriots, he saw the dormant possibilities, but not yet the achievements. In his poem "New Youth," (sec. 2) he attempted to shake his readers out of their lethargy and to challenge them to participate in the world as did German Christians. No longer were they to be "a star that disappeared into the dark," but a morning star who led the way for all to see. Herzl, although unnamed, is a model for this shining light whose "great and quiet word from the lips of a dreamer lifted us up and swept [us] along." Buber knew this from his own experience. He had been caught up in the enthusiasm of Zionism, an enthusiasm he would later berate and belittle. But not yet, for now it was his hope that other young Jews would be caught up in the fever of the new thoughts as he was. "To be a slave or to be free!" that was the question. Buber was quite certain of the answer. Why was not everyone else? It had always been the Jewish way. But since Emancipation the very idea of being a Jew, and not a cosmopolitan European, had been cast into doubt. Buber understood that he needed to transform his young contemporaries' thought patterns toward a new direction.

This new direction included organic images suitable to a renewal in the ancient homeland. How strange to think of oneself not as a merchant, artisan, or peddler, but as the bearer of a seed corn deep within that, when brought in contact with "the pregnant land" will perhaps lead to "the sacred hour of birth" despite fate's mischievous interference. But the acceptance of such a vision by the masses required the success of the literary ploughman now, still far from the shores of the new nation.

Buber did not doubt that changing his young fellow Jews' minds about their purpose in life would not be easy. He understood that one hundred years after Heinrich von Kleist wrote his essay "Das Marionettentheater" (1801) nothing had changed, for young Jews, too, like Kleist's contemporaries, fell into the trap of self-love, totally disinterested in the world and their role in it. Emancipation had also been the birth of "unpolitical man." Comparing the young Narcissus to "a blossom on an overly fragile stem," Buber tried to impress on his contemporaries the danger of narcissism. He warned, "All being seems to you a gentle movement of the waves, untouched by winds and storms." But that is, of course, not how life is. The storms scarcely pass one by forever. Buber described the human need for an ethical imperative that guides one's actions, and he warned this self-absorbed young man (and woman) that some day it would be too late. The moment would have passed to make one's mark on the world, to become the morning star, the gate that was only for one person would have closed. "Then you will die, not as one who has lived fully" but as one who missed his chance to change the world.

One could never accuse Buber of indecision or inaction. He knew how to grasp every opportunity to spread his message, and if the opportunity did not exist—as at the Fifth Zionist Congress—he created it. A young French Zionist poet committed suicide in 1899. Buber used the occasion to "shake up my people" with whatever it took to get them to feel some of the fire of their ancestors. In the poem "Prayer" (sec. 5) Buber tried to persuade fellow Jews to engage in an evangelical "wild abandon" that would point them in John-the-Baptist-like rapture "to the River Jordan," the ancient Jewish homeland.

Buber's carrot-and-stick approach persisted throughout his Zionist period. He was not afraid to stand up to the Zionist leadership, even to Theodor Herzl, and he was not afraid to chastise the masses either. Yet, simultaneously, he would offer the most impressive, gentle, romantic images that one could not possibly find objectionable. "May Magic" (sec. 6) once more preaches the inevitability of a new spring for the Jewish people. This time there is no coercive message but merely a sweet natural evolution from wintry dormancy to "rose-colored fingers" that herald new life and new youth.

Buber's activities for the Zionist movement, which began in 1898, came to a climax at the Fifth Zionist Congress in 1901 where he and his militant Young Turk–like "Young Jews" achieved something of a triumph over Theodor Herzl and Max Nordau. The Fifth Zionist Congress took place in December 1901. In the year preceding the Congress Buber's agitation for cultural Zionism rose to a fever pitch. One of his essays described the Congress as a bonfire similar to those in ancient Israel that announced the arrival of the new moon. Calling "the Congresses . . . the mountaintop bonfires of Zionism," Buber here, in fact, announced the existence, not only the dream, of the new Israel. Again, he mocked those who had not joined the Zionists yet, calling them "people in the valley" while he and the other Zionists had ascended to the top, that is, had become the leaders of a new Israel, pronouncing "the creative spirit of the future." Paraphrasing Descartes, Buber's motto was, "I create, therefore I am." The world, and the future, Jewishly, belonged to the creative individual. The bonfires in the form of the Congresses provided the clarion call to the masses. Images of folk customs such as the night of St. John on June 24 were invoked and the magical, Novalis-like flower that "bestows invisible kingdoms." Judaism was not devoid of such occasions of mysterious enrichment—the Zionist Congresses provided the proof. Buber's somewhat elitist attitudes were abundantly visible in these years. Although "every true Zionist has the same indeterminable high value as every other one," the "mountaintop bonfires require the best." Mixing some undefined folklike images with ancient Jewish spiritual purity, Buber admonished his contemporaries to step before this "long-neglected altar of peoplehood . . . only with a pure and devoted heart," as did Moses before the burning bush. The Zionist stewards (delegates) are at least figuratively returned to the innocence of shepherdship, working together as one big family—an ambitious vision indeed.

Buber reiterated this image of a family celebration in another of his pre-Congress essays, "Festivals of Life." (sec. 8) He subtitled the essay, "A Confession." Here Buber gave a glimpse into his own history, admitting that he once turned away from the Jewish festivals "like a child from the mother, whom he believes he has outgrown, tired of the monotony and desiring adventures." A testimony to Buber's incredible creativity, this essay makes clear that the "old" way to connect to tradition is not the only way. Recognizing the importance of a common bond for the people, Buber attempted to reinterpret the meaning of Jewish festivals in a secular way that speaks to all Jews. "I love you, festivals of my people! Not because God commanded them" but as expressions of the collective Jewish soul: "Now I no longer come to rigid monuments of protective tradition, but to young dedicatory gardens of a young people." Buber saw it as one of the tasks of the Zionist movement to make Jewish tradition, that is, customs and history, relevant to every Jew, regardless of his degree of religiosity.

One of the most important issues in the period was the motivation for becoming a Zionist. Why did people join the movement? Some individuals were "inspired" by anti-Semitism. Buber had no liking for such a "Zionist" because his motivation was "instinctual and . . . egotistical." Another reason was that of "the detached sympathizer," the person who did not feel affected by anti-Semitism but who, from a sense of undefined solidarity with his less-fortunate brothers and sisters in the East, felt the need "to help those poor people." Such individuals, said Buber, do not have "the least comprehension of the ideology to which they pledge allegiance." The third type of Jew who joined the movement identified with the cause. But Buber warned that this identification needed to be nurtured carefully so it would not eventually become "a comfortable, unproductive happiness" that had no teeth. This education toward risk taking for the sake of the cause is of the utmost importance. The right kind of Zionist was one—like Buber—who pulled out all stops in his effort "to produce new values, new works," new personalities, "To allow our individuality to unfold according to a new concept of life!" In the Maslowian scheme of need hierarchies the Jew who joined the Zionist movement for the purpose of self-fulfillment—a peak experience—was properly motivated. Yet, lest this individual become a dreaded Narcissus, Buber acknowledged that there is no Zionism without the Jewish people, the masses, whom he compared to the raw material that the sculptor, the creatively motivated Zionist, will shape.

Just which tasks were most compelling was a question asked not only by Zionists. *Gegenwartsarbeit,* urgent work, preoccupied several Jewish groups who struggled to formulate a program for action.* Buber expressed his own views on the subject, no doubt hoping to influence his readers before the Congress. He felt that there were urgent tasks at hand that needed to be tackled before future tasks could be carried out successfully. His involvement with so many young, initially enthusiastic fellow Zionists made him wonder why some fell by the wayside, while others like himself stayed. Having come up in the movement himself, he realized that the practical work of organization and agitation was not for everyone. Some of the idealists were turned off by these rather mundane activities; they were alienated by them, so they left. Others thrived on these tasks and found them fulfilling. Now, felt Buber, was the time to consider the next step—beyond theory and word. In his view it would be "life and deed," consisting of nothing less than "the reclamation of the 'land of our youth'."

One of the topics still not an official part of the Zionist platform in 1901 was the issue of cultural elevation or amelioration [*Hebung*], a term originally introduced by Friedrich Wilhelm Dohm (1751–1820) in his disputation in favor of Jewish Emancipation provided moral amelioration could be achieved. With the achievement of Emancipation other forms of amelioration took its place. Nordau was still in

---

* See "The Helsingfors Program," in Mendes-Flohr and Reinharz, *Jew in the Modern World*, 423–24. [G. S.]

1901 concerned with ethical, economic, and physical amelioration, whereas Buber focused his full attention on cultural amelioration. The most urgent task, in his view, was a Congressional resolution on officially sanctioned cultural activity. Clearly, Buber uses this venue to "prepare the ground" for a later "significant exchange of views" on the topic. This is, so to speak, a teaser, whetting the readers' appetite for things to come in a new Hebraic language and new Judaic literature and art.

Buber was powerfully affected by his perception of the Jewish renaissance in his time. Paralleling the renewal of the Jewish spirit to the fourteenth-century Renaissance and its effect on European culture, Buber envisioned "a resurrection from semilife to life," the rebirth of a new Jewish spirit that had slumbered underground for thousands of years only to await its time in history. Buber saw Jewish "participation in the modern national-international cultural movement" as the Jewish people's opportunity to join other nations and to share with other cultures Judaism's unique cultural fruits. The channel through which the Jewish renaissance announced itself to its people is Zionism. Yet Buber was quite aware that an internal struggle would precede Jewish unification and participation in a new world renaissance. Just how far the Zionists themselves had progressed in accepting that Jewish culture existed can be seen from Buber's testy response to a newspaper report on the existence of a discussion group on Jewish art and the study of Judaism (sec. 15).

There was little agreement on topics such as Jewish art and the study of Judaism among turn-of-the-twentieth-century Jews. Although rabbinic Judaism was studied and discussed in seminaries and yeshivot (schools for Talmud study), the study of Jewish history and civilization—secular studies—was not widespread. In a two-part essay entitled "Jewish Studies" (sec. 14) Buber tried to disabuse his readers of the notion that they knew what Jewish studies really meant. He presented three possibilities: the study of Judaism in the vein of the *Wissenschaft des Judentums*, the product of a Reform institution in Berlin, the Hochschule für die Wissenschaft des Judentums that had opened its doors in 1872; the study of the Jewish question and presumably its solution; and the study of Zionism. After explaining what he meant by these terms and that "Jewish studies" was none of these, Buber in the second part explained his understanding of Jewish studies very much the way it is understood today, as Jewish scholarship. Buber, however, envisioned a Jewish academy in the sense of a Jewish college, for Jews and by Jews, much more limited than what actually materialized after the Holocaust.

Not only Jewish literature, Jewish studies, and Jewish art were being debated but a Jewish theater as well. Again, Buber used the opportunity to respond to an article in which this idea was discussed (sec. 16). While agreeing that a permanent Jewish theater was impossible for various reasons, he introduced a new idea, the Freie Bühne, a private stage company, which would place much less demand on source material, big money, and audience, and would serve a Jewish public interested in the production of Young Judaic and Young Hebraic literature well.

When the Fifth Zionist Congress finally arrived on December 28, 1901, Martin Buber and his friends shifted into high gear. As delegates or representatives to various committees, they had quite a lot of clout among them. Buber was not only the delegate from Berlin, but he represented the Actions Comité, along with Berthold Feiwel, a German Jewish poet. Buber, Feiwel, Lilien, and others were on the Cultural Committee. In addition, Buber had been chosen as one of the keynote speakers—on Jewish art. The twenty-three-year-old student used the opportunity publicly to rebuke Max Nordau for a breach of trust in his presentation on cultural elevation of the Jewish people. Expecting Nordau to carry the torch in support of Buber and his friends' efforts, Buber was disappointed with Nordau's preoccupation with money and how to obtain it—ethically. Not only provocative in style but in content, Buber countered confidently that "our art will get us money," not a run-of-the-mill idea. Buber also proposed art as an educational tool for the elevation of morals. Again, the notion was repeated that there was enough theory, that now "living facts" were needed. "Jewish art," maintained Buber, "*is* such a series of facts." Although he was well versed in all kinds of literature and deeply appreciative of music, Buber's first love, nevertheless, lay with visual art, perhaps because he was close friends with *the* Zionist artist, Ephraim Lilien (1874–1925), a champion of the work of Lesser Ury (1861–1931), and a great admirer of Josef Israels (1842–1912) and the late Maurycy Gottlieb (1856–1879) as well, or perhaps because this was the most challenging—and controversial—of art forms to come to life Jewishly. "Only in our days has the visual art of our people blossomed in unexpected splendor," he noted. Never had there been an exhibit of Jewish art, scarcely any artists painted Jewish themes, and there was no Jewish museum. Buber and Lilien organized the first completely Jewish art exhibition ever for the Congress.* The traditional explanation for this lack was connected to the Second Commandment with its injunction against idol worship. Just as women over time were excluded from the ritual realm, so Jewish figurative art appeared only occasionally. Yet in this period of emancipation, also in art, human figures, even nudes, appeared among the Zionist artists, and Buber used this creative reevaluation of the Jewish tradition in his fight for the inclusion of a cultural plank—a program to educate the people Jewishly—into the Zionist platform.

Buber's presentation on art to the Fifth Zionist Congress reveals a more than cursory ability to critique paintings and sculptures. The education in art history that he was then acquiring at various universities provided him with the ability to speak ably and interestingly about works of art and the motivation of their creators. One of the artists, Lesser Ury, intrigued Buber to the point that he took it upon himself to write an essay on Ury that he then incorporated into his 1903 book *Jüdische Künstler*, featuring six artists. Ury was one of them. Having been dealt a difficult hand by fate—his father died during his formative years—Ury was a gifted and precocious youngster who found his way to Munich and to Paris and Belgium where he soaked up the influences of the great masters, old and new. Attracted to Berlin, he settled there in the hope of connecting to the avante garde artists. Alas, his penchant for color, so admired by Buber, did not strike a concordant note with his mentor, and his difficult path in the Berlin art world was herewith decided. Buber was not swayed, calling Ury "a promethean nature who looks for a new

---

* I have completed a study of the art exhibit and the artists of the Fifth Zionist Congress. [G. S.]

comprehensive language. . . . He finds it in color."* Ury, who was a herald of a new age in painting, participated in Zionist affairs. Yet he was misunderstood by Jews and non-Jews alike. His art was declared degenerate by the Nazis, and much of it was unfortunately destroyed during the Holocaust.

Buber knew how to use the opportunity presented by a given moment to state his case. So, also during his address on Jewish art, he expressed his displeasure with the Congressional practice of delegates—"especially the cultural lecturers"—to present numerous complicated propositions that could not be discussed properly in the interest of time and, therefore, had to be passed without discussion. Buber tried to predispose his audience in his favor by his dramatic announcement that he would present only one proposition concerning the newly founded Jüdische Verlag, whose financial solvency he hoped the Congress would guarantee. The proposition was defeated, adding to Buber's sense of alienation from and abandonment by Herzl and Nordau.

Events at the Congress are reported by Buber in a two-part essay, "A Word Regarding the Fifth Congress," (sec. 20) in an unusual publication for Buber, the *Jüdische Volksstimme.* The editors found it necessary to print a disclaimer, "We here allow a hardworking colleague to express his measured views without, however, agreeing on all points." What's to disagree? Buber quickly came to the point. Events took an unexpected turn, causing Buber and about forty of his friends to leave the floor. Apparently originally intending to keep silent on the events, he then felt the need to set the record straight. The essay has all the earmarks of an apologetic to place events in a more favorable light for Buber and his friends and, in the process, to disparage Herzl and his high-handed procedures. Although Buber was concerned about appearances, his dramatic presentation on Jewish art and the theatrics of him and his friends regarding the vote on the cultural resolution nevertheless won a victory for Zionism. Not only did he and his friends within one year raise the money for their fledgling publishing house but the Democratic Fraction, as the

---

* Martin Buber, ed., *Jüdische Künstler* (Berlin: Jüdische Verlag, 1903), 142.

seceding Young Jews became known, also won a very great victory for cultural Zionism. The Fifth Zionist Congress passed the cultural resolution that the Cultural Committee submitted, making cultural Zionism an integral part of the Zionist platform.

Buber, however, also damaged his relationship with Herzl irreparably. This rift was still reflected in Buber's writings on the occasion of Herzl's death in 1904. After the Congress, Buber resigned as editor of the Zionist newspaper, *Die Welt,* a post with which Herzl had entrusted him two years earlier. The Congress membership voted thereafter not to hold a Congress every year, and in 1902 district meetings were held in which cultural education received high priority and members of the Democratic Faction participated actively. As a result, much of the rift between the cultural and political Zionists was healed.

During the Fifth Congress Buber had some specific concerns as well. One of his hopes was the creation of a Day of World Zionism when all Jews anywhere in the world could unite in a celebration of the Zionist spirit during not four years of Zionism but "two thousand years of Zionist activity." "All the good and productive things that have happened in these two thousand years were, in the deepest sense, Zionist," focusing as does modern Zionism on a return of the people to the homeland.

The role of the Jewish woman was of interest and concern to Buber as well, no doubt a result of his liaison with Paula Winkler (1877–1958), a Catholic philo-Zionist who became his wife. Paula, an author who wrote under the pseudonym of Georg Munk, had her own ideas on the role of the Jewish woman in the Jewish renaissance.

Although Buber seldom identified the sources that caused him to respond with an article of his own, he stepped out of character with the essay "A Spiritual Center." Ahad Ha-Am, the Russian Zionist and father of spiritual Zionism, first berated young Jews for following Western ideas and leaving behind the ways of the fathers although he himself abandoned his Hasidic upbringing and lived as a secularist. It was also Ahad Ha-am who called for a spiritual center in Eretz Israel, an idea that Buber adopted and immediately adapted to his own agenda. Buber respectfully disagreed with Ahad Ha-Am's position that the spiritual center could flourish only in Eretz Israel, the pinnacle of renewed Jewish existence. Buber argued that Jews have to proceed from above and below at the same time. A spiritual center *within the individual* was needed before the individual Jew could build a national spiritual center in Zion. Once Jewish energies were awakened, they would want to be creatively productive. Arguing for a culture of the masses, Buber believed that all Jews, even the *Lumpenproletarier,* or working class, were capable of art appreciation. Thus, he contrasted the Jewish worker decisively with the Ruthenian or Slavic farmer, who was characterized as dull-witted and practical. The Jewish cultural sensibility did not need to be created. It existed. It merely needed to be redirected.

Just who could motivate the masses was an issue that occupied Buber interminably during this time. A series of mystical/obscure poems, suggesting a connection between Jesus, the baal shem, and Talmudic mystery figures who also strongly influenced their disciples appear during the same period, 1902–3, when Buber argues for a new type of personality, the productive individual. This person is neither intellectual nor artist but a combination of vision and will power. Although there is no mention of Herzl in this essay, a later writing of Buber's on Herzl does make the connection. Both inspiration and will power are the basic characteristics of the "elemental being," a compliment Buber pays Herzl in 1910. In 1902, after his rift with Herzl, Buber would not have been willing to put Herzl in the same spiritual context as the productive person or the Talmudic figure of Acher, even though Herzl very much fit the general typology. "The productive ones," wrote Buber, "are the secret kings of the people. They direct the subterranean destiny of the people, the outer fate being only a visible reflection."

The productive individuals, who are Zionists in Buber's mind, steer the people in the direction of the tasks to be carried out for Jewish renewal. One of these tasks is the development of the Jewish land, the other, the development of the Jewish language. Buber, whose command of biblical Hebrew allowed him to take notes in Hebrew when he began his Hasidic studies in 1905, nevertheless lamented at a 1909 conference on Hebrew that he thought thoughts and spoke words in a foreign language—German. Likewise, although Buber continued to enthuse others about Eretz Israel, he did not himself visit the ancient homeland until 1937 on the eve of his own permanent departure to live there. The ambivalence that marked many a Diaspora Jew about his place in the universe haunted Buber as well.

Ultimately, Buber saw Zionism as one of the historical eruptions of the Jewish spirit in his essay "The Jewish Movement" (sec. 38). Beginning with Jewish rebellion against the Romans, it still continued in his day. The Jewish renaissance, according to Buber, began "during the second half of the eighteenth century" with Hasidism and the Haskalah. It was a time of spiritual liberation although not of physical liberation. Communities in the West that later experienced political liberation fell victim to assimilation. Although Zionism began in the West, the energy and spiritual authenticity came from those very descendants of the Hasidim and *maskilim* in the East.

With the untimely death of Herzl in 1904 the Zionist organization took on a different character. Not only did the group lose its dynamic leader but Buber announced that he was withdrawing from his Zionist activities in order to collect and study Hasidic sources. For five years Buber stayed in self-imposed seclusion, producing two of his most widely read works, *The Tales of Rabbi Nachman of Brazlav* (1906), and *The Legend of the Baal Shem* (1908). Thereafter, his thought was much more mature and powerful and of a synthetic nature. Although World War I shook Buber's faith in humanity and caused him to pronounce less than pacifist sentiments, his place as a world figure, not only within Judaism but among modern thinkers in general, was established. In 1919 Buber's long-time friend and mentor Gustav Landauer was assassinated. Buber then left the arena of Jewish renewal for which he had labored for more than twenty years, turning to the completion of *I and Thou* (begun in 1916) and his collaboration with Franz Rosenzweig in the latter's Yehuda Halevi translation project and their joint Bible translation.

I am deeply indebted to Martin Buber's granddaughter, Judith Buber Agassi, executress of the Buber literary estate, for her kindness, helpfulness, and generosity in granting me permission to translate these texts from German into English. While I was in Jerusalem in 1996, a very special gift came my way with the friendship of Jo Milgrom, who graciously shared her spirituality and poetic gift by collaborating in the translation of some of Buber's poems. Many of the texts in this volume have been in my possession since 1988. I thank Margot Cohn from the Buber Archive, National and University Library, Hebrew University, Jerusalem, and Diane Spielmann from the Leo Baeck Institute in New York for their continuing help in locating needed materials.

Thanks are due the University of Tennessee, the College of Arts and Sciences, my colleagues in the Department of Religious Studies, and especially my department head, Charles H. Reynolds, for his enthusiastic encouragement and support of all of my work. I also thank Joan Riedl for her copy editing, proofreading, and English language expertise, which improved the quality of my own linguistic efforts immeasurably. Bradford Smith, doctoral student in philosophy at the University of Tennessee, Knoxville, and two-time graduate teaching assistant (1995–96 and 1997–98) cheerfully and ably assisted with various phases of this manuscript while the massive task of extensive revisions and organization fell to Barry Danilowitz, my 1996–97 graduate teaching assistant. Debbie Myers, the departmental secretary, supports my work in many ways, always cheerfully. To all, my deep gratitude for supporting this project.

Gilya G. Schmidt

The First Buber

In this poem Buber challenges those who hesitate to join the Zionist movement to take heart and to leave behind their defeatist attitudes. With God's help crowns of thorns will turn to blooming roses if they only believe it.

The Awakening of Our People

By Martin Buber, student of philosophy in Berlin

Ohreh, lamah tishan?
Wake up! Why are you sleeping?
Psalm 44:24

The Call!

A call rings out, a clarion call is uttered,
And our courage has been wonderfully awakened:
Get up my people! The night has ended!
Get up and go forward, for now you will live!

Once you exhaustedly collapsed along the way.
Redemption nears, and morning peers at you,
A burst of sunlight blesses you,
And everyone waits. Take heart, my people, speak!

Answer of the Jewish People

"How can I rise, and how can I go forward?
What meaning do the brand-new songs have for me?
My heart is ill and all my limbs are aching,
My forehead marked from the burden of eternities."

3

"My eyes are blind from many tears
And densely shrouded by impenetrable darkness.
My feet are bloody, torn by thorns;
My hand is ill. No light will come my way."

Encouragement [by the herald]

Your strength returns. My people, you shall recover!
We hold a healing potion in our hands.
Love for you gave us gifts of healing;
We shall wash the blood from your wounds.

We shall take the night from your eyes
And weariness and worry from your body.
Then you will once again with wondrous delight
Proudly feel the Divine fire.

[Israel] Doubts the Wonderful News

The people [Israel] listen excitedly and cannot grasp the dream.
Alas, Israel's head feebly sinks back again:
Don't sing songs of a deceptive happiness to me.
"There is no redemption for me! My God has forsaken me!"

"And even if new strength is promised me,
I shall never find a home or refuge.
When will the dark forces disappear
Who drive me endlessly from place to place?"

Divine Consolation!

They disappeared! We shall erect for you
A house of your own, hallowed by God.
Standing on your own soil, you shall see
East and West and way across the sea!

As in olden times, the golden corn shall greet you
Spread across the field by your own hand,

And once again you shall smilingly see beneath your feet
The tranquil waters of the Sea of Galilee.

God is with us! Do you not see His command
In the hopeful shimmer in our eyes?
He takes the crown of thorns from your head
And adorns you with roses, freshly blooming.

Get up, my people! Your redeemer approaches!
Daylight has arrived and lights our path to deed!

The Awakening!

And when the sun's rays and Israel's glance embraced,
My people were restored in splendor.*

2.

To be a proud Jew was not an attitude with which European Jews felt comfortable—to be a proud German, Austrian, or Frenchman, yes. Buber defiantly challenges his young contemporaries to note the dawning of a new era, to stand up and follow the light that leads to Jewish pride.

New Youth

We were like tired wanderers [*Wandervögel*].
We were young Jews, silent and restless.
Like hunted animals, fearful unto death
Each one of us watched motionless as the world passed by,
And if a spark wanted to light up the eye
It was merely like a star that disappeared into the dark.

* "Unseres Volkes Erwachen," *Die Welt* 3, no. 46 (Nov. 17, 1899): 14–15. Appears as item 3 in Margot Cohn and Rafael Buber, *Martin Buber: A Bibliography of His Writings* (Jerusalem: Magnes Press, 1897–1978), hereinafter cited as *MBB*.

We were like a cluster of flowers
On a fragile stem, squeezed into
The narrow opening of a glass.
Just like a sick eagle cowers,
In a cage, silently yearning, far from
The safety of the nest high on a cliff,
So also our will was only a proud and lonesome pain.

All our deeds bore no results,
Our young yearning remained without hope;
[And even] if life's excitement and golden abundance
Came before our thirsting eye,
Our heart beat faster, but the blood pulsated
Through our hands sluggishly, and there was no hope in sight.

Only sometimes we dimly sensed
The dawning of a different fate,
And no one had so totally lost courage
That he did not experience this happy dream.
When he saw *this* light glide through the darkness,
He was enchanted and wanted to live after all.

And then there was light. A great and quiet word
From the simple lips of a dreamer
Lifted us up and swept us along
It gave us hope and song;
The meaning of the dream that was a hint of our anticipation
Transformed us beggars into wealthy people.

Then our eyes became joyous and bright,
And our hearts gained strength and expanse,
Each rock yielded a well,
Each yearning turned into courageous deed.
The power of the words, "To be a Jew!"
Blessed and strengthened everyone's will.

New life confronts us seriously
And makes us choose: to be a slave or to be free!

We do not hesitate; we stand side by side
And cast off the old shackles,
And our voice calls into the first sunlight,
"We want to be Jews!" *

Martin Buber

3. _____

A young, romantic dreamer dialogues in his mind with the realist who sees no hope for a Jewish future. Buber encourages the notion of a seed corn that may begin to germinate and, who knows, may some day result in an entire field of plants.

The Ploughman

Once I saw a ploughman
Stride silently across dark fields.
He mowed the golden grain of wheat
In bundles for carrying.
He walked so tall, he walked so firm,
A master who allows hope to grow.

I was filled with pure humility
And told myself: "What does your life mean?
Can you give seed to new forms
For your world as he does?
Do you have the strength, as he does,
To grow fresh shoots?

You don't have the strength, you know it well,
You can only dream of your hope.
Or are you the seed corn
That ripens in a dark womb?

* Neue Jugend, *Jüdischer Volkskalender für das Jahr 5661* (Leipzig, 1900) 51–52.
Item 4 in *MBB*.

Will you already by tomorrow have grown to full light,
A yearning that breaks its shackles?

You will not, you know that well.
You will be tied to your narrow existence.
    Are you the pregnant land
      that senses the sacred hour of birth?
    Do you sense in silent bliss
A deep suffering ready for life?

    Oh, my soul, you
Have always been barren and shall remain so.
    You will never happily
      Bring in the yellow harvest of summer seed.
    You are a song that no one sings,
[A song] that does not bring consolation and peace to anyone!"

    Then I saw the whirlwind
Mischievously laughing at the ploughman's work,
    Sending many hundreds of gray seed corns
Into the soft furrowed ground.
    In each already sprouts a tiny soul:
      Cornflower, cockle, wild poppy.

    A nation without seriousness and strength,
Full of unruly gaiety and colorful moods,
Yet I could not help but marvel at the hidden glow,
    At the charm of future blossoms,
      Softly formed and rich in color—
      I saw in my mind's eye each leaf.

    And my soul said to me:
      "Teach your humility to see,
      And a crowned kingdom of flowers
    Will unfold before its eye in you.
    You wild flower, hot and silent,
Who knows and asks nothing of the world!

You cannot satisfy the poverty, thirst, and suffering
Of your brothers with fire and blood,
　　But deep in your heart there lives
　A shiny, strong will to beauty.
Allow it, laden with magnificent gifts,
To nourish the people with fragrance and with brightness.

　And pour the juices of your colors
Onto our dreams, sorrow, and mistakes.
　　Unravel the mysterious play of the
　　　Dark urges with the calm of light,
　　And may all of your flowering be a strength
That is given to the world out of complete happiness!"

　Evening already covered the land.
The ploughman had gone home.
　　I lay at the dark edge of the field,
　　　And all my senses sang.
　　The loud jubilation of the chorus
Proudly ascended to the stars.*

4. _____

To have the chance to be someone, to make a difference in life, and to miss the opportunity because one is so self-absorbed is what this poem is all about. Buber tried very hard to point out to his fellow Jewish students that they did not have to be like their German compatriots, that they had the ability to forge their own futures as Zionists.

Narcissus

[Dedicated to a few young Jews—manuscript only]

You see others shrugging their shoulders
In a useless uncertain gesture, "Whereto?"

* "Der Ackersmann," *Die Welt* 5, no. 49 (Dec. 6, 1901): 24–25. Item 8 in *MBB*.

You see them wander through alien lands
In dull sorrow and aimless searching.
Nevertheless, you quietly enjoy your self-made happiness
And smilingly imbibe your own melodies.
You feel the aura of Greek gods surrounding you,
Joyfully exchanging goblets of nectar.

And each new day is only born
To provide your soul with
New gems and new songs and games;
And each night to weave sweet offerings
Of fairy tales into a colorful veil of dreams.
You never struggle to regain entry into the world,
And if your heart is aglow in a breathless dance of sparks,
It is drunk with the pale wine of illusions.

To be sure; you often think of your people's fire and yearning,
Crippled and twisted from the struggle of existence.
You cradle your head in your hands
Pained by so much useless beauty,
But not the way one formulates passionate oaths
Out of wild fear and tears, with a clenched fist.
Rather, the sounds of your dream of pain
Dissolve like tired autumn sunsets.

And once again your love games and their dallying
Turn inward;
A blossom on an overly fragile stem
You are scarcely firmly grounded.
You already float freely and unerringly from the goal,
Your eyes already enjoy your fantasy land,
All being seems to you a gentle movement of the waves
Untouched by winds and storms.

And yet, also for you someday the painful morning will come,
Illuminated by a dull, autumnlike wilted beam.
Then your spirit will not be shielded
From silent gnawing, from unspoken suffering, by any treasure;

A drink made up of blind queries, puzzles, worries,
Will be presented to you in a sparkling goblet—
No riches and no inner pride will shield you
From a seeping horrible fear.

Then you will thirst for the smell of the soil,
For anger and hope, for the courage to suffer and to enjoy.
You will despair, when the days pass,
And you will be conscious only of your illusion.
You will yearn for commandment and for duty,
For a God who thunderingly commands, "Thou shalt!"
But all the worlds will steadily proceed on their course,
And they will be awesome and silent.

There you will lie at night,
And your energies that you have amassed
In the hope that they shall win victories for you,
Will have waned like a light, untapped.
You yourself, will weave into a crown of thorns
The rosily tinged poem of your youth.
You will see your misery with a clear eye
And know, comprehend, and understand everything.

Then you will die, not as one who has lived fully
And now departs [basking] in the glow of everyone's praise,
[Not as one] For whom the greatest happiness and
The greatest fulfillment is the return to the womb—
No, you will die with inarticulate stammering
As one who does not understand himself anymore. . . .
Once you were magnificent like a star of stars
Submerged in a dense, foglike distance.*

Martin Buber

* The image of Narcissus is taken from Heinrich von Kleist's essay "Das Marionettentheater" (1801). Reprinted in Helmut Sembdner, *Kleists Aufsatz über das
Marionettentheater* (Berlin, 1967) [G. S.]. "An Narcissus," *Jahresbericht der Lese- und
Redehalle jüdischer Hochschüler in Wien über das Vereinsjahr 1901* (Vienna, 1901), 17. Item
9 in *MBB*.

5. _____

Again, in youthful enthusiasm, Buber takes up the pen of Josef Marcou-Barouch, the French Zionist whose enthusiastic poetry for Jewish renewal was well known to the young Zionists.

Prayer

Dedicated to Josef Marcou-Barouch*

Lord, Lord, shake up my people.
Beat them, bless them, savage, tender.
Make them fire and free.
Heal your children.

God, return the lost ardor
To my spent people.
Give them from Your soul
In wild, crackling flames.

See, only a fever can save them
And wild abandon.
Wake it, Father, and point us
To the River Jordan.
(1899)†

Martin Buber

6. _____

In this poem the organic image of nature's greening is employed as an analogy for the renewal of the Jewish people.

---

* Marcou-Barouch was a Zionist poet who committed suicide in 1899. [G. S.]
† "Gebet," *Die Welt* 5, no. 26 (June 28, 1901): 13. Item 14 in *MBB*. In collaboration with Dr. Jo Milgrom, Jerusalem, June 10, 1996.

May Magic

Tree is bare and stiff, still,
But in the uppermost branch
Spring sits and plays
Her fiddle.

Branch does not know whether to green.
Soon it will have to,
For air trembles with song
And earth trembles with kisses.

Even small branch
Kisses as if human.
(Soon) rose-colored fingers
Will tap the green heart.

Young shoots will sprout
From sun-warmed husks,
For earth trembles with kisses
And air trembles with song.*

Martin Buber

7.

Anticipating the euphoria of the Fifth Zionist Congress, Buber whets his readership's appetite for the Congress and lauds its benefits while warning that real work happens in the "valleys"—everyday life. He admonishes the groups of delegates to ensure the expected high standard of the Congress by choosing their representatives wisely.

* "Maizauber," *Die Welt* 5, no. 20 (May 17, 1901): 9–10. Item 34 in *MBB*. In collaboration with Dr. Jo Milgrom, Jerusalem, June 10, 1996.

Mountaintop Bonfires

On the occasion of the Fifth Congress

These lines begin a brief series of articles on the meaning of the Fifth Congress.

The Congresses are the mountaintop bonfires of Zionism. They shine into the world and speak with flaming tongues. They say, here something is happening. They say it in such a way that everybody has to understand. But the people in the valleys cannot believe that there is something alive up here; no, that is unbelievable, they reply to the mighty language of the mountaintop fires. But they will learn to believe. For one fiery signal follows another; the flames first illuminate the meaning of the past, then, the horrible image of the present. A modest, strong program is being forged; dispersing masses are poured into a solid mold, the action tools arise through toil and fire, and the creative spirit of the future lives in the words of productive love that are exchanged. I create, therefore I am*—the mountaintop bonfires signal to those with little faith.

To the courageous ones and to those willing to bring a sacrifice, but who are still distant, the mountaintop fires mean much more. Here, they are no longer only signs of life and work but signal and clarion call. We are fighting, they call, we are fighting for your freedom and ours. Look at this people who arose; can you not see how young this ancient people is? It arose like a wonderful youth, incredibly rich in possibilities, and it yearns for its own life. Can you not feel that this life will bestow riches of new beauty on eternity; can you not feel that here will arise a kingdom of truth and justice? I work for your future and ours; the bonfires proclaim—join us!

But they tell us the most beautiful news themselves. They show us our transformation since we live for our people—stronger, purer, more human. And they show us the precious blossoms that sprout from our people's second youth: our people's lord, the spirit, has shaken off the ghetto dust and has donned the robes of life, and he found stylist and harp, colors and sounds for his language. We cannot

---

* Descartes: "I think, therefore I am." [G. S.]

grasp the abundance of the promise. For me it is like a miracle, and I am reminded of the custom of jovial peoples, who, full of life, on the night of St. John [*Johannisnacht,* June 24], light bonfires everywhere, and how, according to the legend, the most exquisite magical flower will blossom on this night, [a blossom] that blesses the life of the one who plucks it and bestows invisible kingdoms. Our bonfires point to our riches and our joys, and although we have experienced much suffering and dastardly deeds on the way, the silent song of our happiness rises to the dark heavens together with the flames of our bonfires.

Our [Zionist] Congresses are this and infinitely more. And now, when we get ready to prepare for a new one, our will shall be led by the feeling that something mighty and beautiful has been laid into our hands—struggle and triumph, celebration and toil at the same time. These choice days will be great and everlasting.

For this reason alone primarily the most productive ones will meet at the Congress. Of course, in the final analysis—unhistorically seen—every true Zionist has the same indeterminable high value as every other one. But those who represent the people on the most noble, most important days of the galut year, all those need to be capable of contributing something independent and mature. Mountaintop bonfires require the best human beings [*Höhenmenschen*]. This consideration is unrelated to the number of delegates; there are plenty of efficient Zionists, and if the groups of delegates choose carefully, then our notion of this Congress's high standard can easily be realized.

But because, for us homeless people, our bonfires must also replace the mild flame of our hearth, we should be able to feel like a big family at the Congress and not lose the beautiful mood. When independent people, especially Jews, assemble for a meeting, everyone brings his own nuance, even his own Zionism. And yet, all these different sounds must be fully harmonized. Even the most independent person will come to these negotiations with the foretaste of this harmony, with the certainty that the basic nature of the movement will arise hallowed and untouched by all of the differences of perspectives.

And our mountaintop bonfires are also a pure, lively flame on the long-neglected altar of peoplehood. We may step before it only with a pure and devoted heart [as did Moses before the burning bush]. The Zionist whom his brothers are sending to the Congress as their delegate has to prepare for a serious, great task. He should realize that the work during the Congress will be intense, that each one will work silently and with discipline. And so that it will truly be people's work [*Volksarbeit*], he should listen to the heartbeat of the people, to the secret voices that communicate to him the dark, subterranean will of the people, long before the journey—preferably from one Congress to the next. May he be as aware of his accountability as [he is] of his duty to contribute; it is deeper and more serious than in any other parliament on earth, for there is none other so influenced by destiny.

One cannot submit to the majesty of the Congress with enough devotion, and yet we must always remember its limitations. The bonfires are lit on the mountaintops: life itself is lived mostly in the valley. On the one hand the Congresses have been undervalued, but also overvalued, by considering them to be work as such. Nothing could be further from the truth. The Congresses evaluate the existing work and draw the lines for future work; but the work itself is undertaken in the monotony of everyday life, in the slow advance full of sacrifice, in the selflessness of a most unsatisfying struggle, in the breathless hours of building. This realization has gradually broken through and has produced many a beautiful, quietly wrought work during the past year. This time in Basel we will be able to look back [on our accomplishments] with satisfaction.

In Basel—after London that sounds almost strange, yet so familiar; modest, yet with undertones of introspection and turning inward. In our dear Basel we can work and talk about matters of spiritual development, production, peoplehood, economy, but also about inner organization. We hope that it will be a working Congress with a tinge of genuinely productive study [*Wissenschaft*] and at the same time with a touch of intimate beauty that delights and unifies—bonfires that burn within but that also gently envelop those in the circle with a rosy shine as if with a glow of quiet happiness.

Yet the effect into the future will also be powerful. For in Basel great things will happen. Our idea has progressed solidly. It has broken new ground where the most glorious ideas can come to healthy fruition. Already new information has become available that was very substantive despite its formal nature so that those relatively honest ones among our opponents had to accept the ideas while those of ill will had to abandon their pathetic arguments and find new agitation methods among a great deal of hair-splitting and perfidy. The Fifth Congress may bring us words that will express the core of that information.

And the Fifth Congress will bring us various kinds of things and great things. The newly formed organizations in several countries will also result in new perspectives for centralization. The issues of elevation [*Hebung*], which were sketched out in London, will be discussed as one of the most urgent paths to our goal and in the entire multiplicity of their problems. The actual founding of the Jewish Colonial Bank and the foundation of the National Fund will be issues of the first order. In the next few issues [of *Die Welt*] we will share with you some information on these points and some others as well, which will facilitate discussion and exchange of views.

We proudly look forward to the Fifth Zionist Congress. We will do everything to turn it into a celebration of work, of the spirit, and of beauty. . . .

Our Congresses burn brightly like mountaintop bonfires in the oppressive night of the exile. We gaze into the rich flowing play of the flames, most deeply moved. And the blessed dream of a new dawn begins to reverberate gently.*

[Signed:] B

8.

The tenor of this confession is that of a young romantic. During the same time Buber began to write his own version of Zarathustra; alas, only the introduction was completed. The message of this essay is defiance of the traditional concept of the holidays, of traditional Jewish religion. At the same time Buber wishes to reclaim the festivals for himself and for Zionism. He had not outgrown the mother, as he thought, only the traditional mother-child relationship.

---

* "Bergfeuer: Zum fünften Congresse," *Die Welt* 5, no. 35 (Aug. 30, 1901): 2–3. Item 11 in *MBB*.

Festivals of Life

A confession

Festivals, shining like a young sun and yearning like the flood, ancient, eternally first, immemorial, I love you!

Once I turned from you like a child from the mother, whom he believes he has outgrown, tired of the monotony and desiring adventures. You were like the poetry of a prayer whose words the child recites in formulaic fashion, casually, unaware of the meaning, and dreaming of play. So I left you.

Now I return to you like a child to his mother, whose inexhaustible beauty he realizes in a blessed moment, like a child to his mother, who bestows worlds and asks no thanks. Now I return to you like a child to the poetic prayer, whose verses unfold like flower buds.

You are prayer and wish fulfillment for me.

Through you I pray to my people. And I pray for you.

Because I know what the future of my people demands, because I know the invisible turning of its destiny, I pray for you to my people as we pray to a god that he may remain alive.

Oh, names of gods and poems of gods!

The beauty and happiness of my tribal family [Blutstamm] means the world to me.

And I know that my family can gain this only in its peoplehood.

And I know that a people who has no homeland, if it wants to remain a people, has to substitute for this missing unity a living bond of common, meaningful experience. Purely intellectual possessions do not constitute such a bond: we cannot see them, we have no image of them, we cannot touch them. Only visible things that can be touched can create organic unity. They weave themselves into the original life of the people and create a homelandlike mood, a popular character. In this way, and only in this way, do feelings of belonging and deeds of liberation of the people come about. Even if a hostile fate triggers their release, they can only manifest themselves and grow in the quiet, warm atmosphere of a people's traditions, beneath the mild sun of the old, eternally new festivals.

For this reason I love you, festivals of my people!

Not because God commanded them. I have learned to step aside respectfully when Divine statutes approach. But I love you because my people has to command itself to observe you.

You—not as meaningless ceremonies but as a meaningful creation of images, of the old joys and pains in artworks of life. The great destinies march through the centuries to finally end up in this concentrated, second, symbolic experiencing—the festivals.

In you, festivals of my people, the souls of the living and the dead take form, and the collective soul [*Volksseele*] can wake the sleeping seeds through you, seen and loved in you. You are her body, and she acts through you, as only something physical can act directly. But she remains the soul, and the ultimate purpose of her deed is to be soul. In this way the soul derives eternally new life from the body that she created just as the artist creates visible works from the resources of the earth into which he pours his soul's experience and which once again turns into a soul experience for the recipient. Traditions are popular art just as songs and dances are "holy for him who seeks their soul."

Therefore, I love you, festivals of my people, as a child loves his mother.

And I will sit by your feet and listen to your tales and observe the new dedication and importance you experience in our days—how the living harvest wreath of resurrection is placed on your head and how your face changes.

And I will receive from your hands the gift of strength, which will turn into beauty, and the gift of holiness, which does not seek its seat behind the clouds but in the waves of everyday life and contains the gift of maturity, infinity within, and yet lives in our day and time.

And I will go forth and herald your kingdom.

But to you, you good, anxious, shortsighted ones, who always see the matter of "progress" threatened whenever a dream of great art in life emerges, to you I say, that I will not go backward, but surpass you.

For, although I return to the old festivals, they have become new. Now I no longer come to rigid monuments of protective tradition but to young dedicatory gardens [*Weihegärten*] of a young people, not to festivals of the dead past but to festivals of a living future.

This is the privilege of my people: to celebrate that which will be, the future struggle, the anticipated rebirth, the annual cycle of the reclaimed fruitful earth, the history of the stalk and the vine; festivals to celebrate the farmers who have not yet been born; festivals whose old forms have been revived through new contents and values; festivals in which new forms already glow through the dusk like olive branches; festivals, that connect the history of the new land of the Jews to the history of the old one; festivals that tell about the entire destiny of a people's soul.*

Martin Buber

9.

In spite of Emancipation German Jews had begun to understand that their equality was conditional. Buber's subversive message encourages all Zionists to strike the proud posture of Mordecai in the image of Herzl and to celebrate spiritual liberation from the most recent bondage in Jewish history, Germanization.

A Purim-Prologue

By Martin Buber
Esther 3:2.

Today we celebrate a joyful modest festival,
Not one of those days when the heavens
Glow in divine majesty
And golden threads quietly descend
Into human hearts that submit to the Sacred
Humbly trembling and deeply moved.
No, [this is] only a festival of merriment and colors,
A festival of colorful, wild masquerades,
A festival of heartfelt, sincere handshakes,
And of glances happily exchanged.
Yet, our people's entire soul speaks

---

* "Feste des Lebens: Ein Bekenntnis," *Die Welt* 5, no. 9 (Mar. 1, 1901): 8–9. Item 13 in *MBB*.

From this festival's dance, from this smile.
This joy, which you can scarcely grasp,
It seems so strange and distant from your being.
It is the joy of a people, and its hidden power
Has been forged secretly throughout the centuries.
It is the joy of one who has been liberated
After glumly dragging the chains of misery for an entire year.
And now he escapes the yoke for one whole day
And stretches his arms and lifts his eyes to the sun.
That is how our people felt on this festival:
Then they left behind all sorrow,
The degradation of a narrow, breathless life,
And they were proud, dressed in glittering costumes.
They moved their normally sluggish, listless limbs
Joyfully and in dance, forgetting
The great pain of time, the suffering of the days.
This day, it was a festival of lots,
And as the white and black lots
Are alternately cast in play, so, too,
Our people's history may have appeared to some
As such a game of black and white lots.
But did not many a quietly introspective youth
In his soul already anticipate the very call
That he then heard four weeks later:
"Today we are servants; tomorrow we are free!
This year we are confined in a dark land as strangers;
Next year [we will be] in our fatherland!" . . .
And the young dreamer's soul saw
A wonderful image: Inside the gate of the Persian king
There sits a noble man with a grey beard;
Princes pass by him haughtily,
But he does not bow his mighty brow,
The furrowed forehead on which the suffering of the people
Is engraved in ineradicable letters. . . .
The young man's soul goes out to the image,
And his pale eyes whisper passionately:
"I shall not bow. Come, misery, come, agony,
thousandfold pain, overwhelm me,

Envelop me with your arms, press me fervently
Against your bosom, break my heart:
I am a Jew and will not bow."
And from within the moving masquerade
An oath ascends to the blue heavens.

Today we celebrate a joyful, humble festival,
A festival of merriment and rich in colors,
Yet our people's entire soul
Is bound up in this play and speaks from it to you.*

✌︎

(From a Purim celebration of the Jewish national organizations in Berlin.)

10.

Gegenwartsarbeit [urgent work] was a term in every Jew's vocabulary. It usually, however, meant minority rights in the Diaspora. Buber adopted the term for the state of the Zionist movement, whose leaders, he felt, had not yet learned the art of tapping people's talents for the "great and radical education of the [entire people]." Buber hoped that his concept of "applied Zionism" would involve "all modern national Jewish movements within the [Zionist] movement." Not "catchy slogans" would lead to a transformation of the Jewish spirit, but "productive activity."

---

* Printed in "Ein Purim-Prolog," *Die Welt* 5, no. 10 (Mar. 8, 1901): 10. Item 23 in *MBB*.

Urgent Work

By Martin Buber (Berlin)

1

Zionism is entering into the phase of urgent work [*Gegenwarts-arbeit*].* This should not be understood to mean that those program issues that have to do with the work of the future will become less important. These new perspectives have emerged precisely because of the strengthening and refinement of our active faith in the future. When we young ones joined the movement as a living manifestation of our yearning, with glowing, trembling hearts and hands that yearned feverishly for action, our faith was a brand new enthusiasm, a flame that shot heavenward, nothing more. There was something mighty in our enthusiasm but also something dependent and helpless. We allowed ourselves to be captivated by the cause and wanted to receive gifts. We reached out our hands and asked for assignments. For many this was the best that they could do for their own development and that of the cause. But for others it was robbery of their selves and of their future achievements. They pleaded for assignments. They conceived of work in the sense of their ideas, which were expansive, wonderful and unrealizable. They were given assignments, efficient, productive assignments within the organization and in promotion. But this did not turn into an organic whole for them, no real results and no real joy. Was that their fault or the fault of the assignments? They were individuals with strong willpower and potential achievement; it was a beautiful and rich area of activity, but they just did not fit together. Too little attention was paid to the uniqueness of the talents. That is why some left, some stayed but without the satisfying purposefulness that one experiences in serving a great ideal. Until gradually, here and there, the thought began to emerge that there might be other Zionist activities which are just right for these people.

* Although this installment is marked 1, there are no additional writings on this subject. [G. S.]

I already stated how this thought developed among the young Zionists—for it actually evolved from their midst—from the transformation of their faith in the future. In the beginning this faith was utopian and full of fantasy, more deductive [from ideas] than experiential; dipped in poetics and fiery [romantic] feelings, but vague and without any firm content. Here the promotional activity that fostered so much empty rhetoric and slogans [*phrasenselige Gedankenträgheit*] educated in a two-fold way: positively, because it familiarized the young enthusiasts with the realm of facts and gruesome reality; negatively, because it left them unfulfilled and caused them to look for another, more meaningful form of activity. Our faith began to follow in the paths of historical necessity and to assess present conditions with a clear, uninhibited eye. In addition, a self-knowledge matured that enabled us to set the parameters of our Zionist tasks ourselves, in as far as they were related to our subjective inclinations. Internal and external knowledge complemented each other; we became more independent in relation to the movement. We went different paths, but one idea united us: we are part of a movement in which politics is only the last inevitable consequence, which requires strictest and tightest centralization, and for which organization and promotion are only remotely connected and indispensable aides which must be quite decentralized and in the hands of those chosen for this task. Conversely, we see the essence and the soul of the movement in the transformation of the people's existence, in the education of a truly new generation, in the development of the Jewish tribe into a strong, unified, independent, healthy, and mature *Gemeinschaft* [community], that is, in those processes that are as yet expressed unsatisfactorily in such slogans as "elevation" during the London Congress.*

Two groups come to this result in different ways. One group thinks that the reclamation of the "land of our youth" can occur only on the basis of a reborn Jewish culture, as its fruit and consequence; the others, who attribute cultural productivity only to the soil and the landowning people [*Volk*], seek only an improvement and ennobling of our human resources. But this difference is purely academic; action as such is not influenced by it. In any case, an exceptional movement such as ours, which strives for a unique and ultimately in-

---

* The Fourth Zionist Congress was held in London in 1900. [G. S.]

comparable kind of liberation, necessitates an exceptional program, a great and radical education of the [entire] people. Only the beginnings for this program exist now; it has to be developed. I think of it as a program of applied Zionism: based on the foundation of scholarly knowledge, concrete, full of life, practical in the best sense of the word, without formulas, considering all directions, employing all resources, far-reaching but focused, demanding the ultimate in activity, at the same time offering the highest fulfillment.

It suffices to indicate the goal of this program. Above all, we expect it to collect the loosely and sporadically paralleling efforts of national elevation, to strengthen and guide them; to educate the educators and inspire those who are uncertain. It shall unite those who were not able to satisfy their need for involvement in the area of the conventions and who fell away. This program will accommodate all modern national-Jewish movements within the [Zionist] movement and, thus, lay the groundwork for a broader Zionism. May it expand Zionism by uniting all spiritual aspects of rebirth and deepen it by leading from a rigid and superficial combination of catchy slogans to a living understanding of peoplehood and national activity. Finally, the verbal propaganda will be replaced by the already currently effective propaganda of productive activity.

We see in our time an all-around replacement of theory and word through life and deed. Modern natural science no longer wants to explain but to describe, the latest development in art replaces trends through personalities; the political parties more and more turn away from abstractions and theoretical slogans and toward the economic demands of our time; and finally, individuals are tired of the religious and ethical patterns and demand laws of individualism in life, and new life bonds based on individual choice—they all are witnesses to this great transformation which occurs in our days. Zionism enters into this overall development by proclaiming Jewish activities for the present. Precisely from this point of view one could argue that no program of action is needed. But our young movement needs a unification through deeds, a common focal point for all of the people's desires that becomes the source of the commandments. Only a program of intensive activity, as we conceive of it, can exercise the awakening and stimulating power that has always emanated from the manifestos of triumphant life and transformed worlds. Only such a program can educate our people to spiritual freedom and independence that will someday lead us beyond the need for programs.*

11.

Perhaps aware by now that cultural questions are still a thorny issue, Buber, under the pseudonym Baruch, through Die Welt *intends to provide a platform for discussion of cultural questions. First elucidated by Friedrich Wilhelm Dohm, the question of* Hebung *—amelioration, elevation, improvement—took on ever new meaning. At first amelioration was political and economic, now elevation was associated with the improvement or renewal of Jewish culture.*

The Congressional Platform

We shall provide a platform for the Fifth Congress not only for the practical questions, which are part of the program and are no longer new, but also for the theoretical problems expressed therein. For example, what a construct of fine and meaningful realizations is the thought complex that we call cultural questions [*geistige Hebung*]!

Why and in which way do the Jewish people need to be ameliorated? And what is the purpose, meaning, boundary, and tool of this amelioration? What has happened up to now with which we can preface our [current] activity? What, based on the much too European orientation that is now directed entirely elsewhere? And what [has happened] that has for years been practiced naïvely and partly unconsciously, occasionally also in programmatic fashion by long-term Zionists? What is the deep historical genesis of these questions? Which name shall we give to the great history of suffering of the Jewish spirit and, when we speak of cultural amelioration, which martyrdom, which storms, which tragedies do we inherit? What do our words "spiritual amelioration" mean? Are they not merely the conscious expression of a development that occurs independently of our influence, and is it not merely our task to state the

---

* "Gegenwartsarbeit," *Die Welt* 5, no. 6 (Feb. 8, 1901): 4–5. Item 15 in *MBB*.

mighty strides of our people? Or are they not supposed to be the living concentration that summarizes what occurred and inspired new productivity? To be sure, we do not conquer new worlds for the Hebrew language and give the people's literature to the people forever; we do not produce monuments of national art and set them before thousands of shining human eyes; and it will not be our joy to describe, analyze, explain the immense, wonderful being of our people. This all will be accomplished by the productive ones, our brothers. But we speak about that which has been created; we announce very quietly that which needs to be produced; and therein lies direction. And all of this greatness, all this power, all this beauty we will introduce to the people and we will familiarize them with it, give them the true use of their strength when they become conscious of it, give them the moral certitude of quiet waiting, of readiness for the ultimate—that we call people's education, and that is our actual activity. But to what degree these are of necessity merely means and may never exceed that function, and how we define tasks and methods of such a people's education in detail, these, too, are questions that need to be discussed thoroughly.

We can dig even deeper. For today, let these intimations, taken from one weighty example, suffice. They merely point to the need for a lively topical as well as personal dialogue on the basic questions of the Fifth Congress and our movement on the whole. He or she who is a Zionist believes that the idea will form the reality. Therefore, no Zionist will question the importance of honest theoretical communication. For this discussion we will provide a platform in these pages. Acceptance into this platform will not be based on this or that direction but only on the objective value of the contents, breadth, and depth of the viewpoint. We hope that [from this exchange] a discussion will result that is a step ahead of any Congressional debate in quiet, deep objectivity, a clean separation and comparison of the problems, a high level of quality. We hope for some clarification and improvement of the Zionist idea and for the Zionist movement as well.

At the beginning I noted that this platform will also address practical Congress questions. A resolution [to this effect] of the large Actions Comité will facilitate this. We expect that the presenters will announce their topics considerably in advance of the Congress so that they may be discussed in our pages and in the individual's clubs and groups as well. We can already prepare the ground now for this significant exchange of views by a preliminary theoretical discussion [of the topics]. Everyone who has something to say will have the opportunity to speak, to inspire, to promote. Everyone who has something coherent and genuine to present, whatever its nature, is welcome. The barriers have been lifted. May the productive struggle begin!*

[Signed:] Baruch

12.

For most of his life, I. L. Peretz had been a Yiddish poet. Horrified by the 1881 Odessa pogrom, Peretz turned from Jewish Russian writer to national Jewish poet. He began to write in Hebrew, and was venerated by Buber and other cultural Zionists as an example of Jewish cultural renewal, illuminating the Jewish Worpswede. Hard-core Zionists such as Ahad Ha-Am (1856–1927), Hayyim Nahman Bialik (1873–1934), Micah Joseph Berdyczewski (1865–1921), and Joseph Hayyim Brenner (1881–1921) considered Peretz a galut mentality and refused to count him among the Zionist writers.

I. L. [Isaac Leib] Peretz [1852–1915]

(A few words for his twenty-fifth anniversary as a writer)

In Germany there is a place called Worpswede.† Only a few years ago it was unknown to tourists and travelers. But if someone wound up there through some wretched coincidence, he would hurry to leave again, for he would not find a thing of beauty there, not in nature and not in the people; everything looks grey, heavy, and dull.

---

* "Die Congresstribüne," *Die Welt* 5, no. 36 (Sept. 6, 1901): 1–2. Item 12 in *MBB*.

† Worpswede is an obscure mining town in Germany. Buber's son Raphael happened to go there to join "Vogelers Siedlung," in preparation for making *aliyah* (emigrating to the land of Israel) and living on a kibbutz. See Grete Schaeder, *Martin Buber Briefwechsel aus Sieben Jahrzehnten*, (vol. 2 Heidelberg: Verlag Lambert Schneider, 1976) 152 [G. S.].

But one time a few young artists arrived with a fresh sense of adventure and the blessed eyes of youth, and, gifted with that artistic strength that works wonders, they explored Worpswede and—they saw it. For the first time this silent, dark place was seen. The young painters sat down, looked, and painted. For years. And when the pictures that they had painted reached the world at large, suddenly everyone agreed that Worpswede was a beautiful piece of the earth. And those who had previously moved away in irritation now were the most charmed admirers.

Jewish national life is the Worpswede of the nations. It developed quietly and unknown, according to its own laws. No one knew of its beauty, not those who lived it, the pressure of everyday life had obscured their view, and not those who looked in from outside, their glances rested on the surface and grasped only that which was gray, dull, and heavy. But then came a man who had the eye and the hand of an artist. And the deep, surging light made itself known to his eye, and his hand awoke the slumbering [beauty] to clear, visible life so that the great beauty of Jewish life was visible to all, [even] in its misery and its wild, yearning struggle.

For this we would like to thank him today from a warm and loving heart, and we send him the best wishes of which our heart is capable—greetings in the name of Zion. Even if radical Zionists denigrate him because they do not consider him a Zionist, for us young ones who treasure people more than words he is more of a Zionist than all the hardliners together; for he has lived Zionism. Others gave us ideas and a program, but he gave us beauty, and the beauty of our own world. Those who give us such things are Zion's most faithful fighters, for Zion is for us the kingdom of future Jewish beauty.

Someone else will write in the name of Jewish experts and writers, that is beyond my scope. I speak only in the name of a few young people. We love all who see into the Jewish soul and put it into words. For this reason we also love you, poet of our people, and praise you on the day of your remembrance.*

Martin Buber

---

* "I. L. Perez: Ein Wort zu seinem fünfundzwanzigsten Schriftsteller-Jubiläum," *Die Welt* 5, no. 18 (May 3, 1901): 9. Item 16 in *MBB*.

13.

Buber, who was very enamoured of German culture, used Goethe's dream of a world literature, albeit a world literature based on commonalities, and he transformed it into a dream for the twentieth century, focusing on a nation's particularity, its "innermost essence." The Jewish people has a place among the nations; it participates "in the modern national-international cultural movement" that Buber envisioned for the future.

Jewish Renaissance

By Martin Buber

We live in a period of cultural gestation. On the one hand, we see forerunners of a great general culture of beauty. Many signs of the hour point in that direction: the artistic feeling that awakens everywhere, the development of modern arts and crafts, the infusion of everyday life with a sense of beauty, the diverse attempts at an aesthetic education for our youth, and the effort to socialize art.

On the other hand, we see nationalistic groups assemble around new flags. They are no longer moved by a basic impulse of self-preservation or by the need to defend against hostile attacks from the outside. These nations do not wish to exercise their desire for territorial possession and expansion, but their individuality. It is a self-reflection of the national soul. They wish to make conscious the unconscious development of the national soul; they wish to condense the specific qualities of an ethnic group and use them creatively; they wish to bring out the national intuitions and thereby lead them to greater productivity. Here there is an attempt at a national culture. Goethe's dream of a world literature takes on new forms — only when each people speaks from its innermost essence does the collective treasure increase.

In this way we see an amalgamation of universal and national culture in the deep unitary evolution. What the greatest spirits of our time envision is a life saturated with beauty and positive energy in which every human being and every people cooperates and from which each benefits, each in his own way and according to his value.

That segment of Jews who feel a part of the Jewish people is part of this new development and is electrified by it as are the other groups. But the character of its nationalistic participation [in the evolution] is unique: muscle flexing, taking note, awakening. The word *resurrection* comes to one's lips: an awakening that is a miracle. To be sure, history knows no miracles. But history does know rivers of ethnic life that seem to dry up, but continue underground, only to break forth once more thousands of years later; history knows seeds of peoplehood preserved for thousands of years in dull royal crypts. The Jewish people are on the doorstep of a resurrection from semilife to life. That is why their participation in the modern national-international cultural movement is seen as a renaissance.

It seems to be the nature of slogans to be misunderstood. This seems to happen because slogans are usually taken from one viewpoint of an event that simultaneously provokes repercussions from the other side. So it was also with the "Jewish renaissance."

When we think of renaissance, we think first of all of the great period in the fourteenth century. This renaissance, too, was misunderstood for a time: it was seen as a return to the forms of thinking and speaking of Antiquity, as a renewal of the classical lifestyle. But as its history was examined more thoroughly, it was understood that renaissance does not mean return, but rebirth: a rebirth of the complete human being from the dialectical narrowness of Scholasticism to a broad pantheism, to a flowing feeling of life, from the constraints of sects and guilds to the freedom of the personality. This period is guided by the secret of the new, the rich sense of the discoverer, the free life of risks, and the overflowing desire to create. It is the psyche of this time that speaks in Marlowe's hero, Mortimer, who declares at his execution:

> Do not bewail my death,
> The death of him, who, despising this world,
> Now will explore new lands like a true wanderer.

That time is marked by the symbol of "new lands"; no, not return, but also not "progress" in the very boring, conventional sense of this word. Everywhere new lands are discovered. Everywhere sleeping worlds emerge like green islands from the depths of the sea—within the soul of the individual human being, within the structure of societal reciprocity, in the artistic birth of works and values, in the external spheres of the cosmos, in the ultimate mysteries of all being—all things are renewed. Bathed in young light, the old earth sees with new eyes, and the rebirth celebrates its quiet sun festivals.

Jewish renaissance—this has been interpreted to mean a return to the old traditions that are rooted in peoplehood and a return to their linguistic, moral, mental expressions. We merely need to compare this concept to the fourteenth century Renaissance to understand its smallness and insufficiency. Such a return would in no way deserve the noble designation "renaissance," this crown of historical periods. We must dig deeper if we wish to understand the future of our people.

In our time those people who have a sense for what is coming, John-the-Baptist personalities who recognize in their own pain the evolving formulation of a new human life, are more numerous than in any other time. Those visionaries are today privileged to witness the heralds of a new renaissance. From the fermentation of a cultural movement, which I tried to describe at the beginning, they see future forms emerging. They suffer as once did the prophets because they are knowing and lonely and because they see more beautiful, happier developmental conditions in the future that they, however, will not experience. We must trust their prophecy, which is born from suffering. It points us to the approaching of a rebirth in which every person and every people will participate, each according to his kind and his values: a rebirth of humanity, a rule of "new lands."

It will be more difficult for the Jewish people than for any other to enter into this rebirth. Ghetto and *galut*—not the external but the internal enemies by that name—hold them back with iron chains: the ghetto, the chained spirit and the pressure of a senseless tradition, and the *galut,* the slavery of an unproductive money economy and hollow-eyed homelessness, which destroys all harmonious will power. Only from a struggle against these powers can the Jewish people be reborn. The salvation from the external ghetto and *galut,* which can happen only through a much more radical transformation than today, has to be preceded by an internal one. The struggle against the impoverished episode [known as] "assimilation," which ultimately degenerated into verbose and impoverished wordplay, will be replaced by a struggle against deeper and more potent powers of destruction. This struggle will transform latent energies into active ones, qualities of our tribe, which were manifest in the liberation history of our autonomy but fell silent in the suffering of the Diaspora, present them [the energies] again to our modern life as its form. Here, too, no return, [but] re-creation from ancient material.

At this point I would like to hint only at the most general points of view; we hope that the quiet cooperation of fellow Zionists [*Mit-strebenden*] will in time evolve into a positive, solid program of action, not the program of a party but the unwritten program of a movement.

This movement will above all restore a unified, unbroken sense of Jewish life to the throne. This is a slogan against pure theorizing. Once, when we were the small people of that strangely blessed corner of the earth that moved worlds, we created theories, but we were filled with a strong, expansive sense of life that often overflowed, and that, when our own law did not allow it, tried to find expression in the alien orgies of the unproductive neighboring peoples. In truth, it is just from this sense of life, resting loosely on the law like lilies on the water, that our great creations of the spirit unfolded. Exile acted like a torture instrument: our sense of life became distorted. The external slavery of the "host people" and the internal slavery of the Law contributed in equal measure to the deflection of our sense of life from its natural expression, from free creation in reality and art; it lost itself in pathological manifestations such as *chutzpa* (nerve) and Hasidism. The movement that begins in our time will once more encourage Jews to feel like an organism and to strive for a harmonious unfolding of their strength, to invest as much energy into walking, singing, and working as in the analysis of intellectual problems and to take pride and joy in a healthy and perfect body. The movement will eliminate the dichotomy between deed and thought, the inconsistency between enthusiasm and energy and between yearning and sacrificial courage, and will once again restore the unified personality that produces out of a burning will power. The movement will remove the dust and cobwebs of the internal ghetto from the soul of our people and allow Jews to peek into heart and nature, to teach them to call trees, birds, and stars their brothers and sisters, and to measure their own individuality against the individuality of all be-ings. Through training of vivid seeing and through concentration of our creative powers the movement will reawaken the gift of Jewish painting and sculpting, and the movement will place the fiery column of resurrection before the dull efforts of the young Judaic poets. The movement will bestow a second youth on the festivals of our tradi-tion. We will learn to celebrate what will be our future productivity, the intimated rebirth; the movement will lead us from sterile monu-ments of a protective tradition to the young offerings [*Weihegärten*] of a young people. The movement will grant us the simplicity and in-tegrity of a free way of life. The movement will create for us an inter-nal home before an external one by collecting Jewry in a new unity and thereby granting us rest in the brotherhood of hearts; by giving us a modern language in modern Hebrew that alone will provide us with the true words for the joy and sorrow of our soul; by entering into a covenant that is the ancient one yet new. Our days shall be crowned with the glow of a new beauty.

This national movement is the form in which the new culture of beauty announces itself to our people. We are faced with an internal struggle before we can go the way of other nations. We have to re-move many an ailment, subdue many a hindrance before we will be ready for a rebirth of the Jewish people, which is only a branch of the stream of the new [human] renaissance.*

14.

Just as there was no discipline of Jewish art, no Jewish museums or anything else that was wholly Jewish before the turn of the twentieth century, there also was no agency, with the exception of the Reform-inspired Wissenschaft des Ju-dentums, that dedicated itself to studying Jewish life. The discipline of Jewish Studies, as known today, had not emerged. Buber, who did not see eye to eye with Reform philosophy, wanted the Zionists, and especially the cultural Zionists, to take on the responsibility of a Jewish academy. In this essay (pts. 1 and 2) he struggles with the meaning of a "Study of Judaism" that would be inclusive.

* "Jüdische Renaissance," *Ost und West,* 1, no. 1 (Jan. 1901): cols. 7–10. Item 18 in *MBB.*

Jewish Studies

1

The program order of the Fifth Zionist Congress included among the questions of spiritual amelioration [*geistige Hebung*] also the item, "Jewish studies." * Many a loyal Zionist may be clueless on the point of what Jewish studies is. To what purpose and how does one engage in it? Where does it exist? What does it have to do with Zionism? And what [does it have to do with] the questions concerning the spiritual amelioration of the Jewish people? All this is not self-evident. We have to try to clarify the meaning of Jewish studies and its relationship with our [Zionist] endeavors.

Jewish studies may have a threefold meaning. According to its point of departure, it may either be [1] the study of Judaism [*Wissenschaft des Judentums*], [2] the study of the Jewish question, or [3] the study of Zionism. In the first case its point of departure would be the historical and present reality of the Jewish people; it would aim to describe and explain the facts and would pursue no practical aspect other than, perhaps, tracing consistent developments through the maze of contradictory phenomena. In the second case it would have to deal with the "pathology" of contemporary Jewry and with the anomaly of their relations to other people. These studies would find it more difficult to remain objective than would the study of Judaism, for already the choice of material would be influenced by the purpose. It would be even more difficult for the study of Zionism to be objective; its point of departure would not be a question, but an answer, an answer that in most cases was not arrived at by a scholarly method, but by intuition or, in any case, subjectively, and must now be justified; here the purpose would not merely determine the choice of the material but also its arrangement, its interpretation, and its evaluation.

---

* See "Martin Buber, Jewish Scholarship: New Perspectives (1901)," trans. J. Hessing, in Mendes-Flohr and Reinharz, *Jew in the Modern World*, 1st ed. (Oxford: Oxford Univ. Press) 241–43. It contains lengthy excerpts from this two-part essay. The translation presented here is complete and my own. [G. S.]

The two latter concepts seem even less satisfactory if we consider them from another broad point of view. Let us consider an analogy. These two concepts are reminiscent of the scholarly investigation of timely sociopolitical themes, in one case by a naïve economist, in the other by a political scientist. We shall here ignore the distinction between the two cases. But, if they do not flow from the major traditions of social life, both are obviously only fragments of a temporary nature. They must not presume to be more than addition and transition. And only when they do not wish to be more than that are they important. The study of the Jewish question or the study of Zionism likewise must not want to be more than addition and transition. But addition to what? And transition to what?

In truth there can only be one type of Jewish studies: the study of Judaism. Partly, at least, it would naturally result in a scholarly treatment of the Jewish question and of Zionism (because it would explain opposing conditions historically and sociologically), and would partly be complemented by it, just as the theory of political economy is complemented by that of economic policy. But where is this study of Judaism happening?

One might respond to me: It does not exist. And one might add: And it cannot be created.

That is correct. It does not exist. And it cannot be created. It does not exist, for there is no defined area of study that belongs to it nor one specific methodology that is systematically applied in its study. And it cannot be created, for true inquiry does not evolve from plans, schemes, and programs, however well-intentioned they might be, but from the farsighted and yet narrowly circumscribed research of the person of knowledge. Plans and programs are only the top of its house, not its foundation.

Yet we do not only speak of an academically pursued Zionism but actually of Jewish scholarship. Admittedly, this expression is not quite correct; it is to be retained merely for practical reasons. But if one accepts our definition for our purpose (I shall presently try to prove its relative justification), then the answers to the question about where this science might be found will also not turn out to be quite correct.

For, if we wish, this scholarship does exist. A small part of it is embodied in what is presently called the Study of Judaism [*Wissenschaft des Judentums*];* its larger part can be found in various other disciplines. And it is not a matter of creation but of detachment and linkage. This process of detachment and linkage, however, must not take place to create an independent discipline, valid according to the principles of the philosophy of science—an independent subject matter without a valid methodology will never suffice to establish a particular discipline—but to collect that which belongs to us, to build up a continuously developing inventory of Judaism, to see what we are, what we have, and what we are able to do. Even if this, too, is a practical point of view like those I have previously mentioned, it will not diminish the objectivity and completeness of the scientific body under consideration.

The parts pertaining to Judaism should, therefore, be detached from the relevant disciplines and then linked to the so-called Study of Judaism. It is to be hoped that through these efforts and related organizational work, and through the development and the deepening of the Jewish national movement as well, the interest in the newly defined resources will be enhanced, and that Jewish scholars will study the exposed problems in the respective fields.

But what about the so-called Study of Judaism, which will serve as the focus of the nascent body of materials?

It is not entitled to its great name, that much is certain. To be sure, it could always claim outstanding men. To be sure, it has developed its method with critical subtlety and heuristic acumen. It also has demonstrated eagerness in its research, comparison, and analysis. But inevitably, it has always remained what it was from the beginning, a branch of philology. Its object was ancient Jewish literature; its method of research was philological. It is not even entitled to the name Study of Judaism to the degree that German Studies [*Germanistik*] deserve the name Study of Germankind.

To be sure, laymen also grouped other scholarly creations under this heading. But a history of the Jewish people surely is part of the historical discipline, a treatise on the legislation in the Bible or Tal-

* See chap. 6, "The Science of Judaism," in Mendes-Flohr and Reinharz, *Jew in the Modern World*, 182–85. [G. S.]

mud is part of the general jurisprudence, studies of Jewish legends and customs are part of folklore, the monuments of ancient Jewish art are part of archeology and the history of art. The studies of the development of the Jewish people as an ethnic group, of our psychophysical uniqueness, of ancient Jewish economics, of our social stratification, of the evolution of specific customs and morals, of the Jewish spirit and Jewish culture—all these studies, to which we are looking forward, will not belong to that discipline which depends on the philological method but to anthropology, ethnology, economic, social, moral, and cultural history, disciplines with a different purpose and, therefore, with different methods.

These two areas—Jewish philology, on the one hand, and the Jewish chapters of anthropology, history, and the social sciences, on the other—can never be fused theoretically, only practically. That this is possible we can see in our days by the strange and valuable example of the Jewish encyclopedia,* which we shall discuss in detail later. But this Jewish encyclopedia is only an incomplete example, or only one example, no matter the monumental nature of the work. Especially as an encyclopedia this is no purely academic undertaking: it will include scholarly meaningful papers, but no scientific whole; that is against its structure, its system, its task. As far as details are concerned, it will be thorough, even exhaustive, rich and deep in interpretation; it will not be able to draw the overall conclusions that are the final goal of scientific inquiry; it will not be able to produce a complete picture of any given side of the Jews. To do so it would have to deviate from the law of its nature and develop into a series of large, independent works. This seems impossible to me and to anyone familiar with the structure of the work. The Jewish encyclopedia, which many see as the end product, can in truth only be characterized as a great preproduct.

If we consider further that the encyclopedia does not, and perhaps cannot, consider some of the above-mentioned disciplines suffi-

---

* The first Jewish encyclopedia undertaken in the twentieth century was published in the United States, in 12 vol. 1901–6, and edited by Isidore Singer. *Encyclopedia Judaica*, (Jerusalem: Keter Publishing House, 1971), 2: 732. [G. S.]

ciently, for example, the social sciences, we understand where we need to begin.

More on this in a second article.*

Martin Buber

Buber envisioned a new discipline that would go beyond the existing, Reform-based Wissenschaft des Judentums [scientific study of Judaism]. Buber here explores the complexities of combining the study of Judaism, of the Jewish people, and of Zionism into one academic discipline, and examines its corollary, a Jewish college.

Jewish Studies

2

In my previous article (no. 41 of *Die Welt*) I tried to show that there can be no valid Jewish scholarship in a strictly methodological sense, but merely a scholarly body of Jewish materials that could be organized by isolating the areas pertaining to Judaism in the various disciplines and by systematically linking them to the modern philological Jewish studies. Having said this, I shall call this body "Jewish studies."

This largely answers our first question, "What is Jewish studies?" Actually, we already know its purpose as well. We shall engage in Jewish studies in order to learn about the Jewish people—their origins, development and present situation. This has a dual purpose. First, to understand that which we love, but then also to learn from

* "Jüdische Wissenschaft," *Die Welt* 5, no. 41 (Oct. 11, 1901): 1–2. Item 19 in MBB.

the facts what our people need and what they might expect—our people's needs and possibilities. The former and the latter [are needed] to be able to create a scholarly foundation for the grand design of Jewish politics, that is, to address that which we have called the "study of the Jewish question."

The purpose is a theoretical-practical one. The practical [purpose] may even predominate. It is, of course, self-evident that it would not make any sense if all concerned would work their way through all affected disciplines and extract that which is Jewish. That would be a waste of energy and time that we cannot afford. Rather, we have to find ways for all to study Jewish subjects coherently and systematically. Among these ways I would like to single out two: the task and the college. They correspond to the dual function of the discipline: the active and the contemplative.

I already explained why the Jewish encyclopedia can only be considered a precursor. We will have to set a task for the discipline of Jewish studies that would be carried out according to an academic plan and not encyclopedically (or even by examples). Biographies and generalities would have to make room for a strict organization of facts and relationships in the natural sciences, history, and sociology. This task I consider a collective creative effort in which the best-known Jewish scholars would participate, each conscious of his task as a mission, each one presenting his findings independently and self-contained, and yet everyone together and interactively. Upon completion, this task would be a chapter of the intellectual endeavor from which we might try to see into the future of the Jewish people.

Recently, the idea of a Jewish college has come up repeatedly.* The thought is alive in some of the best of today's Jews. The idea was presented at the [Fourth] Zionist Congress, and then it appeared repeatedly in periodicals;† then, in a positive way, in the

---

* See M. Buber, B. Feiwel, and Ch. Weizmann, *Eine Jüdische Hochschule* (Berlin: Jüdische Verlag, 1902). [G. S.]

† See "A Spiritual Center" (sec. 25) and "The Jewish Cultural Problem and Zionism" (sec. 39), pt. 3. [G. S.]

United States, through the personality of a herald connected with the [Jewish] encyclopedia; and then, again, discussion in periodicals. Out of all of this some guiding principles formed for me that are in definite contrast to the American [encyclopedia] project. Briefly and precisely stated, they are: (1) a Jewish college is a necessity as the primary means to educate a modern, Jewishly thinking generation, as the preparation for future Jewish Studies, as the center of the efforts of an intellectual amelioration of our people. (2) The curriculum material of the college of Jewish studies in Jewish studies or the study of Judaism as defined by me. (3) The curriculum does not consist of the traditional, insufficient structure "history, literature, theology" but will be subdivided according to modern academic methodology (such as anthropology, history, including history of literature and history of religion, and the social sciences). (4) The present location of the college can only be in Europe; only here does the necessary humanpower exist. (5) The college will be run by an administration appointed by the Jewish academy (discussed below).

The Jewish academy under discussion here would be the institution in whose work the "task" and the college would coincide.

We have seen what today is still almost entirely missing in the "task"—a systematic plan, the parameters and organization of the material, the design of the structure, the organization of the workers. Likewise, the college is still lacking nearly everything. All of this cannot be supplied by individuals but only by an association convened for this purpose. This association I would like to call the Jewish Academy. Its function would be to lead Jewish studies from monographs and scattered activities to the task of education. Today task and college are still impossible. It would be the responsibility of the academy to make the college possible and to take on its administration. But more on that another time.*

Martin Buber

---

* Jüdische Wissenschaft," *Die Welt* 5, no. 43 (Oct. 25, 1901): 1–2. Item 19 in *MBB*.

15.

Written in the Spring of 1901, Buber here defends the existence of a group that learns about art and the Jewish people in the Zionist context.

A Group for Jewish Art and Jewish Studies

In a report, [which appeared] in no. 11 of *Die Welt,* entitled "The Berlin Zionists," a "Group for Jewish Art and Jewish Studies" was mentioned. First, I would like to correct the name, for this is not only a pipe dream but something absolutely essential. I cannot even imagine Jewish art, and our group also does not deal with the honorable "Study of Judaism" either. Jewish art means the living art of a living people; Jewish studies is the study of Jewish life. In our group both words have a broader and deeper meaning, that of Zionism; a movement of our *Volk* soul's creativity and a movement of ideas shall become reality. Our section is, as it were, above politics [*reichsunmittelbar*], focusing on the great movement that surrounds and reaches beyond the established [Zionist] party as well. Thus, the programs presented so far have been by men who are generally seen as outside the "party": Matthias Acher [also known as Nathan Birnbaum (1864–1937)] and Ahad Ha-Am [Asher Ginsberg (1856–1927)]. The next evening program (Monday, the 25th, in the "Münchner Hof"), will present Max Nordau [1849–1923], who will speak on "Challenges of Zionism." There will also be a discussion of issues concerning our current activities. Visits to studios and art demonstrations and additional lectures will follow. Our group is limited to a small number, but precisely for that reason we hope for continued elevation of the discussion level and sophistication in the tone of the discussion. Soon more about the necessity of such institutions.*

[Signed:] M. B.

---

* "Eine Sektion für jüdische Kunst und Wissenschaft," *Die Welt* 5, no. 13 (Mar. 29, 1901): 9. Item 26 in *MBB.*

16.

Here Buber picks up the torch for a Jewish theater from Pantarhei, an anonymous Zionist writer. Lending his voice to this discussion, Buber hopes to encourage the creation of a Freie Bühne, a private stage company that would produce plays for members only. Buber feels that the resources of material, money, and people would be available for such a limited theatrical undertaking under Zionist auspices.

A Young Judaic Stage

In an article in no. 43 of *Die Welt* entitled "The Promotion of Jewish Drama" Pantarhei [pseudonym] encouraged the founding of a Jewish stage, which would present Jewish situational drama in German and also some of the dramatic products of a blooming original Jewish literature. Surely this idea is seen by some of our readers as a fantastic idea that cannot become reality here and now. Others will have reflected on the obstacles more thoroughly. Then they may have concluded the following: (1) we do not have a public; (2) we do not have a repertoire; (3) we do not have any money. And with these three reasons the undertaking is finished.

Initially, it appears that those who argue in this way are right. For if we are considering a permanent Jewish theater, we indeed do not have any of the three things mentioned above.

We do not have a public. We think here in the first place of the West European [cultural] centers. If we do not, on the one hand, count the indifferent bourgeoisie, which we would have to cultivate very gradually, nor the classes of little means who would attend holiday performances at reduced prices, then there indeed does not remain a public who would suffice to maintain such a complicated establishment as that suggested with its two groups—one German and one Jewish.

That certainly cannot be the case when the repertoire will be such a small one as that of our stage initially. I agree that a Jewish stage would awaken many talents and direct many toward drama. But in the beginning, when it will not yet be a sufficiently known and recognized institution to exert such an influence, the number of available pieces for production will be small. There will not be enough to fill even the shortest theater season.

But this tiny repertoire includes another great difficulty as well. As Pantarhei wrote, this repertoire will consist of alternately German and Jewish pieces. For this, two groups will be needed: one who speaks German and the other, Yiddish. I will not even go into the difficulty of the composition of these two groups here. From a very basic financial point of view it is completely impossible for a theater that cannot yet count on a steady audience and whose season is extremely short to maintain two groups. Or, to put it briefly, we will not be able to raise the necessary capital for the establishment and development of such a theater in the near future.

I have prefaced my affirmative discussion with the words, "if we are considering a permanent Jewish theater." In this case I find it impossible to disagree that those three reasons—lack of an audience, a repertoire, and money—exist, at least for the initial, decisive period of the theater.

But we are not thinking in terms of a permanent theater. We are thinking in terms of performances by a Young Judaic stage company [Freie Bühne] producing plays for members only, which can occur at regular intervals or spontaneously. And therewith the three preceding arguments lose their validity; they are completely untenable in connection with a stage society.

What is a stage company? It is a private theater company that, from time to time, offers select dramatic productions for its members, mostly artistically valuable pieces that for some reason are never, or only seldom, produced for the public theater. A stage company offers the following advantages: (1) it has a regular audience, that is, members of the society who can be counted on to come [to the performances] and to whom we can add random individuals for specific performances. (2) It does not need a large public because a smaller but guaranteed one suffices for its purpose and means. (3) It does not need a large repertoire because a small but select one suffices for the relatively few performances. (4) It does not need a steady troupe [of actors] because it can procure its personnel from the public theater and attract and train artistically gifted dilettantes (amateurs) for the roles. (5) We do not have to explain any further that it does not need large funds, and the subscriptions of the members will enable it to match the offerings to the circumstances.

If these principles, gathered over many years of experience, would be applied to the project under discussion, we would first need a committee consisting of experts and fund-raisers for the establishment of a Young Judaic theater. This committee would be charged with three tasks:

1. The founding of the organization
2. The selection of the repertoire
3. The composition of the personnel

Naturally, the founding of the organization would be conducted on a strictly professional basis.

For the selection of the repertoire we should also consider a contest as Pantarhei also suggested.

For the composition of the personnel (actors) of the Jewish section we would have to focus on the cities where visiting theater groups already give performances (here I am thinking partly of appropriate remuneration, partly of matinee performances) or of groups from the Yiddish theater who would, of course, have to be educated for their new task.

✂

In spite of all of these possibilities, I do not expect this plan to become reality in the near future. But I am convinced that this idea will catch on sooner or later and be realized.*

A small step in this direction may already be undertaken this coming winter in Vienna—the organization of evenings and matinees that will at first be dedicated to lyrical and epic poetry within a framework of Jewish music but will, by the very presence of [Jewish] talent and the creation of a first artistic platform, also mediate the promotion of Jewish drama. It just came to my attention that similar plans are also underfoot in Berlin, independent of our efforts

---

* In 1917 the all-Hebrew Habimah Theater was begun in Moscow. The group of actors settled in Tel Aviv in 1937. Today it is the Israeli National Theater. [G. S.]

and without any knowledge of them. This minor occurrence signals to me everywhere the budding desire of Young Judaic literature for recognition and exposure.*

Martin Buber

17.

Buber, who was at odds with the cultural committee of the World Zionist Organization (WZO) as it had originally existed, here has his first chance to present to the entire Zionist body besides the many guests in attendance his views on Jewish art. Buber, who organized the "art exhibition" at the Fifth Zionist Congress together with Ephraim M. Lilien and B. Feiwel, had a particular interest in championing Jewish art and artists. But he also understood the unifying power of Jewish literature and Jewish music. In this keynote speech at the Congress he pleads for an appreciation of Jewish culture and appeals to the audience to support a Jewish publishing house, the Jüdische Verlag in Berlin. The latter project would come to fruition in 1902, but not with the support of the Zionist Congress. Here the proposal is voted down.

Address on Jewish Art

By Martin Buber at the Fifth Zionist Congress

PRESIDENT DR. HERZL: . . . Mr. Buber now has the floor for his presentation on Jewish art.

MARTIN BUBER: Honored Delegates, Today Dr. Max Nordau spoke to you on the question of cultural amelioration of the Jewish people in a way that made a most painful impression on my friends and me. And may I point out that my friends and I represent a good portion of the young generation of Zionists. As Zionists, we have shown Max Nordau love and admiration. Precisely for that reason I must here point out that we have been hurt in our deepest sensibili-

---

* "Eine jungjüdische Bühne," *Die Welt* 5, no. 45 (Nov. 8, 1901): 10–11. Item 20 in *MBB*.

ties, in the core of our psychic connection with Zionism, by the way in which Nordau treated our concerns. Dr. Max Nordau declared that it is irresponsible and dreamy to debate the issue of spiritual amelioration here. But he did not take into consideration that these issues concern nothing less than the wonderful budding of a new Jewish national culture. (Applause.) Shall we here, in this unique assembly, in which the Jewish people recognize themselves, become conscious of themselves, decide about themselves, shall we, in these unique Zionist days in the *galut* year indifferently pass by this, recently still unknown, and daily continuing transformation? Shall we here not take a position [in relation to this transformation], shall we not try to further it as far as is in our power? If we do not do it, if we do not have anything to say about this resurrection, does this Jewish parliament then fulfill its task? Are we then not like human beings who see nerves and muscles, bones and veins, in a human organism but do not recognize the soul? (Applause.)

But if, for some reason, these perspectives do not apply to us, the recognition of that which is necessary so that our movement can develop and grow demands that these questions form a major item on our agenda. Let us take Jewish art, the topic of my talk here, as an example. I would like to remind you that Dr. Nordau himself showed in an article, "The Zionism of Western Jews," that Jewish art is a first class propaganda tool suited to win the productive ones and the great circles of the intelligentsia as well for our cause. Ordinarily, I am not swayed by the demands of propaganda. But if Dr. Nordau explains here, "We first of all need money," then I respond, "Our art will get us money." (Applause.) And finally I ask Dr. Nordau whether he believes that Zionism will affect only our destitute proletariat. Zionism is for all the people. And truly, we need spiritual amelioration especially for those of our classes who are not completely destitute. We need to educate especially the propertied classes, spiritually and morally, before they will be a capable and respected human resource for Palestine. (Applause.) And we wish to suggest to you here means of education that will improve large groups of our people, strengthen our movement, and lead new and valuable resources to our national cause. Jewish art is such a means.

Honored fellow Zionists! We suffer from theory. Today, in speaking to you about Jewish art I want to stay away from abstract schematic theory and to speak to you of powerful living facts, which are great and overwhelming.

Jewish art is a series of facts.

For thousands of years we were a barren people. We shared the fate of our land. A fine, horrible desert sand blew and blew over us until our sources were buried and our soil was covered with a heavy layer that killed all young buds. The excess in soul power that we possessed at all times expressed itself in the exile merely in an indescribably one-sided spiritual activity that blinded the eyes to all the beauty of nature and of life.

We were robbed of that from which every people takes again and again joyous, fresh energy—the ability to behold a beautiful landscape and beautiful people. The blossoming and growth beyond the ghetto was unknown to and hated by our forebears as much as the beautiful human body. All things, from whose magic the literature spins its golden veil, all things, whose forms are forged through art's blessed hands, were something foreign that we encountered with an uneradicable mistrust. At times only the half-lost sound of a song darted across the dark and narrow alley, rushed by, only to die in the thickness of night. The very thing in which the true essence of a nation expresses itself to the fullest and purest, the sacred word of the national soul, the artistic productivity, was lost to us. Wherever the yearning for beauty raised itself with tender shy limbs, there it was suppressed with an invisible, merciless hand. Wherever a young bud stretched toward the sun in fear and expectation, it was suffocated by the existence of the most terrible destiny.

The great transformation became possible when Judaism entered Western civilization. We see its first fruits in our days. I would like to emphasize this because recently a peculiar ghetto sentimentality emerged in some Zionist circles. In remembering the tender, unusual beauty of the unified national life that we led in Europe until the eighteenth century we forget the significant fact that the modern national-Jewish movement, that Zionism, could not have been born without that strange stage in the development of our people that was erroneously called "emancipation." Emancipation usually means the more or less arbitrary actions of individuals and national representatives. But this was only the expression of a great historical transformation that, for the nations, led to the struggle for human rights, for us to an inner move closer to modern civilization. To be sure, due to the character of our *galut*, this move took on an abnormal, leap-like form. It did not create that blind adaptation to modern civilization, which we know by the name assimilation, but to the peculiarities of individual peoples—a sad episode in our history in which we learned the whole seriousness of our degeneration. But when, in the life of Europe, the healthy national self-consciousness stepped into the place of a bloodless ideal of humanity, when the attitude had registered that every person and every nation best serves the public in using their own talents for productive activity, when the social consciousness of that which should be was being fused with the national consciousness of what is, then it was our marriage to Western civilization, after all, that made it possible for us to unfold our ancient desire for national existence—a desire that for centuries had expressed itself in dull, yearning waiting or in wild, messianic ecstasies—in the modern form that we call Zionism. (Applause.) And it also was that marriage which allowed our yearning for beauty and action—a yearning that was again and again tortured to death in the ghetto—to mature to a young power in whose unfinished present form we venerate the great future and to which we have given the name "Jewish art." This energy means the rebirth of productivity in our people. We no longer translate the overflowing movement of our soul into isolated intellectualism but into an activity of the entire organism and, through this activity, into lines and sounds, into living being, which again awakens living appreciation. (Applause.)

But the fact alone that we once again have artists—and by artists I understand not only sculptors but also poets and composers—is not enough to confirm the existence of Jewish art. Recently, we have gone beyond this first step, the mere existence of artists of Jewish descent. This happened because an artist here and there paid tribute to the muse of his people and was inspired by it. In the eons of our national life a wealth of fine secret spiritual values accumulated, and our artists began to draw on this treasure. Some went even further; they used what the people had created, themes and material. On the way to a national art this production and utilization will become ever

finer and deeper. Even if we are, on the one hand, completely immersed in modern civilization, we cannot, on the other hand, give up
the things in whom the soul of our people expresses itself: language,
customs, naïve folk art of songs and *nigunim* [melodies], of menorahs
and *talesim* [prayer shawls]. But we must not see these things as
something sacred that we look at with reverent awe but as material
from which we build a new beauty—not as statues that we may admire from afar but as a valuable block of marble that waits for our
hand and our chisel. (Applause.)

But this stage of Jewish productivity, the fact of the national consciousness of our artists, does not yet mean the existence of Jewish
art in the strictest sense of the word. If we understand by Jewish art
something existing, finished, unified, and not something in the making, developing, unfinished as I do, then I would have to answer the
question about the existence of national art with a no. [For a national
art] we lack the unifying association of the artists among themselves
and with the people and their ideals. A national art needs a soil from
which it grows and a sky to strive for. We Jews of today have neither. We are the slaves of many different soils, and our thoughts rise
to different skies. In the deepest depths of our soul we have no soil
and no sky. We have no homeland that harbors our hopes and that
lends support to our steps; we have no national sun that blesses our
seeds and brightens our days. A national art needs a unified human
community from which it arises and which it represents. But we only
have pieces of community, and only gradually the parts awake to the
idea of one body. Only in connection with the continued rebirth can
Jewish art come into being and develop. (Applause.) A whole and
complete Jewish art will be possible only on Jewish soil, just like a
whole and complete Jewish culture as such. But what we have already today are cultural buds, artistic seeds; and we have to nurture
these here in the Diaspora with a tender, loving hand until we can
plant them into the soil of our homeland where they will be able to
unfold fully. (Applause.) What we call Jewish art is not being, but
becoming, not fulfillment, but a beautiful possibility, just as Zionism
today is a becoming and a beautiful possibility. Each one of us can
contribute to the growth of both in his kind and manner. Each one of
us can prepare the way for Zionism and for Jewish art.

There will be some who will not understand why the development of our art is such a big and essential deal for us—surely not those who stress the international nature of art. In a recent letter the Swedish painter Richard Bergh responded in a very sensitive way to the great writer Ellen Key. He admitted that aesthetic appreciation does not care about nationality. "But," he continued, "the momentary bliss is not the most important thing for the human being, rather, his desire to create is, his yearning. In a completed garden one desires to enjoy and to rest, but when we see uncultivated soil, we wish to create new, strange, never before seen gardens, may they be large or small. "Ubi bene, ibi patria" [Where there is well-being, there (is your) homeland]* is an old lie. Not the land that we enjoy the most is the best but that where we are the most productive. May Jewish art be such a new, strange, never before seen garden. (Lively applause.) For in artistic creation the specific qualities of the nation express themselves most directly; everything that is particular to this *Volk*, the uniqueness and incomparability of its individuality, finds concrete, living form in its art. Thus, our art is the most beautiful path of our people to ourselves.

As I have already indicated, the rebirth of the Jewish *Volk* is at the same time the form in which this nation participates in the great cultural movement of today's humanity. Zionism and Jewish art are two children of our rebirth. What does Jewish art mean for its older brother? What does it mean for us as Zionists?

First, Jewish art is for us a great educator. It is a teacher for a living perception of nature and people, a teacher for a living feeling of all that is strong and beautiful, a teacher for this perception and feeling that we lacked for so long and that we may now recover through the visual and poetic productions of our artists. And it is essential for us as Zionists that our *Volk* will regain this living perception and feeling, for only fully developed, complete human beings can be full Jews capable and worthy of creating a new homeland. (Lively applause.) But our art is an educator to true Judaism in an even more direct way. No language is as urgent, as suggestive as the language

* Many thanks to my colleague David Dungan for the translation of this phrase. [G. S.]

of art; there is no language that can reveal the nature of life and the nature of truth as can the language of art. And our art will also become a strong herald of a resurrected Judaism, it will grip all slumbering hearts with the power of forms and melodies, with the power of noise and visions, and it will bring the song of the becoming Zion to them like a storm. (Lively applause.) Our art will arise, and if one should say—these people are dead—art will strike his eyes with a powerful beam so that he will see and behold their beauty and recognize that these people are fuller of living juices and overflowing living energies than any other people on earth. (Lively applause.) As our most wonderful cultural document, our art will witness to the outside that a new Jewish culture is beginning to emerge. Our art will also educate us, even us Zionists. The deepest secrets of our national soul, the great mystery of Jeshurun, will become evident in it and shine with the fire of life eternal. We will behold and recognize ourselves. We will behold it and recognize our treasure. I expect a wonderful enrichment and spiritualization of Zionism from Jewish art. (Applause.)

We have great and undeniable responsibilities toward that art which means so much to us and which can become so much more. I would like to speak to you about these responsibilities today. I would like to speak to you about the three great areas of art: music, visual art, and literature. I would like to discuss one after the other. I would like to present one after the other to you. First, I would like to sketch what we did in this area during the *galut* period [70–1901 C.E.], then touch on the most important moments in the current phase of development, and, finally, deduce from these the duties that we have to fulfill in this area. Accordingly, these duties are two-fold. They concern, first, the collection of the historical art treasures of our people, no matter how modest they are because future productions will always draw inspiration from this ethnic particularity. Second, they concern the incomparably more important amelioration and nurturing of the currently arising new art, the mediation between the artists and the people, and the aesthetic education of the people. The first of these responsibilities, to our past, is already being fulfilled in non-Zionist circles in an admirable way but without unity and without the great idea of development that inspires us. The second set of responsibilities concerns the actual duties of art for the present and the future; to think of them in terms of production, that is our responsibility. May we be worthy of the task that history has bestowed on us!

I can say only little about Jewish music. I am not trained to deal with music as an expert and must confine myself to appreciating it. But my love alone is not sufficient to speak to you thoroughly on music because I do not wish to move from the language of facts, which alone is appropriate here, to the language of the heart.

You know that there have always been two forms of Jewish music: liturgical melodies and folk songs. It is peculiar to see how in the latter, the naïve artless song of the people, the elements that we designate as Jewish music are strongest. Those scales and chords, unique to our people, are purest in the folk song; the specific Jewish scale, which has been researched and written about recently, emerges most clearly. We are a singing and music-loving people. This is often overlooked. A song comes to our lips during all kinds of experiences and activities. It is, however, quickly silenced by the worries of daily life. During all those strange eruptions of our forcibly repressed zest for life—known in our history by the name of messianism and in recent history and currently as Hasidism—the wildest yearning of the soul rings out in song. Our beloved Isaac Leibisch Peretz tells us that there are areas where one can recognize the number of male family members in a Jewish household by the number of fiddles in the house. The Klezmer is the actual hero of modern Jewish folk literature and the first great, ever recurring symbol of our sobering yearning in song. For instance, we find a fiddler and a singer in the center of the two incredible novels by Shalom Aleichem. And everywhere—in the home and in school, in the synagogue and in the street—a song, no matter how monotonous, mixes in the hallowed or busy rhythm of the hour. Music in the galut has become the essential form of art, a real folk art.

This seems to be the reason why Jews became active in the field of music when they entered the European art development at the beginning of the nineteenth century. It produced many significant composers.* The people's singing comes down to individual personalities.

* Jacomo Meyerbeer and Felix Mendelssohn Bartholdy were such composers. Richard Wagner composed diatribes against Jewish artists that unleashed anti-

And it is once again interesting to see that composers, again and again, consciously or unconsciously, reach back to Jewish themes, to chords and melodies of their people. They know instinctively that here are the roots of their strength and that they can only blossom if they nurture and develop this ancestral gift.

After having said this, what we can do for Jewish music is collect the existing material. Here, in addition to the Hebrew songs and so-called Syrian-Palestinian songs, we speak primarily of the folk songs in Yiddish. Until now we have had few in writing. Two years ago a small collection was published by Warschawski that, in spite of some mistakes, contains much valuable material. In it we find many a splendid folk theme that waits for choral or orchestral adaption. Some have already successfully been used in this way. Such collections provide a rich texture of simple melodies [*nigunim*] that Jewish composers can use for contemporary music. It would be important in later collections to preserve clearly the popular character [of this music]. We can expect this from the proposed musical section of that very significant collection of folksongs whose texts were recently published by "Woschod" and which I plan to discuss in greater detail.

From the previous we may infer that we may expect a true upsurge of Jewish music, especially of lyrical songs.

Until now, the visual arts have developed only like a seed, like a hint in our people. Art was employed primarily in the decoration of ritual objects, and many old synagogues are wonderful repositories of such art products. Until very recently all of these works were dispersed; a few years ago systematic collecting began. It is the achievement of the Society for Jewish Research and Conservation of Historical and Art Monuments in Vienna, the Society for Research of Jewish Art Documents in Frankfurt, and the Society for Jewish Folklore in Hamburg to have erected centers in which all items produced by the naïvely shaping hand of our people over the course of centuries are collected. All these institutes form one collection of an-

---

Semitic hatred, claiming Jews are incapable of art. See Mendes-Flohr and Reinharz, *Jew in the Modern World*, 327–31; also Eduard Levy, "Richard Wagner und Felix Mendelssohn-Bartholdy," *Ost und West* 6 (June 1905): cols. 393–406. [G. S.]

cient Jewish art, a collection to which also belong sheets and books that our friend, Dr. Chazanowicz, has donated to our National Library in Jerusalem. (Applause.) In these collections we may recognize the dark, laborious groping of a nation for whom visual art is not a natural form of expression but who, nevertheless, desires beauty for its surroundings, at least during times of celebration.

Only in our days has the visual art of our people blossomed in unexpected splendor. It is not possible here to trace the historical causes of this wonderful upsurge. I can only say what happened. Our tribe, which has for so long produced scholars who hated life, began to create artists. And one by one these artists turned toward the destiny of their people. They did not only express the soul of our tribe in their creations externally, in materials and themes, the Jewish character was also deeply embedded in the perception and form of these works. I also cannot go into more detail on this here. But look only at the items that we have collected for this Congress as a small token of our great art. (Lively applause.) Pay attention to the peculiar appropriation of light and shadow, the play of the atmosphere around objects, the integration of individual items into the surrounding environment, the broad concept of space, the strange inward movement. Everywhere you will recognize elements of Jewish perception and formation.

First among our artists I would like to mention the great master, Joseph Israels [1824–1911], known by everyone in Europe. (Lively applause.) Several of his ingenious etchings are based on Jewish sources, the most important of which are "David and Saul" and "The Son of an Ancient People." Not only in these works but in all of his work there is something deeply Jewish. He belongs with his entire soul to the ancient tribe. For him the quiet, steady continuous production is as normal as the quiet, invisible learning for the Talmudic Jew. He also often emphasizes his living Judaism in words; so, for example, in his book *Spain* in which he characterizes in a warm, soulful way his encounter with Spanish Jews—the dark fire of their figures, the poor, sorrowful mood of their environment and the strong, heartfelt yearning sounds of the mutual Hebrew greeting. (*"Gam ani Yehudi mi erez hollande,"* [I am also a Jew, from Holland] he calls to them.) This occurred recently with some Zionists with whom he shared his deep empathy for our movement, for our ideas. And if the

Jewish figures that he creates sit or stand ever so peacefully, there is mystery in their lines and tragedy in the rigidity of their poses. Eons speak out of these silent, motionless individuals and a yearning that is trampled by fate. Yes, it is the gigantic, dark-as-death hand of fate that hovers above them like a gray, heavy cloud that absorbs all light. But beyond that cloud, invisible to our eyes, yet aware of the master's sweetest dreams, the first hint of redemption stirs, a redemption that will be victorious.

Israels reaches into our time from previous generations. We are the first generation that understands and appreciates him. During his lifetime a tender, young artistic life shot up but soon died. I am speaking of Moritz Gottlieb, who died at age twenty-three. He was a chosen bearer of our people's tragedy as if the spirit of our history bestowed on him the kiss of suffering and death. Once he painted himself as Ahasverus with a golden band across his forehead. And the kingdom of wandering and of pain possessed his soul. He came too early. He felt the new Judaism [Zionism] before it existed. He was a herald type, and his fate was the fate of the herald who dies all too soon, who is not blessed to behold the promised land himself. His Jewish paintings, of which I wish to mention "The Praying Jews [on Yom Kippur]," "Shylock and Jessica," "Uriel Acosta and Judith," are monuments on our journey. We love his young, struggling, melancholy figure. We identify with his struggle and his suffering. May his memory be for a blessing.

In the type of art he produces Max Liebermann approximates Israels. He is a great artist. He is not nearly as much of a Jew as is Israels, but he feels the deep old sources of his being, even if he lacks the regal pride with which Israels embraces his people. Unbeknownst to him, the Jewish element breaks forth again and again in his work. The way he sees the vast, fading landscape and the way he populates an area with individual simple objects and the way he amasses quiet shadows around the human body—this is a hidden Jewish trait. Whenever he draws on our people's book for material, he becomes consciously Jewish. Here the eternal power captivates him.

Lesser Ury stands completely in contrast to Liebermann.* (Lively applause.) His superhuman will power is his greatest attribute—a

---

* See "Lesser Ury" (sec. 18). [G. S.]

fiery, stormy will power in which lives the yearning for boundlessness, a will power that bursts all bonds and attempts to express the
inexpressible. In him, the incredible suffering of our people breaks
free, not in complaints but in accusations, not in questions but in wild
attack. In his great paintings, again and again, a living power rebels
against dark powers of fate and demands redemption. He has found
monumental symbols for our fate. In his "Jerusalem" he painted the
entire Jewish people in a small group of wandering Jews who rest
on a bench at the ocean and the entire history of our people in one
painful evening when heaven and ocean face each other in yearning.
In his "Jeremiah" he painted the prophet who was made to bear the
entire history of our tribe and who is brought low by the burden of
an eternity. In Lesser Ury a mystery has become a revolution.

The most conscious among our artists is one of the younger ones,
Ephraim Moshe Lilien. (Lively applause, which turns into a joyous
spontaneous ovation for the artist, who is present.) He penetrated
deeply into the miracle of our people; he has recognized meaning and
value of our old themes and appropriated them. He experienced
Zionism on his own body, internalized it completely. Precisely because he belongs to the young generation, he is one of us. I even expect much more from him than he has accomplished. He has drawn
wonderful sketches. His technique is rich and mature. Yet his art is
more promise than fulfillment just as the striving of our new generation in general. His book *Juda* and his Hebrew ex libris (pl.) earned
him our full admiration, and we put all of our hope in him, which is
more than all the praise in the world. He is more than an honored
master, he is our friend, our brother.

Jehudo Epstein [1870–1946] is one who combines in his works a
wonderful sense for a strong color effect with a pregnant characteri-
zation. (Applause.) We are exhibiting one of his most recent and as
yet unfinished paintings, "Job and His Friends." Currently, we can
see in his studio a large-scale group of Maccabees, portraying the
scene where Mattathias rises before the idolatrous altar to avenge
the Lord. I had the opportunity to admire another, earlier painting,
"David and Saul," at the home of Theodor Herzl. These colorfully
expressive works with their tight, soulful designs make him one of
our foremost artists.

I could mention many more. Here I can mention only a few more names: first among them is S. J. Solomon (applause), who brought a peculiar Jewish nuance into traditional modern English painting. Here we are interested in his works, "Simson's Imprisonment" and his portrait of Israel Zangwill. [I will also mention] the portrait painter Leopold Horowitz, who has shown a noble and sensitive concept of the modern Jewish facial type; Isidor Kaufmann, whose fine groups and scenes from Jewish life we know; [Eduard] Bendemann [1811–1880], who painted Biblical scenes in a pathetic, much-praised style; Alfred Lakos [1870–1961], whose [painting] "Mourning Jews" is exhibited here; the very talented young etcher Hermann Struck, who possesses a rare understanding for the soulful portrayal of Jewish heads and from whom we may still expect much that is beautiful; Hirzenberg, who created superb realistic moods of modern Jewish life and a moving Ahasverus; [Ssolomon J.] Kischinewski [1863–1941], who has portrayed Russian Jews in a sharp, characteristic manner; Henry Levy, who has created numerous lithographs portraying Jewish life; Wilhelm Wachtel, who produced pretty decorative pieces.

From our sculptors we should name Marc Antokolsky, indisputably the most important sculptor, who has gained worldwide fame and whose "Spinoza" is the most interesting Jewish piece. Henryk Glitzenstein, a richly gifted artist, laureate of the Munich Academy, whose "Abel" is a symbolization of suffering Jewish idealism; Frédéric Beer, with whose Congressional medallion you are all familiar; Aaronson, whose group, "Le berceau d'amour" portrays an ancient Jewish saga in a tender, delightful way; Bernstein-Sinaieff, who created an "Ezra," among others; Alfred Nossig (applause), who created an "Eternal Jew," a "Maccabee," and some portrait plaques, among them that of Max Nordau, and whose best work is probably a mask of King Solomon on exhibit here; Boris Schatz's "Mattathias," and others.

I only emphasized works with Jewish contents here because they interest us already externally, even though they are not always the most Jewish products of these artists. I was not able to discuss many of the ones I truly value, let alone mention all of the names in question. But I do hope that I was able to give you even a faint idea of the developing Jewish art. It is remarkable that most of these artists joined the Zionist movement and have gratefully devoted their creative energy to the movement. (Applause.)

Let us consider the question, What can we do for our visual art? What can we contribute so that our people recognize our artists and our artists their people? In this direction we need to act in a threefold way. First, we will organize exhibits of Jewish art in the larger cities; I hope that we will already be in a position to make a worthy beginning next winter. Traveling exhibitions will also be a possibility. Second, we shall endeavor to create publishing houses and distribution centers of Jewish art wherever these promise to succeed; in this context, we welcome the recently established Jewish art publisher "Phoenix" in Berlin and the art publisher "Aesthetik," which is underway in Warsaw. Third, we shall endeavor to create an artistic-economic organization of Jewish visual art, the establishment of an association, which will work for the unified and centralized application of Jewish productivity in this area and which will, through its leadership, exert a certain influence on the exhibitions and publishers previously mentioned. I express the hope that already at the next Congress we will have before us the statutes of this necessary and important organization. (Applause.)

The third major area of our art is Jewish literature. Before I begin to speak about this, allow me to say something very personal that may, perhaps, have a more general, representative character after all. Of all the indescribable riches with which the modern Jewish renaissance movement showered us nothing moved me so strongly, so magically, as the renaissance of Jewish art. Nothing has brought to my attention as overwhelmingly as Jewish literature that a new land has been born, that we have received new strength and a new voice. First, a short review. Until a few years ago there were three kinds of literature: first, the literature of West European Jews, who wrote in different languages without being conscious of a connection with an existing or developing Jewish culture, without thinking of another association than the literature of the host nation in whose midst they lived and in whose language they wrote; second, the literature of the East European, mostly Russian Jews, who were either epigones of the Bible or imitators of western Europe; third, the folk song. The folksong was, for a long time, the form in which the Jewish psyche expressed itself poetically in the purest, most genuine, most direct way. To be sure, our song could not compare with other peoples in the manifoldness of themes, in the richness of moods. *Galut* life was not capable of producing poetic excesses. But in its modest, sparse way our song is an equal testimony to the inner life of a great, enslaved nation. Until recently, we did not have a usable collection of Jewish folksongs. Only recently, an exemplary collection was published by the "Woschod" publishing house under the direction of Ginzberg, which is limited to Yiddish songs in Russia but which contains more than one thousand pieces and which contains absolutely valuable material from the perspective of a cultural historian besides that of artistic appreciation. It is the result of voluntary and joyful collaboration of likeminded individuals, and we might point out that the participants were largely Zionists. This collection is merely a beginning. Soon others will have to be produced, especially in Galicia, Romania, and Turkey, and then we need to expand the research to the specifically Hebrew song besides that in German in some western countries. Here, too, the research offers rich themes to emerging artists in all areas of creativity—documentation of our soul's history with which they can begin and on which they can build.

This was the state of the literature until a few decades ago. But during these and simultaneously with the great national-Jewish movement, and in constant connection with it, a particular, powerful literature emerged and has so steadily developed that we must not see it as an accidental occurrence, but as a living organism. (Lively applause.) This literature develops in three great branches: modern Hebrew literature, Yiddish literature, and literature in foreign languages. This threefoldness is indicative of the fragmentation of today's Jewry; behind these different languages lies something like a division of the soul. And still there is a remarkable richness in this quality of Hebrew and Yiddish literature. To be sure, it is not a native treasure, not the richness of the peacefully blessed, the peacefully joyous person, but it is the richness of danger, richness of wandering, the richness of a king in exile. And in this twofoldness we see once more the gigantic dualism that runs through our history in gigantic struggles, as a fateful presence—the dualism of spirit and of zest for life. In general, Hebrew literature is as alien-to-life, idealistic, unworldly, as Yiddish literature is happy, realistic, earthy. But precisely in the latest phases of both literatures I see a valuable and promising approximation. The twofoldness serves the expression of all nuances in any case; that which the soul of the contemporary person cannot express in Hebrew, it may be able to express fully in the vernacular [Yiddish] and vice versa. I see Jewish literature in other languages, however, as something abnormal, tragic, almost a sickness. But just as there are human beings, animals, and plants that have achieved a magical beauty because of their illness, as the pearl can only be born from the disease of the shell, I see much luster, much peculiar beauty in this literature. I consider it to be a power equal to other forms; I look to its development with happy anticipation. (Applause.) I must refrain here from discussing the Hebrew and Yiddish literature in detail. To characterize this third group I will merely mention some names. First, our ingenious friend and comrade, Israel Zangwill (lively applause); among those who made a name in German literature are Georg Hirschfeld (applause) and Jacob Wasserman (applause); among the budding poets, M. J. Berdyczewski (applause), who is also significant in Hebrew literature. Some of the young talents were introduced in the most recent Pesach and Maccabee holiday issues of *Die Welt* but in an unorganized, uneven series. The Jüdische Verlag hopes to publish an anthology of current Jewish literature in all of its forms of expression.

What can we do for our literature? First, the transformation of our press, in the sense that it will, in the future, include more good modern Jewish literature, thereby educating our reading public to better understanding and contribute to the creation of a literary public that so far does not exist. Second, through contests for novellas, poems, dramas, and so forth. Third, through public readings from Jewish literature that will gradually develop into a theater. Fourth, finally, through the foundation of a modern Jewish publishing house. (Applause) I would now like to say some more about this project, the subject of my only Congressional proposition.

We can summarize our work in the service of our art essentially in these words—aesthetic education of the people. I realize that this does not do much for the numerous disenfranchised and destitute individuals. This means first that there is much work left to do and, second, that if our plans pan out, we will already soon be able to distribute many simple, modest, generally comprehensible works of art among the general population. We envision that there will be Jewish art in Jewish homes, Jewish music, Jewish paintings, Jewish readings, which is, at the same time, good and genuine art. Foreign [art] shall be relegated to second place; that which is poor and aesthetically unsatisfactory will be completely displaced. (Lively applause.) That is internal national education. This also means the empowerment of the creative forces. And it means large-scale propaganda. So far we have agitated* through words. Now we also want to agitate through life. Words can influence people. Only life can serve life. Words can create shekel payers. Only life can create true Zionists. Words can compel to profess an idea. Only life can compel to live the idea. (Lively applause.) That is why we wish to agitate through life. And we do this in more ways than one by our activities through a publishing house for Jewish art. First, we will win over many artists who create through life and who do not consider working with us because so far they have not seen a possibility here to be creative. We strengthen the ties between us and those artists who have joined us by giving them the opportunity to express their Zionism in their own way. We win additional intellectual circles who have so far kept their distance because they see in our movement only political slogans and do not know the deep modern-cultural content of our program. We publicize our ideas in the works that embody them. And finally, our own people become true, complete Zionists. *(Applause.)*

Dear Assembled!

At earlier Congresses it was the custom for each lecturer and especially the cultural lecturers to present many very complicated propositions so that there was no choice but to accept them only as resolutions that fell victim to parliamentary procedures. To avoid this I would like to present only one proposition. As previously mentioned, this proposition concerns the newly established Jüdische Verlag. You have the pamphlet that describes this publishing house. I do not wish to repeat its content. I would merely like to emphasize that this publishing house, if it succeeds, will be in a position to bring together and closer to completion all that which will happen in the field of Jewish art in the near future. This publishing house is the re-

---

* *Agitieren* at that time did not have the negative connotation it has in English today. To agitate meant no more than to publicize. [G. S.]

sult of years of planning by individuals who have given all their energies for this project. It is a purely idealistic undertaking, and there will not be any personal gain for the organizers. At the same time it is based on a solid, ideal-practical basis, namely subscription. The subscribers pay twenty marks annually and in return receive publications valued at thirty marks; groups will receive twice as much material for the same price. With the support of organizations individual subscribers may pay their subscriptions in installments.

Half of the surplus will be used to build up the publishing venture. In addition, we would like to publish primarily important books that stand outside the regular range of publications; among these I stress the often-suggested school books for Palestinian* school children that have been rejected by all existing publishers. The appropriate Zionist Congress will decide what to do with the other half. To facilitate the establishment of the publishing house as soon as possible certificates guaranteeing the fund at one hundred marks each will be distributed, 50 percent of which will be repaid from subscriptions. We ask Congress members and guests to sign up for the guarantee fund, to subscribe, and to solicit their friends for signatures and subscriptions.

I further submit to the Congress the following resolution:

The Fifth Congress resolves

1. To guarantee two thousand marks for the guarantee fund of the Jüdische Verlag, which will be repaid with 50 percent of the subscriptions that we will receive.

2. To empower the Actions Comité to send pamphlets of the Jüdische Verlag to all organizations, local groups, and representatives by mid-February 1902 with the request to sign up and thereby support it most sincerely.

Dear Congressional Members!

We do not ask you for a subvention, only for a loan that will allow us the speedy beginning of our work. And we would like to ask for strong moral support.

Please keep in mind that here a positive cultural undertaking awaits realization. It will depend on your decision whether Jewish

---

* Meant here are Jewish children living in the land of Israel. [G. S.]

art, which has blossomed so wonderfully, so promisingly, in such a short time, will wilt in a corner like a misunderstood and neglected stepchild or whether the doors will be opened wide so that she may enter into her kingdom—the young, lovely royal daughter—and sit on her throne, bestowing sunshine and rain on all who behold her face. Confidently, we put our affairs into your hands.*

(Lively, long-lasting applause and clapping. Speaker is congratulated.)

18.

Martin Buber literally discovered Lesser Ury. Born in Birnbaum, Posen, Ury had made his way to Berlin via Paris, Munich, and Belgium. Upon his arrival in Berlin, however, he fell on hard times because of a disagreement with Max Liebermann, who controlled the Secession. It was only after Liebermann's retirement from the Secession that Ury was made an honorary member and his works were exhibited in major galleries. Ury was known as an impressionist-expressionist, and he aroused enthusiasm and bitter opposition as well because of his strong colors. Two of the works described in this article, "Jerusalem" and "Jeremiah," were included in the art exhibition at the Fifth Zionist Congress organized by Buber and Lilien.

Buber wrote the article on Ury for the artistic Zionist journal, Ost und West.† *It was picked up by the Zionist newspaper,* Die Welt,‡ *and in 1902 Buber reused the basic material from the article for his book,* Jüdische Künstler, *that featured six artists and was published by the Jüdische Verlag in 1903.*§

---

* "Referat über jüdische Kunst," *Die Welt* 6, no. 3 (Jan. 17, 1902): 9–11, and no. 4 (Jan. 24, 1902): 6–9. See also in *Stenographisches Protokoll der Verhandlungen des Zionisten-Congresses in Basel,* Dec. 26–30, (Vienna: 1901) Erez Israel, 179–80. Items 25 and 42 in *MBB.*

† Martin Buber, "Lesser Ury," *Ost und West* 1, no. 2 (Feb. 1901): cols. 114–28, with the permission of the publisher. Item 22 in *MBB.*

‡ Martin Buber, "Lesser Ury," *Die Welt* 5, no. 14 (Apr. 6, 1901): cols. 7–13. See pts. 1–3, col. 1, below.

§ "Lesser Ury," in *Jüdische Künstler,* ed. Martin Buber (Berlin: Jüdische Verlag, 1903). See pt. 1, pt. 2, col. 2, below.

Lesser Ury

By Martin Buber

[Text in *Die Welt*.]

[*Text in Jüdische Künstler.*]

1

The strongest testimony to life is productivity, and the most direct form of productivity is art. That is why those of us who announce a life of the Jewish people inquire into the possibility of Jewish art.

Is Jewish art possible today?

To this we only have one answer, a clear and harsh one —no.

National art needs soil from which to develop and a heaven toward which to flow. Today's Jews have neither. We are the slaves of many earths and our thoughts fly upward to different heavens. In the deepest recesses of our soul we do not have a heaven or an earth. We do not have a national land that harbors our hopes and might provide steadiness for our feet, and we do not have a national sun that blesses our seedlings and brightens our days.

National art needs a unified human community from which to stem and for which to exist.

1

Lesser Ury is the most unusual colorist in contemporary art. He belongs to the Promethean natures who look for a new comprehensive language because they find the old one flat and insufficient. He finds it [the new language] in color. Form does not say anything about reciprocal relations, the reciprocity of things. But this is the essential. The thing is nothing in itself, but everything in the universe. The thing is effect, not substance. Close it off and you kill it. The most personal rests in the relationship to the other. Connect a being to all beings, and you tease out its most essential. Place an *individual* into the world, the walls fall, the rigidity dissolves, the soul awakens, the great plan is reborn. The artist uses color for this purpose. Form separates, color unites. Only color can tell about air and sun, fog and shadows: it puts the thing in

But we only have pieces of a community, and only gradually is there movement in the arts to form one body.

But without these natural preconditions national art cannot arise—this has to be said again and again—it cannot be created. It is not a greenhouse plant, either, but a healthy, juicy plant life in a free, homey atmosphere. No artificial conditions can be created for it; it has to become and to grow together with our rebirth.

The question of external conditions, of *one* earth and *one* community, is not part of these considerations. But to know whether Jewish art *as such* is possible we have to ask the question and try to answer it. It is certain that our people has at no time possessed a true national visual art. Did the historical development awaken and prepare the capacity for art in secret? A deeper scholarly discussion of this question, if it is at all possible, would have to trace the development through the centuries. I would like to follow another simpler path. Let us ask the question this way: Are there Jewish artists today? That is, are there artists who in their being and in their

context; it awakens the underlying harmony.

Ury may not know all of this—he does it. But not in the way that we use a tool and discard it. He is no reflective, superior man. He is an ecstatic. Dionysos lives in him. He is obsessed with color. It becomes God for him, an everpresent God, whom he sees in visions. What he paints is not "a piece of life," but visions, his life in his God.

He does not limit the area of color; he wants to present everything as color. His work is an abstraction of everything that does not have color value. This is the reason for his onesidedness and for his power. Here he goes further than anyone else, here he often goes beyond our senses, and here he creates the intoxicating suggestion of his shades of color.

It has been rightfully said of him that he dedicates himself to portrait art to carry out certain coloristic observations in the appearance of the human being, the naked landscape, in order to be able recklessly to accentuate pure color in its changeable phases, the great image of phantasy in order to develop an artistic language of works express Jewish ethnicity? If we can answer in the affirmative, we can also affirm the inner possibility of Jewish art. Usually two elements are needed for a national artist to evolve: a national lineage and a national environment. The first is temporal, not experiential, but subconsciously inherited, the second, spacial and (to a certain degree consciously) experienced. Because as we have seen, in today's Judaism even under the best of circumstances merely the material and the beginning of a new formation are given, a Jewish artist today would have to take his national being primarily from the qualities that he inherited. But this would prove that in the Jewish tribe the capability to act lives beneath the ashes and today merely requires personalities endowed with creative energy, personalities in which this capacity concentrates, multiplies, and is turned into deeds so that there will be Jewish artists.

Are Jewish artists possible today? In response it suffices to show that there are Jewish artists today. This fact will best be shown in an artist who made his way through the wilderness independent of outer formulas

the most general style from the colors.

For this reason he is least his own self in portrait painting and also technically least perfect. He wants to dissolve the uniqueness and emotional states of the represented being in color nuances. But reality confronts him with too much form and limitation. The individual, apart from his environment, has firm, rigid lines that cannot be dissolved. He does not stand out from his background as color, but as form. Sometimes Ury struggles against this fact by giving colorful life to the background. But this approach can never lead to a real overcoming where the subject must be only the individual as such.

The most significant artistic achievement of Ury's, if not the most personal, is in his landscapes. Here everything is present as reciprocity in nature. Here color is the indisputable sole ruler. Here he can truly communicate the soul of the landscape, which reveals itself in the reciprocal effect of the elements, in the reciprocal shades, musings, clarifications, and deepening. The soul of a tree is the continual transfor-

and rules, who had nothing in common with schools and cliques, and who was guided alone by the law of his own being, who was hard as iron ore vis-à-vis the temptations of external successes and only soft and pliable as wax in the hands of his muse. Only such an artist, who is cradled as safely in his will as a child in his or her mother's womb and who is led by the internal motivation that creates human beings, will be able to teach us that the Jewish spirit, the old image maker, has been reborn to a second youth and will also be represented in visual art.

The following expositions are dedicated to Lesser Ury.

2

The life of this man was like the expression of his being — abrupt, eruptive, restless, filled with struggle and revelation. He, who is today not yet forty, has experienced all of the suffering of the individual, the lonely one, the artist, the Jew, the spiritual proletarian, the dreamer, the visionary. And each pain that took hold of him propelled him upward. And every pain gave even greater

mation of the tree. A moment in which a thousand lifefloods are mixed — that is Ury's landscape. The sun commands, and the enchantment with the sun kindles matter beyond its essence, but at the same time things set each other afire. The sun sets, things return to being just things, but at the same time things exchange their being. Not only light participates in the creation of the coloric values of a thing, but all of nature.

Ury is most personal in his large compositions. Here he achieves mastery [of the material] that is denied him in his portraits. Here, too, he and his idea are confronted by the brutal form of the individual. But he masters it without disregarding it; he integrates it so completely into the impersonal environment that it begins to yield, to dissolve, to fuse. The outline remains, but its meaning disappears. Human beings are not different from all things, they are integrated. What is all tension vis-à-vis the power of the heavens, air, and earth? What is the energy of one being compared to the energy of all being? And even the giant is only one point in which the energies take hold, struggle with power to his eye to see and even more red-hot energy to suffer and even finer strength to create with his hand.

His life developed volcano-like. Again and again, something that had boiled and bubbled for a long time and that he did not understand himself would suddenly burst forth with passion, lash out and tear down everything, and then take hold on shaky ground.

Already, in his youth, he struggled with external constraints. He left his family and the burdensome sales business at age seventeen and went to Düsseldorf to paint. There he soon experienced a great thunderstorm, wild and incomparable; it burst open the gates to his invisible kingdom, to the world of colors that only he could see. Now he experienced the natural light, which was yet to come to Germany from within himself and for himself. He went to Brussels, saw and rendered the soul of the Belgian landscape in the new color tones. The Paris and Munich art centers developed him. Artists met him and learned to appreciate him; the masses were silent and without comprehension. Then, in 1887, he

each other, become active; his activity is a consequence. He remains the giant, and Ury paints him in his full splendor; yet we feel that he is only the point of energy. The problem of the simultaneously absolutely free and absolutely unfree will is here resolved in a purely artistic way.

It is foolish to repeat before Ury's paintings the old objection against "nature." Here, too, the pattern of the three steps applies: to seek nature, to represent nature, to poeticize nature. On the first step we do not yet identify with the source, on the third no longer. This is where Ury stands. The essence of his art is the coloristic poeticization. At Lake Garda we may not see *this* color mood; in front of the picture we experience it with all of the selectivity and concentration that is contained in it. The artist has created an ecstasy from the material that is denied to the material itself; we enjoy only the consequences, not the precondition, in a moment of heightened life. And this is a grace that obliterates all criticism even if it is justified in a narrower context.

came to Berlin. For years the city and the people remained strangers to him. He always had a hard time fitting in with life. Here he worked on himself with a granitelike seriousness, refined his form more strongly and more delicately. He studied the changing images of life everywhere—in the forest, in the street, in cafes. He was criticized for painting cafe scenes. All too many among the public and the critics turned this into a label, which they attached to his name. At first Italy, which he visited repeatedly, did not provide the right material for his eye; he had to create *his* Italy. In 1892, in Holstein, he discovered the lyricism of his landscape, that language of the slender trees that he retained; in the following years, on the island of Rügen and in Hamburg, this tender mood tone developed into a great, soulful landscape style—a shy, young trembling reverberates through his forests, and sometimes a muffled cry of nature knocks and glows in the branches.

But suddenly it seems like a bursting of locks, the plummeting of a flood, the birth of a world, a gigantic creation of the hands of fate. Old dreams take

2

Ury's landscapes are so beyond content, so visionary, that we can only see and feel them, and not discuss them. An analysis of the larger compositions is more likely. I am also choosing them because they are the most controversial of Ury's pictures and also those that speak to the innermost part of our soul. In the life of the forty-year-old they appear only very late: "Jerusalem" in 1896, the triptych "The Human Being" in 1897, "Adam and Eve" in 1898, "Jeremiah" in 1900. After that, "Paradise Lost" and a plate to "Moses" were created. A representation of the biblical topic, "Jacob, blessing his son Benjamin," already created in 1883, was later destroyed.

on form, at first wildly and laboriously, then, with triumphant certainty, the deepest experience takes on monumental form on an extended plane. Ury's great paintings emerge: "Jerusalem" in 1896, the triptychon "The Human Being" in 1897, "Adam and Eve" in 1898, "Jeremiah" in 1899. And only in these paintings do we grasp what Lesser Ury means to us.

3

Ury's first great composition was the treatment of biblical material painted in Brussels in 1883, "Jacob, blessing his son Benjamin, before he sends him to Joseph." Five years later, in Berlin, the artist destroyed this picture in a fit of artistic conscientiousness that often makes him suffer excessively because of a small mistake. He himself stated that the painting showed the influence of Diego Rivera. The way I understand Ury's soul, surely old Jacob's words, "But I have to be as one who has been robbed of his children," provided the foundation for this work.

[From this point forward the texts of the article in *Die Welt* 14 and the essay in *Jüdische Künstler* (1903) are the same.]

But already two years before this [1881 in Brussels], another Jewish historical idea had appeared for the first time in Ury's art—the image of the destruction of Jerusalem. First, he only intended to place a historical moment into a mournful landscape in his own way, not through the theatrical pathos of "heroes" but by means of the deeper and more elegant pathos of a group of nameless people whose simple and artless posture greeted us with the sacred power of a great fate, precisely because it was so simple and natural. There are two sketches from the year 1881 that testify to this first concept of the painting "Jerusalem" as a modernly conceived and scenically tinted history. The first shows the destroyed Temple on the left: a large, freestanding set of stairs, Jewish women and children sitting in silent mourning among the corpses of the defenders, the broken sacrificial vessels, and the torn priestly vestments. On the right we see the ruins of the city, slain warriors among the stones of their homes, and in the background a group of women and children with knapsacks on their backs, their gaze wandering into an unknown future. A similar image is given by a second, later sketch, only more concentrated, condensed, and more eloquent. Again, in the foreground, stairs with a corpse; all the way in the back, a shattered hall with pillars with large, motionless senior citizens who, in death, seem to behold a miracle; in the middle between the bodies is a bare, long bench with some women, some bent over, others staring into the distance. Almost fifteen years later, this bench formed the basis for the work. The inner path from these sketches to this painting is the way from the historical to the monumental. The historical presents a moment in history, whereas the monumental presents an eternity in a moment. History presents the relative aspects of an image, the monumental its infinity. The historical is determined by capability; the monumental is enhanced beyond the immeasurable value of capability by will power that, more than eye and hand, is a unique, one-time, human soul. It is likewise impossible to describe the painting "Jerusalem" adequately in words, just as a reproduction cannot possibly communicate the colors in the original. Ury speaks in colors, and that is a language that cannot be reproduced. One has to see his works; there is no other way to him. When we speak of them, we merely direct [the views to Ury].

The bench in this picture has grown secretly over the years until it has become the foundation of a large picture and the symbol of a world. Now it stands above the ocean before the steep shore. Evening comes, rich in yearning and beauty. The greenishly glowing sky is dotted with small, pale, tenderly red clouds, and licking flames of color play on the waters. But he who gives this painting his full attention sees the tone of the painful puzzle and the vibration of an unquenchable yearning in the sky and in the ocean. That is Ury's tone and motivation.

The long, bare bench stretches with the heavens above and the waters below. Two slender trees reach upward, reminding of slender, shy juvenile arms. A late [afternoon] sun shines through its branches. But these late rays are tired and do not quite reach the bench. It stands there, shrouded in shadows and fog, and one senses, stretching behind it, a joyless land with poor fields and a difficult, dull struggle for life. In front of the bench is a mighty roar between heaven and earth as if from mighty wings; behind it lies the shadowy area like a prison.

On the bench sit human beings—Jews. A short rest on a great journey. A moment between past and future. This moment is in reality no longer than that other one before it or the one after. Visibly, there is nothing that would lift it above the others as [for instance] that time of first sorrow among the ruins of Jerusalem. The people have traveled many long bleak days; now they sit here. Soon they will rise and continue to drag themselves through the dreary sorrow of desperate times and lands. Yet this moment is an eternity, for it reveals the souls in burning self-revelation. It is an evening like many others and Jews among many Jews. But these people are the entire Jewish people, and this evening is its entire history. That is Ury's long, blessed path of struggle from the sketch to the work: he intended to paint the Jewish past, and he found Jewish eternity.

Eternity speaks from these silent human beings, who sit *next* to each other, not *with* each other, each enmeshed in his own fabric of dreams, yet, in the deepest life of his pulse, bound to all else. Eternity speaks from his soul.

[Eternity speaks] from the old man on the right with his skinny, intertwined hands, which are quiet yet completely animated by the struggle of the age-old prayer, the lower lip protruding from his mouth like the defiant sign of one, sure in his faith who, with half-closed eyes, gazes without direction as if toward the Beyond from where the Invisible One listens to him. With his elbows resting on his legs he sits in a heavy, somewhat listless, submissive loyalty. His faith has blinded him to the entire course of his fate; he only knows that God's punitive hand descended on him and his loved ones. He expects everything from this hand, the best and the worst; his hands, the finely crafted, bony ones, only know prayer. He will die believing. He is one of many, but eternity speaks from him.

And [it speaks also] from the one next to him—young, daring, hopeful, through whose noble Semitic head [*Rassenkopf*] flows the fresh strength of the people like a fiery stream, arousing visions, ideas, plans. He knows the abyss of suffering and of danger to its ultimate depths, yet, his free, proud gaze roams over the waters, to far lands, to new beginnings, to new struggles. Here we see freedom, daring, strength, future. His gaze is ready to engage in battle, looking for victory, and his body is as if molten from ore, yet agile like a young palm tree.

Next to him sits a veiled female figure, totally turned toward the ocean, familiar yet secretive. Her left hand is pointing left as if she glimpsed a far-off land in surprise. She is full of despair and full of hope; she is no longer here, but over there, in the land of our yearning. She knows nothing about the development of fulfillment, but she knows its existence. Wonderfully we can see here Ury's simple, powerful way of painting a visionary and his art of turning hands into the bearers of the most secret emotions.

On the ground sits a boy, only partially visible, thin and dreamy. His questioning gaze, resting half in the heavens and half in oblivion, does not yet understand; it tells of a joyless, careworn childhood, a timid helplessness. Here the great suffering is still question, still unconscious burden. The boy lifts up his hands, lightly folded, not intertwined like those of the fanatical old man; he does not know to whom he is praying.

Eternity speaks from all of them.

Farther in front, turned to the right, sits an old woman, a broken matriarch. She broods, dully, almost unconsciously, her head in her hands, with crossed legs, incredibly tired. Her cheeks are sunken, her dull eyes, robbed of their lashes, have no more tears left and know only dull, empty sleep and a dull blank stare—eyes for whom the colors of the world have died. The oppressive exhaustion of the destroyed maternal soul reaches all the way to the rough pleats of her cloak. But her naked, crooked feet display noble lines, and her small fine hand, which protrudes from her wide sleeve, is like a magic mirror in which the foggy image of erstwhile beauty is reflected. The people, on the whole, have Semitic hands [*Rassenhände*] in form and in expression. But this old woman's expresses destiny. The history that is visible from the hand—how it has become so poor and so meaningful—is a testimony to the most silent and greatest tragedy. Ury often puts the unspeakable into the forms of a noble hand.

Eternity . . .

Next to her is a young woman, bowed, wiping her one eye with the hem of her dress. The other eye stares downward with a tough but confused expression. Her wild hair, her distorted facial features show the influence of a terrible life on one who is fit for life [*Lebensfähigen*].

And farther on, an older man covers his face with his hand. He is a pious one, who mourns silently, who knows how to collect his pain and to live it within. He is one who reflects on the pain, and who thinks beyond the pain. Maybe he is one of the line of those strange Jews who have remained almost entirely unknown, with the exception of Spinoza, who step from the ghetto into the cosmos without transitions.

On the left in the foreground a figure crouches on the ground, a furrowed, tormented one around whose neck hangs insanity. Here we see degeneration, but the specific Jewish degeneration that created a sick, half-clever, half-crazy desire for life and a sick mysticism. Here we see the horrible wounds of the eons and the stupor that shook Shabbatai [Zvi]. Here we see the strongest representation of the *galut* type in his peculiar pathology, which is completely filled with crippled possibilities, a horrible inner field of corpses. In the sketches we saw the fatalities of an hour; here we see the destruction of millenia of our people's spiritual powers. He who looks into this face, inspired by the mercilessness of a great artist, understands that next to the Jewish decadence every other decadence looks almost like a harmless game.

Eternity . . .

On the extreme left, completing the scene, sits a dreaming young man. He holds his head in his hands; his gaze is in another world. He does not see anything; his soul is filled with poems of the past. Perhaps even a poem of the present is born. He does not mourn, he does not seek, he does not recognize, he does not despair; he submerges the horrors into his full mood. But in this mood is mourning and cognition, despair and desire of discovery; his mood unites him with the heavens and the waters. This long, narrow riverbank carries a diversity of life, but here, at the quiet water's edge, a song is born, a song that grips and expresses all souls, the song of the new Jerusalem.

Eternity has blessed this dream.

And it has blessed Ury's dream, which, in the struggles of a difficult solitariness, became this work.

In one of its basic relationships, the painting is related to Leonardo's "Last Supper." In both [paintings] several individuals react, each in his manner and revealing his own manner, to something common—in one case to the terrible word of their master ("Verily, verily, I am telling you that one among you will betray me"), in the other to the one common destiny that affects them all. In the speaking Christ Leonardo represents what is coming and will affect the soul; Ury paints fate in the bodies of those sitting and in the surrounding space.

Destiny. The destiny of his people and his own. For he experienced it on his own body and created it from himself in this painting. In his work lives the great necessity of history and the rules of battle of a true artist's life, a complete national soul, and a complete human soul.

4

One year after "Jerusalem," Ury presented his triptychon "The Human Being," whose original concept reached back into the same time period as the Jerusalem sketches, into the youthfully overflowing inspired Brussels days.

Viewed after "Jerusalem," this threefold picture is surprisingly simple. It represents the course of human life in three powerfully experienced, encompassing moments. Three moods, three cross sections, spread them over the course of time and a composite will result. And it does. We see these three moments as a whole, as the fullness of life itself. We do not miss a mediating action or explanation, we do not demand connections; we see continuity, unity, the whole history of a destiny. Here our usual perception of individual images leaves us. In these three pictures we see the human being as such, something superindividual, nameless, and we feel here is life, bow your heads!

In the first picture the youth lies in the spring forest, which is flooded by the light of an early sun, submerged into a thousand colors, and he dreams soft, cloudlike, formless dreams for which there are neither images nor words in the world, only tender, quietly reverberating sounds. This young body is pressed into the young grass; both are permeated with moving and growing, both are carried by one strong wave of life. His dreams fly heavenward on light wings toward the birds, resting with them for a while on thin, suckling branches, then soar way beyond them into the infinite. He follows them with his eyes in surprise.

In the central picture between two columnlike tree trunks stands the man. He braces his right foot defiantly, crosses his strong arms in a fiery show of will power and raises burning, knowing eyes to the heavens. A gigantic hand seems to descend to his head from the heavens, his head having been shaped into hard, solid lines by the struggle. He feels the burden of the gigantic hand and concentrates all of himself in the countermovement. Everything within him is ready for an eternally renewed, silently hopeless struggle.

But time, which gives birth to and devours all being and struggle, continues on its course. In the third picture cowers an old man with dead eyes, exhausted body, with no will power left, in a desolate, impotent state of brooding. His path ends without a goal. The sun sets behind him, the heavens glow as on the first day.

The artist's quietest hours, dreams, struggles, and agony of doubt created this triptychon, whose meaning is the tragedy of the solitary one. This youth who, apart from all community, in the magic of the forest, reflects on his flights of fancy, not on love, not on friendship, is a lonesome one. A lonesome one is this man, who confronts his fate here by the seaside, his gaze and will power lifted heavenward. And this aged one prepares himself for death as a lonesome one turned from all human bonds.

The human being! But actually only—a human being. One who speaks a unique language incomprehensible to all, who lives a separate life shared by no one. One from whom there is no bridge to the world of humanity. One who does not rise beyond himself and who sinks, shattered, into the great tomb of becoming without having received the deep peace of sharing from a creative life bond and without having gleaned a final blessing from the continuation of his movement.

But Ury reaches beyond this song of loneliness. Again, one year later, he produced "Adam and Eve." Here he deals with biblical material in a new, nonbiblical way. These are no longer the two rueful children, who sinned half-willing, naïvely reaching like children and who are now chased from paradise, before they could enjoy it, with an array of flaming swords and words wholly incomprehensible to them. Ury shows these young world conquerors. They wanted to know, with their senses and their souls. It was forbidden to them, but they did not obey because they wanted to live according to the law of their own being and not according to strange laws. They recognized and grew in their knowledge, and when they were banned, they left tall and strong to build their own world. These are no longer silly, romantic children; these are two human beings and much more than that—a pair of human beings. This is how Ury painted the two.

Here the young, fresh, innocent earth reaches to the sea. Evening descends. Adam and Eve stride driven from behind by a storm, the only sign of the angry elements. In surprise the two look at the unfamiliar rocks that their feet touch, at the mysterious, deep-blue sea and the incomprehensible distant horizon. He, self-assured, with proud compressed strength surveying and exploring all possibilities, she, taken aback, but trustingly snuggling up to him and ready to act. Above them, in the shining heavens, is a song of songs of colors; in their shining souls is a song of songs of human energy and human love.

5

It is remarkable that Ury is again and again attracted to Jewish themes. In them he seems to be able to live his personality more easily as if these figures came toward him, as if they demanded to receive from the national artist a new life.

His first great picture resulted from a scarcely intimated biblical scene. In "Jerusalem" he created an eternal expression for the entire tonal scale of the Jewish people. After "The Human Being" he returned to the gifts of the Original Book [*Urbuch*]. He gave us "Jeremiah," and, beyond that, his soul produced "Moses."

But first he painted a small picture of most general content that again showed Jewish types. He called it "Finity" [*Vergänglichkeit*]. We see autumnlike, yellow-reddish evening sky above a hall of ruins from which three columns reach heavenward. In the background is a woman with her child, looking at the sun, in the foreground two men, one of them bent over, hopeless, the other, an ancient man, his hand lifted toward heaven as if he wanted to pull down justice for himself.

Approximately at the same time, "Jeremiah," already conceived at the time "Jerusalem" was completed, is created.

This most mature work of Ury's, which still stands in his studio, known only to a few and understood by even fewer, already in its design signifies an event, a document of artistic development. As it were, the main figure is immersed into the surrounding nature, and for that reason stands out all the more; the separating lines are almost obliterated, but only to allow the psychic border lines of the individual to be appreciated fully. Later on, we will see the way in which a Jewish essence is present in this great conception.

The ruin of style in our time has conditioned us to see an effectively dressed old man when hearing "Jeremiah," who, with pathetic gestures of mourning, sits on stagelike ruins. Now we step before this "Jeremiah," a broad night sky filled with all the awe of eternity above a small, ugly piece of earth. A peculiarly illuminated midnight fills the gigantic picture in all gradations of blue and violet. Above, we see wreaths of countless intensely white stars, somewhere, invisible, the moon, whose flood of light washes over the room and seems to tease a different color out of each bit of air. But below, on this small, naked piece of rock is a brown clump surrounded by a violet hue, at first barely visible. A strange rock formation that grows out of the earth, a pile of this gruff, wild earth? We stare, we grasp it with our eyes—a human being! And now we suddenly see him clearly. A quiet, old man lies on the ground. His purple gown is immersed in shadows, his blackish brown mourning coat tinged by the bluish shading of this unique night—the clothing of a pilgrim and a wanderer, falling in crisp, heavy lines. His head reflects the blue of the universe. His eyes carry an enormous question into the limitless distance. His mouth is tightly shut; we can see his struggle with a superhuman pain. His right hand supports his large head sculpted in large-scale lines. His left hand, however, rests, casual and yet massive—large-boned, lined, gigantic, suffused with soul power up to the gray, tight skin—the hand of a prophet and a revolutionary. And when we have immersed ourselves in this picture with our greatest intensity, it seems to us as if the unmentionably deep blue of the night nestles itself around this wonderful hand, as if the hand creates the blue from its golden power of desire, this kingdom of blue, this kingdom of a thousandfold space-fulfilling yearning. The blue envelops the figure of the prophet brightly like a gown of light; it gets darker and darker toward the top, deeper, unworldly. On the horizon, in a peculiar deep relief, is a hint of distant human habitations.

A critic compared the painting to the poet of Lamentations.* Nothing could be more wrong. The one who lies on the ground is the lone and powerful one for whom prophecy was a burden and an inspiration—painful, draining burden and freest exaltation. He is the strong one whom the Lord fashioned into a strong iron wall against

---

* See "Jewish Art" (sec. 19). [G. S.]

his people; the wanderer who had to leave his house; the knowing one, whose heart pounds in his breast and who finds no rest because in peace times his soul hears the sound of the trumpet and the cry of battle and murder above all else. He is the lost one who lives among others in a barren land and in the light of day beneath a dark sky. He is the honest and upright one, who assaults the rulers with his mission and stands up to their anger. He is the shunted and abused one, who is tortured and incarcerated in jail and thrown into the mud pit, whose speeches are burned and of whom priests and loyal prophets say to the people, he deserves to die. He is the passionate one, who desires revenge against the masses, but whose heart nevertheless beats with the people; the chosen one, whom God trusts, and who says to his master, "Lord, You convinced me, and I allowed you to convinced me. You were too strong for me and you won." [It is he] who, in the pain of his calling, rebels against his master and thinks, "Well, I will no longer think of him and preach his name" and in whom the word, nevertheless, jumps and vibrates like a fiery stream that he cannot resist.

ৡৣ

[The conclusion of the essay in *Die Welt* 14.]

Ury, who says little but whose words are always the result of long, heartwrenching labor that penetrates into the very depths of his being and carries the stamp of an incomparable genuineness, sometimes looks at his "Jeremiah" and whispers, "Those who know me know who lies on the ground here." Those who followed the outline of the prophetic figure as I characterized it understand these words.

[The conclusion of the article in *Jüdische Künstler.*]

From the final period we have "Paradise Lost" and a plate to "Moses." The first is a strange appendage to "Adam and Eve." The same two people sit huddled together. She holds her child in her lap and both look at him or her, she with the eternally unconscious, knowing love of a woman, he with the deep infinite surprise of the first man. The human world begins—all is wonder, and everything is necessity. The color

6

This is how Ury's great works appeared to me.

But he has plans as well— far-reaching, mature plans. One of them, which I only want to hint at here, he shared with me. He wants to paint "Moses."

Michelangelo created Moses as he confronts a dull and indistinguishable mass rebellion. He sees the lowly doings of the masses, he wants to stop it, but he desists. Before him, Hermann Grimm felt "as if he [Moses] has Divine thunder at his disposal, but contains it before he unleashes it," and Conrad Ferdinand Meyer wrote,

"You grasp the beard with a sinewy hand,

But you, Moses, do not jump up."

Ury wants to represent the next moment: a Moses who jumps up to assault the stiffnecked, wayward people—this generation that grew up in slavery, which may hear the words at Sinai but may never see the promised land, destined to die in the wilderness, as Ury says,

problem in the picture is not new, only a complement of the other one.

We can say little about "Moses" today because he is missing the color that is Ury's strength. But the chosen moment is characteristic: Moses confronts the stiffnecked, wayward mass of people, this generation who grew up in slavery and who may hear the words at Sinai but may never see the land of redemption, destined to die in the desert, and he throws the first, most sacred tablets of the Law, written by God Himself, at them, says Ury.

5

We survey these works once more.

Energy surges, a living energy rebels against dark powers of fate and seeks redemption. The individual fights against the world. That is the "content." All things are connected; all things awaken each other, develop each other. Each reveals to the other its self, draws it out. Each lives off the other, in the other. That is the "form."

In reality both are united in

in a voice that vibrates with anger as well as love.

7

In what way is Ury a Jewish artist?

First, in his way of painting, in his colors. I mean here not only his preference for glittering, light-drenched colors — which he does not compose through choice of pigment, which he instead derives from nature as a result of his talented eye — a preference that has been traced to oriental influences. (Franz Servaes once said of Ury's works: "It is again and again the Hallelujah of color which approaches us like a rousing psalm of praise. And we stand, unable to move, overwhelmed, drunk before this biblical power of the coloristic vision — Yahweh lives in these fiery colors!") More than that I mean the reality of extreme colors even in the form in which Ury shows them. These colors do not wish to prevent an outline of things, but their nuances, the way they emerge from the interaction of light and air. The stress is on the delicate reciprocity of beings and ener-

each of Ury's works indissolubly, world struggle and world harmony, revolution and pantheism.

It is not harmonious pantheism, perhaps a cyclopslike pantheism. It is a pantheism of storm, of movement.

We do not understand something intellectual by that, no "idea" — only a basic relationship of life, a revelation of life, presented as pure art.

Lesser Ury is a Jew. He is also truly a Jewish artist. A yearning struggle of boundlessness and the feeling of the boundless world unity; these were at all times the basic powers of the Jewish people. Infinity without rest. A Divine Kingdom that can neither be dissolved by the personality nor by the movement.

Spinoza forced it [the Kingdom of God] into formulaic form too soon. Its embers glowed beneath the surface, touched by his system. Only in our days did there appear forceful but true prophets: Alfred Mombert, Lesser Ury. They have no formula and little clarity. They are first ones. They feel their way. They stammer. But they do not only speak gies, not on their external appearance, but the softening of external boundaries occurs only for the sake of an internal individualization as we saw in "Jeremiah" (if, indeed, we can speak of a softening where we have only a representation of the natural). This way of seeing the world is genuinely Jewish. This one can see if one experiments with Jewish and, let's say, Germanic imagery, or if we compare the descriptions of the Hebrew Bible with those from Greek Antiquity. Everywhere in Judaism perceptions are formed on the basis of spacial, overall relational observations rather than on forms. This does not mean, however, that the possibility of Jewish art is questioned. But I believe that it will develop primarily out of sculpture. Jewish sculptors achieve the finest, most intimate, most Jewish effects with their works as did [Alfred] Nossig [1864–1943] with his mask of King Solomon.

As a Jewish artist Ury is a revolutionary, one who originates movement, transformatory movement. He is such an artist alone because he preceded the general artistic devel-

fragments, they are fragments of this deepest Volk mission, of this cosmic message: not just nature, but *natura naturans* is everywhere, in me, in you, from me to you, from you to me.

opment by creating out of himself a radical impressionism and
then the modern monumental
style in painting. Not only did
he anticipate and prepare the
new, as Jews have always
done, but he is above anything
revolutionary in his way of creating, which is an ongoing
struggle and which knows only
one unforgivable sin—qui-
etude. He says, "To will is to
love, to do is to die," and that is
Jewish. And he is a revolutionary in his paintings in which
living energy again and again
rebels against dull fate and
seeks redemption. The Jewish
tribal spirit marches through
time as such a revolutionary.
The Jewish spirit began human
history with a rebellion, and
even if it branded Jewish history, all of the rich beauty of
human life is based on it. In the
Palestinian period this revolutionary tendency becomes visible in personalities, the most
developed of which is Job, and
in the objections of the prophets against the will of the people. In the Diaspora this poetic
national revolution is narrowed
down and diverted into becoming pathological messianism;
next to it and above it the basic

movement develops into a human surge for redemption. We now live in the transition to a third time period. [Unfortunately], especially the most hopeful one has to be shamefully silent about its revolutionary aspects. But in Ury's work all phases found unconscious, tentative expression.

Ury is a Jewish artist who is the poet of the Jewish soul. Far from everything literary, occupied only with the creation of coloric values, he painted the poetry of Jewish suffering and Jewish yearning. He represented the lyricism of today's new Jew, who is angry with his people because he loves them. I expect more from him in the future. But today let us greet him thankfully as that which he is: Lesser Ury, the master of the sunniest colors of the movement founders, the poet of our anger and our love.

19.

Few evaluations of matters Jewish illuminate the deep misunderstanding of the Jewish spirit by German Christians as clearly as the assessment of Ury's "Jeremiah." Nearly one hundred years ago, Buber argued the lofty nature of Ury's "Jeremiah," very much in contrast to Bendemann's or Rembrandt's renditions and in total opposition to this art critic's perception of Jeremiah as "cursed."

Jewish Art

On Lesser Ury

In the *Berliner Börsenkurier,* dated November 5, B (apparently Professor Dr. Oskar Bie) writes on Lesser Ury's "Jeremiah," at present exhibited for the first time:

"Of the imagination-inspired paintings, the powerful 'Jeremiah' which has been in the works for some time, is exhibited. I do not think I am mistaken when I assume that this work, like his first, the 'Mourning Jews' (here the painting 'Jerusalem' is referred to. Ed. [of *Die Welt*]) will speak to all those who are interested in ethnicity* in art. If we see year in and year out the modest attempts of established artists to develop historical material into great vistas, we feel that we are viewing genius without any banality at all. I hope that Ury will someday become for the Old Testament what [Fritz von] Uhde [1848–1911] has become for the New. As Uhde, the great expert, shed a new light on the social and human matters of Christianity, Ury lives the old sacred flame of the Orient, the hot breath, which washes over the rough earth, the gigantic figures of elemental creatures before the grand background of an immeasurable expanse. His Jeremiah is not the hero of old Düsseldorf, but a piece of the miserable earth. A cancer of the earth, he lies crouched on the ground like a gigantic piece of misery, beaten, bent, crushed, only a dark line [against the horizon]. A terrible image to the person who is up close, who encounters him suddenly, a great old Jewish, deep and heartfelt curse. Above the cursed being the night sky extends, from eternity to eternity in its silence, and from it smile down the bright stars, incomprehensible to the stricken one."†

---

* The term *race* (*Race* or *Rasse*) was used frequently at the turn of the twentieth century, not yet tainted by the negative connotation it has today but comparable to *ethnicity, nationality, peoplehood,* which I prefer to use. [G. S.]

† "Jüdische Kunst: Über Lesser Ury," *Die Welt* 5, no. 46 (Nov. 15, 1901): 10. "On Lesser Ury" (Über Lesser Ury), 190. Item 17 in *MBB.*

20.

This two-part explanation of events at the Fifth Zionist Congress gives Buber's view regarding the friction that had become public during this time. Buber, who was estranged from Herzl from this point to Herzl's death in 1904, was anxious to present his side of the story regarding cultural Zionism, the Congress proceedings, Dr. Max Nordau's relationship to cultural Zionism, and Theodor Herzl's authoritarian approach to Congress matters. Buber was particularly interested in presenting his understanding of the actions of the Democratic Faction, a secessionist group within the Congress.

A Word Regarding the Fifth Congress

> They thought: at the beginning is money.
> No! At the beginning is the idea.
> —from Theodor Herzl's opening address at
> the Fifth Zionist Congress

After returning from Basel, I would like to say a few words of explanation on a matter that is widely misunderstood.* When the Congress decided to interpose the elections of the Actions Comité and the standing committees before a vote on the proposals of the Cultural Committee, about forty delegates decided to leave the room and returned only when the idea that they had proposed was dealt with to their satisfaction. The reasons given for this "Secessio in Montem Sacrum" (we accept this mock expression gladly by adhering to its literal meaning) are so abstruse, the rumors spread so ridiculous, that I found it necessary, at least as far as I am concerned, to break the originally intended silence.

The Fifth Congress was one of the best although the debate, especially on the first day, was not too profound. All negotiations, however, were characterized by a great seriousness and an unflagging willingness to work. And we achieved much. Individual achieve-

---

* The editors of *Jüdische Volksstimme* noted: "We here allow a hardworking colleague to express his measured views without, however, agreeing on all points."

ments were governed by more modern attitudes than at earlier Congresses. Overall, we young ones warmly supported the reforms of the organization, the directive for the bank, the creation of the National Fund, and were pleased with most of the resolutions concerning these matters to whose creation we contributed sincerely. Besides these productive achievements we would like to mention first the very important address by Israel Zangwill [1864–1926] against the men of ICA.* Finally, we have to acknowledge that a modern spirit informed the work of the committees. Notable are the propositions of the Bank Committee, the Colonization Committee, and the Cultural Committee. In these propositions could be seen a positive inner development of the party, a development toward a popular Zionism. We only lament that the committees who were elected by the Congress to prepare some topics and proposals for presentation did not get to word adequately or had to watch as their proposals were only acknowledged by the president and then "turned over to the Actions Comité" after a summary presentation rather than being voted on according to the customary parliamentary procedures. In these cases the Congress seems to have forgotten that these committees exist not for the purpose of "honor" but to ease Congressional responsibilities and to prepare complicated specialized questions for the vote. When there is no vote, the raison d'être of these committees ceases. It is totally ridiculous when the committee with the most members, the Publicity (Agitations) Committee, does not get to speak at all. If it is superfluous, it should be abolished. I was told of one delegate who approached the chairman of a state delegation and intimated that he would not mind [having] a position. Because the satisfaction of such honorable aspirations is not one of the essential purposes of the Zionist Congress, only necessary committees should be elected, but they should then be listened to and their proposals voted on.

Of the three major addresses on the bank by Francis Montefiore [1784–1885], on the question of amelioration by Max Nordau, and

* ICA is the Jewish Colonization Association, a "philanthropic organization established in 1891 by Baron Maurice de Hirsch with the aim of settling Jews in agricultural settlements in North and South America. In Palestine . . . it took over (1899) from Baron Edmond de Rothschild the task of consolidating the settlements he supported." From *Encyclopedia of Israel and Zionism* (1994), 759. [G. S.]

on organization by Theodor Herzl, I found only the last truly enjoyable; it contained overall sound, useful suggestions for reform. My friends and I responded less satisfactorily to Montefiore's speech on the bank. Sir Francis Montefiore not only carries one of the best names, he is also a superb individual, but he understands no more about our Colonial Bank than a well-informed lay person. He is aristocratic and elegant and will always elicit a storm of applause, especially when he mentions the name of his great uncle. But this address was in no way suited to initiate a factual debate on the present and future of a Jewish National Bank, whose viability was proclaimed to the Congress previously. For such a significant moment in the history of the party, a knowledgeable expert should have been chosen. I will not even mention that we were painfully touched to hear of an "Israelite" bank instead of the well-known Jewish National Bank and to be classified as a "fellow religionist" rather than as a member of the tribe; this assimilatory jargon might have been avoided here, even if it is the result of an inadequate knowledge of the German language. Above all, Sir Francis Montefiore told us nothing, nothing at all on the real situation and on the developmental possibilities of the bank. From the official bulletin we already know that it will be fully protected (the only thing that was said), and even without that [we know it] from the absolute confidence that we have in the directorate and the board of directors. This lack of content and objectivity in the address bore bitter fruits: the discussion turned haphazard, uncertain, illusory, and only gradually became solid after some of the explanations that should have been in the speech had been provided by the leadership. Thus, important points could not be appreciated sufficiently while hours of valuable Congressional time were squandered in the back-and-forth of clarification.

As always, [Max] Nordau's speech was an oratorally magnificent achievement. Concerning content, we were disappointed. Instead of addressing the questions of the physical, cultural, and economic elevation of the Jewish people, it only dealt with one of the economic questions—the fact that the Jews do business without capital, that they enter the intellectual professions without money, and the consequences of this fact. Nordau developed this thesis with an admirable logic as if carried by golden chains of thought. But to solve a problem it is not enough to squeeze it into one formula, no matter how brilliant. This could be seen in the practical suggestions that followed and that cannot be seen as adequate. This was confirmed by the speaker himself. It is more significant that Nordau criticized the majority of Jewish students more sharply than they deserved and disproportionately to their difficult situation, full of struggles, which grows worse by the hour. This, apparently, was not intended. Nordau was merely enraptured by his thesis. It seems to me that it is even more significant that Nordau discussed the question of cultural elevation merely from the perspective of his thesis. "Whatever can be said on this subject is empty rhetoric as long as we lack the basis for a thorough, well-rounded national culture, namely money." With these words he condemned everything that had been said on this matter at previous Congresses, all that had been said by lecturers at this Congress on Jewish scholarship, Jewish art, Hebrew language and literature, national culture, and national education. All that was a priori judged and damned. And with what justification? First, it would have to be proven (1) that we do not have any money, (2) that everything is only empty rhetoric as long as we do not have money, and (3) that money is not one prerequisite but *the* prerequisite for a thorough, well-rounded national culture, and, finally (4) that the questions of cultural elevation are identical with national cultural education. I will try to prove the opposite of all these assertions.

First, we have to stress the obvious that a thorough, well-rounded national cultural education cannot be created overnight, but gradually, from many small projects, [that it will] develop gradually from the slow uninterrupted collaboration between many organizations. National culture is a typical example of organic development. It is the responsibility of the Congress to act as the doctor to the organism—to create the unifying, summarizing, energy-saving hygiene, the plan of action.

Do we really not have any money? If I find money in our organization, I know it is not the shekel.* I am not so deluded that I do not know that the shekel barely can sustain our complicated organiza-

---

* Every member of the World Zionist Organization paid one shekel membership annually. [G. S.]

A Word on the Fifth Congress

2

A few days before the Congress, a conference of Zionist academics —
also called "Day of Young Zionists" * — took place in Basel. This conference, barely noticed by the official party press but discussed in the
Hebrew and Yiddish press almost as thoroughly as the Congress itself, is an uplifting and encouraging fact in the development of Zionism. The quality of the lectures equalled that of the Congress, but the
level of discussion was a higher one. The great significance of the
conference was something else, however, the living realization that
Zionism encompasses a large number of opportunities and a re-
spectable number of workers but that both did not engender that
broad and intense activity which alone brings a movement to its goal.
This did not happen because the voice is missing that would assign a
task to each strength and would combine all to one unified, great
production. This lack is all the sadder as the opportunities that people lack are made up of the innermost living conditions of the movement, and the workers who do not have adequate work are the
Zionist intellectuals. Consequently, although we publicized and organized freely during five years of Zionism, nothing substantial, certainly nothing unified and centralized, emerged for the education and
preparation of the people for Palestine. On the other hand, the intellectuals, the persons of the mental initiative, withdrew more and
more because the rug was pulled out from under their ideas, because
there was scarcely a place for them in a movement that had become a
party in such a short time. This latter fact is in glaring opposition to
the development of other modern movements to which the intellectuals flock in ever greater numbers, for here they find the arenas of
power and activity and here they can realize their ideas in a harmo-

---

* Jungzionisten are cultural Zionists. The terms *jungjüdisch* (young Judaic)
junghebräisch (young Hebraic), and *neujüdisch* (new Judaic) are used interchangeably
when discussing the efforts of cultural Zionists. [G. S.]

nious, supportive community. Our work is also in crass opposition to the activity of other nations who are emerging from darkness and subjugation to a national rebirth. For them, the spiritual and ethical regeneration is at the center of all activity, even the most acrimonious agitators pay at least lip service to the cultural treasures of the nation. For us, who want to free the people who are most in need of regeneration, the desire for an increase of numbers in the party has become the driving force. The view that it is the holiest task of the Zionist to bring money and people into the party, rather than to affect the life of the people in all its moments, was preached until it became a negative dogma, hostile to life. We work more for the party than for the people. But no charter will work when the people are not ready to enact it. The kind of unique settlement that we have in mind requires human beings who are strong in body, mind, and morals, human beings who are strong enough to tackle the most difficult and laborious tasks, to resist the most precipitous dangers, to stand up to the least productive disappointments. To turn the people into Zionists is only part of this incredible task to energize the people. The belief in Zion is not motivation enough. What is needed is a freezing of the bound instincts, a revitalization of all functions, a transformation of national life. A revolution, if you will. Those prophets who wished to educate the people in exile for a new Palestine were also revolutionaries; they did not succeed because they were individuals without organized support.

For the indicated inadequacy of contemporary Zionism, the hypertrophy of external propaganda at the expense of real national work, there is only one remedy in the present circumstances—the creation of a study group [*Arbeitsgemeinschaft*] that will in part take on and carry out what has so far been neglected and in part influence the party in this direction. This is the awareness of the Day of Young Zionists [*Jungzionistentag*], and its achievement is to have taken the first steps in the formation of such a study group. From this conference arose a group to which already now belong the best elements of our youth and whose specific program of action will only be determined later this year at Easter. This group, which carries the preliminary and misleading name of Democratic Faction (the cute expression "f(r)action Zionists versus black-tie Zionists" [a play on

words in German: *Fractionisten gegen Frackzionisten*] has already
achieved popularity), counts among its causes the independent cultural activity and the organic-scientific justification of Zionism. I
tried to indicate the significance of the first. Most are probably convinced of the scientific foundations of our ideas. As long as we do not
have these [scientific foundations], there is no backbone and no
steadiness in our work. In our propaganda we present unexplained
concepts, assertions for which we lack the statistics. It is even more
important that our own Zionism is full of gaps and does not allow for
a consistent world-view. Everywhere we lack positives. Other parties were preceded by great theoreticians; Karl Marx's *Kapital* [vol. 1
in 1867] served as the ideational system of a worldwide movement.
We can only show beginnings. Here, too, we have to achieve enormous feats. The preliminary activities need to focus on two main
points—the two sides of our program—people and land, one an of-
fice for Jewish national statistics and the other a scientific expedition
to Palestine.

These points of view and the views of the faction on other issues
(bank, organization, settlement, etc.) were expressed in the committees and in the Senate of the Congress by the representatives. Of
these, cultural work and national statistics belong to the domain of
the Cultural Committee (composed of representatives of all groups
and geographical delegations). The committee decided, based on the
points of view expressed, to present to the Congress a general resolution and some special resolutions. The resolution read, "The Congress considers the cultural amelioration, that is to say, the national
education of the Jewish people, as one of the most important aspects
of the Zionist program and obliges all fellow Zionists to participate
in this endeavor." Special resolutions concerned the underwriting of
the National Library in Jerusalem, the establishment of a paid Commission for Statistics, explorations regarding the establishment of a
Jewish college, the promotion of the newly established "Jewish publishing house" (Berlin), the transformation of the standing cultural
committee into distinct committees.

Naturally, the resolution that the Congress accepted and whose
acceptance sanctions cultural work was most important.

At previous Congresses the debate and partially also the decision regarding cultural work were postponed with a persistence that bordered on the systematic. The reports were always politely listened to, but the feeling was that that was enough. When it came to discussion and evaluation of the proposed items, the Congress suddenly remembered the order of the day. The work on human sources, the education of the people to a power factor (for that is the deepest meaning of national education) had to yield to the "living necessity of the movement," that is, the hubbub of the party. An objective discussion, in which points of view could be clarified and in which the perpetual misunderstanding that cultural activity is opposed to religion could have been cleared up, never happened. Either no decision was taken, or, because of the "advanced hour" (the hour was always advanced), the positive resolutions were adopted in the form in which they were included in the first article, a form that did not obligate the party executive in the least (for what reason would have existed not to accept them in this form?). I must note that some individual proposals were also brought to the vote, but the enactment of these was not much better than that of a resolution.* The reader should refer to the Congressional minutes to confirm the correctness of these assertions.

The cultural issues at the Fifth Congress met the same fate. The "questions of amelioration" were on the calendar for the second day. But already on the previous morning the order was to be changed, only Nordau should speak on the second day; then immediately the agenda would move on to "organization," and the questions of elevation were to be discussed whenever there would be an opportunity. We, on the other hand, demanded that a night session take place after the first day, which would be dedicated to the bank, that the special reports on the elevation issue take place immediately after Nordau's speech and, thus, form its practical completion (Nordau's talk disappointed this latter assumption as it took a definite and a priori oppositional position to most of the special questions). This proposition passed. The discussion should now have followed the re-

---

* An exception is the monies approved by the Congress, of course. [M. B.]

ports.* Instead they moved on to the topic of organization. When this debate was broken off, they moved on to the National Fund. When both were finally concluded, it was Monday, and now the bank questions needed to be concluded. When this was finished, it was Monday evening, the last session of the Congress. We had quietly waited after the presidency declared that the question of amelioration would be settled before the elections. And our expectations seemed to be met; the two representatives of the Cultural Committee, two Factional Zionists, Dr. [Chaim] Weizmann [1874–1952] (Geneva) and I, were given the floor. We read the propositions and provided the necessary explanations. After us, either the first of the respondents to the amelioration question should have been allowed to speak (there were no fewer than sixty) or general speakers. Instead we had to listen to the two Russian rabbis [Reines and Rabinowitch] who were present at the Congress. It is possible that they were the first who responded. Perhaps this was also supposed to provide a degree of parity. We did not know. But when the debate was suddenly stopped and they announced a switch to the elections, we protested, reminded the presidency of its statement, and demanded either a continuation of the debate (proposed by [Ephraim] Lilien [1874–1925]) or a vote on the propositions of the cultural committee (proposed by Buber); at least we demanded the acceptance of the general resolution (proposed by [Leo] Motzkin [1867–1933]). Before us was the ongoing fate of the cultural question, this eternal ignorant postponement and fragmentation, all of this blind hostility and apathy in regard to the development of the national soul, this unending sin against the spirit. The Congress was finally to recognize and acknowledge that the idea was not only in the beginning, but has to be in every moment and above all of our deeds, the determining mistress, the idea of all modern movements, the idea of development. Zion cannot be produced, we have to grow toward Zion—thus cried our hearts. The Congress, as the Zionist Legislature, was to recognize and sanction the work of the people, the work of the soul. We

---

* The course of the Congress taught us that the reports should not be presented orally, but in writing, and that the main emphasis should be placed on the discussion. [M. B.]

demanded that. And because we had waited long enough, we protested against all further delay.

Our protest was denied—partly by the presidency, partly by the Congress. When this had happened, we and our friends left the hall, without prior arrangement, without sign, all moved by the feeling, now we are no longer able to participate in the work of the Congress. From the gallery, we followed the elections, for which propositions had been prepared by the permanent committee and which were adopted nearly unchanged, but with much fanfare.

After the elections, the president made an absolutely supportive and pleasant statement on the cultural propositions, supported them with all of his influence, and our resolution was accepted (without our vote) after the responses of four adversaries. At this moment we returned to the hall.

Now, two possibilities exist: either it was originally not intended to bring the cultural resolutions to a vote or they merely wanted to get the elections completed beforehand. If the former was the case, we had a point; there is no need for discussion. But if the latter was the case, this merely meant—in a session that took place at night, the last night of a long and incredible busy Congress—for the elections we need a relatively "alert" Congress, for the cultural propositions, a tired one is good enough. Otherwise there would be no reason not to complete the latter first. And here, too, no comments are necessary, I have said it all. The cultural propositions dealt with the spiritual fate of the movement. The elections concerned the confirmation of the names agreed upon by the standing committee.

I have only one more thing to say. In an interview with a reporter from the newspaper, *Echo Sionist,* Dr. Max Nordau mentioned that the [Democratic] Faction contains the *galut.* He said that Zionism created unity, the Faction introduced the type of division that is characteristic of the *galut.* I would never have expected that of Dr. Max Nordau, who, at the First Congress, presented that incomparable psychology of the united and unified ghetto. In all the years that I have spent contemplating the essence of our exile, one thing has become all the clearer to me—the outstanding peculiarity was unity at all cost, unity for the price of individuality, a unity for which we sacrificed all young buds, all brave creative powers, a unity hostile to the soul. And it was necessary as protection against the penetration of the enemy, the subversive. But now, in the new land of the spirit, which we have created for ourselves, we no longer need a protective wall at such high cost. May individuals grow, participate, prevail, receive their due, realize their dreams. Yes, we, too, want unity, but only a unity that arises out of a harmony of free, full voices.*

Martin Buber

21.

When Buber and his friends had succeeded in creating the Jüdische Verlag, they feverishly published high-quality illustrated books of a cultural nature, Ephraim Lilien's fabulous Lieder des Ghetto *(1902),* Ost und West *(1901),* Palaestina *(1904), among them.* Jüdische Künstler *contained biographical sketches on six Jewish artists. This introduction addressed mainly the issue of the absence of visual art throughout Jewish history. In 1920 it was reprinted with adjustments under "Kunst und Judentum" as the postscript to the second edition (1920) of a collection of Buber's works under the title* Die Jüdische Bewegung.

Jewish Artists

[In *Jüdische Künstler* only]

It was still possible for Richard Wagner to deny Jews the sensual capability for producing representative artists. The proof of his assertion consisted almost exclusively of a group of insignificant imitators. When we today point to [merely] a few Jewish artists, we are obliged to inquire into the causes of that unproductivity.

[From this point forward the essay is identical in *Jüdische Künstler* (1903) and in the postscript to *Die Jüdische Bewegung* (1916), "Kunst und Judentum," 2d ed. (1920), 245–51].

* *Jüdische Volksstimme* 3, no. 2 (Feb. 15, 1902): 2–3. Item 46 in *MBB*.

We may explain the absence of visual art in ancient Judaism through the ethnic characteristics of the people. We, however, should not forget that these ethnic characteristics are not something final and unchangeable but merely the product of the soil and its climatic conditions, of the economic and social structure of the community, of the life forms and of the historical fate created at the time of the formation and determination of the race, developed over thousands of years, strengthened through heritage, and, finally, matured into an almost unchangeable power. This also explains why the Jew of Antiquity was more of an aural person than a visual one and more a temporal than a spacial person. Of all of his senses, his hearing contributed the most to the formation of his world-view. The strongest descriptions of the ancient writings are of an acoustical nature.* Music [sound] is an adequate form of expression. The Jew of Antiquity could create only on the basis of the rhythm of original art. He was incapable of experiencing an even development of the [national] organism and therewith of a complete world-view. Of course, his soul was not yet developed to the point where he could turn suffering into virtue—to be able to see the world as time, as happening, as flowing, as movement, even as soul. He was, therefore, satisfied with a world that was more time than space and with a world-view that contained more impressions of experiences than actual experiences. His space was impoverished, nearly two-dimensional. In the literature, our only document, we find little physical representation. The descriptions, if they appeal to the eye at all, encompass movement and size, almost nowhere is there color and form.† The epithets, Homer's basic relationship to nature, are missing. We learn about differently named substances, which extend to a greater or lesser degree and which move more or less quickly, but we do not see them. Visual life, the raiment of attributes that truly makes the world into nature, is missing. What exists we might call mathematical vision. And what is, per chance, communicated as form is poor spacial drawing; and the sparse colors appear in a bright, jarring peculiarity.

* For example, Isaiah 5:26–30; 16:6–12; 24; 30:27–33. [M. B.]
† Compare Job 41. [M. B.]

All of this is situated beneath a sun that moves things into the distance, dissolves the shape, and does not grant a harmonizing nuancing of colors. This sun gives vision but not sight. At no time is there a faithful bow to a subject, never the dedicated absorption into the dark growth of a being, never the nameless capture of a unique and incomparable single item.* Everything is relationship; the substances do not become visible, only the relationship; nothing is seen as such, everything is seen only in relation. The Jew of Antiquity does not see graphic absolutes in the individuals, as does the contemporary Indian, nor closed figures like the Greek; his work is a world of relations. From here paths lead to his talents for mathematics and music and to his utilitarianism and intellectualism; he who sees everything visual as relation will live his life as a chain of I-relations as easily as a chain of utilitarian purposes. On the other hand, he will sever the activity of his mind in its search for the absolute from everything visual. Precisely this is the reason for the inability of the antique Jew to create visual art. Where there is no representation and no commitment to what exists, a purely subjective art form develops, an art form of the nonvisual emotional expression—lyricism. Of all the objective arts only that can develop which does not originate in nature—architecture, and even it could not reach its peak among the Jews because even architecture can achieve this only within the framework of basic forms.

And something else. The Jew of Antiquity seems to have been endowed with an inheritance from the desert nomad whose existence consists of a sequence of exaltation and deflation. It appears that this inheritance gave the Jew's emotional life its precipitous, eruptive character. He was incapable of giving form to an emotion that overcame him. Horror and bliss convulsed in him, burdened his chest, choked him. He had to scream them into the world. He had to unload that which affected him. And in this scream, in this unloading, was the greatness of a passionately wracked human soul, without harmony but full of inner energies. This is how the Jewish pathos, the Jewish art of pathos, was born. The ingenius Jew of Antiquity

* The comparison of the Song of Songs is a characteristic example for this. [M. B.]

had to become a prophet or die from the fullness of his passion. He was not capable of producing an image: his feelings were too wild and the distance too great. Just as there was no bridge from the senses, so also there was no bridge from his innermost soul to representative art.

The Jew of the Diaspora is touched by a new personality not so much in the ghetto as in the wanderings to which he is subjected again and again. He takes in impressions that seem to dissipate on the threshold of consciousness and yet exert the most lasting effect for generations. In his life, which has been shaken in its foundations and which is ruled by the most silent despair, ever so slowly and gradually new shoots arise, a subterranean work of eons. Without his noticing it, a vision awakens within him, and his senses become ever more conscious of the space that he traverses breathlessly. But the budding inclinations cannot unfold. He cannot learn to relax because his suffering and his insecurity are too strong and too old. His forcibly exclusive occupation with money does not allow him to make the transition from a life in relation to a life of objects; money, the symbol of the most unfruitful relations, suppresses all urge of young desire. In connection with this narrowness and misery in life his sense of being separates more and more from reality, flees farther and farther, ever more distant from the world, into a rigid tradition incapable of development and into a spirituality totally estranged from life. Only now religious Law becomes absolute. The human body is shunned. Beauty is not appreciated. To look is sinful. Art is sinful. And the Law of this concept reaches a power as no law possessed it in any people and at any time. Education of the generations happens exclusively as a tool of the Law. All creative effort is stifled in its beginning.

But the new, nevertheless, grows invisibly and unconsciously, and it breaks through. In Hasidism the subterranean reveals itself. The secretly sprouting powers shoot up. Hasidism is the birth of a new Judaism. Reverence of the world is expressed in the human body; beauty becomes a ray of God; beholding becomes unification with God. The Law is not the purpose of life; the purpose of life is love. It is the goal of humanity to become a law unto itself. Creation continues today; the human being participates in creation. There is no sin that separates us from God. Everything physical that occurs with a pure heart is service to God. Ascetics is confusion. All joy of life is a revelation of Divine love.

The evolution of the new Jew had found its language. The gate to art was open. The emerging Emancipation merely cleared away obstacles by softening the pain, by expanding life, by restricting the money economy and by making it productive, by breaking the rigidity of the tradition, by opening new areas, by making possible appreciation of nature and artistic creativity, and at the same time by awakening the will power to these activities. In this way the relational human being begins the development to a total human being. The quietly emerging energies that found religious activity in the mystical and yet earthly fire of Hasidism, flicker towards the production of contemporary Jewish artists.

This total humanity [*Vollmenschentum*] is merely a new phase, not a dissolution of Jewish ethnicity. According to the nature of popular art, the first art form to develop in our time was music, the art of the aural sense.

[Here is the end of the postscript in *Die Jüdische Bewegung*. What follows is the conclusion from the introduction to *Jüdische Künstler*.]

In the ghetto it had remained alive in synagogal and popular music, and now it adapted easily to the new forms. In Jewish lyricism subjectivity blossoms. Almost all poetic creations of Jews are of a lyrical nature. The modern Jew realizes the explosion of ecstasy, the pathos of excitement as an actor.

Last came visual art, for the new representative sense needed time to mature to representation. When visual art emerged, it, too, became the bearer of national characteristics. Here, too, relativism lived on in new forms. But it is precisely this relativism that may have made it possible for these people, who began to conceive and to create figures without any trace of them in their national consciousness, to contribute new and inspiring elements, especially at the threshold of a period that seems to dissolve substance into relations and to transvalue them into spiritual values.

These artists are a beginning. We are, therefore, better off to show their creations and to point to their characteristics than to theorize about them. That is the intent of the collective work presented here. It points to the representational capabilities in modern Judaism. Once in a while, we will also be able to discern national characteristics in the nature of the artists and in their works. A summary of this subject will have to wait. Our book will have achieved its purpose completely if it contributes to the creation of a consciously Jewish art public that knows and loves its artists.*

Martin Buber

Vienna, June 1903.

22.

Buber did not mince words when he intended to chide his readers. Here he criticizes all those who are Zionists for the wrong reason. As so often, he sees the Jewish people as an unhewn block of marble to be sculpted into shape.

Ways to Zionism

By Martin Buber

There are different types of Zionism and different approaches to Zionism.

The most common approach is the one inspired by anti-Semitism. X does not have a good life here; he is being discriminated against and insulted; life in Europe does not further his desire for comfort and his "human dignity." Now an inner process takes place, the result of which someday will be a full-fledged "Zionism": the good man yearns to leave to a country of his own where no one will dare to discriminate against him and insult him without punishment, where he can flaunt his comfort and his human dignity unhindered, and, because he has heard of the Jewish state, he accepts this proud desig-

---

* Martin Buber, ed., *Jüdische Künstler* (Berlin: Jüdische Verlag, 1903), 7–12; idem, "Kunst and Judentum," in *Die jüdische Bewegung* (Berlin: Jüdische Verlag, 1916, 2d ed., 1920). Item 51 in *MBB*.

nation for his proud dream. This is the way in which a prolectarian of
the so-called intelligentsia yearns to escape from his misery to the ex-
tolled state of the future.

Another approach, less instinctual and less egotistical, but, therefore, not more valuable is that of the detached sympathizer [*ab-
seitsstehenden Mitgefühles*]. Y is quite happy here, but because a
smidgen of solidarity remains in him, which he often cannot understand, he occasionally gets upset that "the poor Jews in the East are
at such a disadvantage." If he is no more than a satisfied bourgeois,
he alleviates this uncomfortable feeling with philanthropy. But if he
belongs to those who do use their brains on occasion, even if they do
not think original thoughts, then his noble reason for becoming a
Zionist is, "We have to help those poor people." Let's remember
those empathetic "socialists" who do not have the least comprehension of the ideology to which they pledge allegiance.

Considerably more honorable is the view that Zionism is real because the people suffer and, therefore, must be saved. This simple
synthesis, "the people," is a desirable development. Z, who sub-
scribes to this view, is lifted way beyond the minor worries that serve
as the basis for X's great songs and also beyond the mollusklike
benevolent superiority of Y. He identifies. He perceives himself as a
member of a great organism even if he does not have any sense of its
uniqueness and peculiarity. And he feels that Zionism is the Jewish
people's vital issue. That is a person with whom we do not waste our
breath. But that is all. And I do not even mention that such a Zionist
could very easily be misled to see one of the means — economic amelioration, for example — as an end in itself and be satisfied with a par-
tial solution. But, above all, this point of view is much too narrow
and much too utilitarian. It corresponds to that of those naïve English moralists to whom the greatest happiness of the greatest numbers seems to be the highest ideal.* How pitiful the beautiful word
happiness sounds spoken by one who is toothless! And it resembles
that armchair perspective [which advocates] letting the world run its
course so that as many people as possible are comfortable! If ever
great values of life derived from happiness, it was a happiness mixed

* John Stuart Mill. [G. S.]

with deepest tragedy and unspeakable suffering. And is it possible to strive for such happiness, the happiness of personalities?

Let me express as clearly as possible what I mean. If I had to choose for my people between a comfortable, unproductive happiness, as some of our neighbors knew it in ancient times, and a beautiful death in a final effort at life, I would have to choose the latter. For this final effort would create something Divine, if only for a moment, but the other [would create] something all too human.*

To create! The Zionist who feels the whole sanctity of this word and lives for it, seems to stand on the highest rung. To produce new values, new works, from the depths of our ancient uniqueness, from the unique, incomparable strength of our tribal relations, which for so long were shackled in unproductivity—that is the ideal for the Jewish people. To produce monuments to our character! To allow our individuality to unfold according to a new concept of life! To set before the eyes of eternity a new way, a new form, a new play of possibilities! For new beauty to unfold before those who thirst for beauty, who wait in the dark, allowing a star to rise in the magical night sky of eternity! But first, to struggle, with bloody hands, with a courageous heart, to discover our own nature from which all of these wounds will emerge. To discover one's self! To find one's self! To struggle for one's self!

This approach means to seek our people because we love them and not to recoil from any unpleasantness that we find. To see in our people the material for a statue and not be confused because the material is not marble from Paros or Carrara, but tough, clumsy stone which resists. This approach means to want a life for our people, but not a life that is satisfied with just being life, rather a rich, full, creative, continually productive life.

I have only tried to outline the main approaches. There are still other paths to Zionism, detours. Perhaps the most peculiar among them is the approach of a social scientist who wants to use us to try

* Friedrich Nietzsche, *Human, All Too Human*, trans. Marion Faber (Lincoln: Univ. of Nebraska Press, 1984). [G. S.]

out his ideas. To him, Zionism seems to be the possibility of a giant social experiment. But even these men who come to us, usually without true appreciation for the entire beauty of our national idea and incapable of achieving such appreciation, nevertheless are a creative impetus. They contribute new elements to our discussion; they force us to take a positive position vis-à-vis the great trends of our time.

The other approaches appeal to diverse interests. There is the approach of the Judaic scholar, who wishes a secure place for his scholarship; the approval of the artist, who seeks appreciation and usefulness for his Jewish creativity; the builder, who wishes to help his people build a modern life and simultaneously senses great possibilities of free activity supported by all. There is the approach of the one who vacillates, who has found his environment and holds fast to it, and the approach of the young semi-sceptic, who happily reaches for a familiar world-view. There is the approach of the historiographer, who receives mysterious hints from the past, and the approach of the politician, who peers into Asia's wonderful future. There is the path of the religious person and the beautiful, dreamy path of the romantic, who loves the ancient, soulful traditions and their calm existence differently than does the religious person. There are contemptible, base ways that we do not want to mention. But there is also the grand approach of the hero, who has been born into a world without laurels. There is the inconsiderate approach of the dreamer who wants to live his dream. And there also is the *via dolorosa* [*Schmerzensweg*] of the poet-prophet, overgrown with young roses, enveloped in the singing of the larks, with the glow of a young morning sun shining upon him or her, yet he will die without having beheld his yearning.

◈

Yet the Zionists, who carry within themselves more than Zionism, [more than] the shining Zion, did not follow any of these approaches. They are the ones who did not have to follow a path. They are the Jewish people.

This people is the material [I spoke of] for our sculpture. They do not at all become unpliable because of their Zionism. But they are enveloped in a great white light that resembles that of marble. Our hope goes forth from this light. And from this [hope] our creation goes forth.*

("Jüdisches Jahrbuch")

23.

Because Buber did not dare sign this call for a Day of World Zionism with his own name, one may assume that the idea of such a day was unpopular with the leadership. Buber, always the builder, hoped to engender a feeling of pride in those who would attend and to win new adherents to the cause.

A Day of World Zionism

Miraculous powers are revealed in the joint effort of the masses.

Take ten shock [10 × 60 = 600] of individuals, combine them, give them something to do: more will certainly be achieved than these same individuals could have done individually during the same time, but it is the same *kind* of work [as that of the individual].

Now observe a group united by instinct or enthusiasms. It, too, is only a collection of individuals. Yet they feel completely differently than each member would have felt individually: they move differently than the other group; they achieve completely different things, one could say, from another world, than the others could ever achieve.

Through instinct or through enthusiasm the external effect, the level of tension, and the amount of the ebbing energy may in both cases be the same; soul, meaning, and value will be incredibly different. Instinct is the raw beginning, the confused, vague point of departure of the general development, enthusiasm [is] its zenith and its crown. In the fusion via the instinct the masses sink to the level of their lowliest member. In the fusion through enthusiasm it cannot rise to the noblest level—for this is forbidden to the masses—but it then embodies the most beautiful elevation of a totality; it presents it-

* "Wege zum Zionismus," *Die Welt* 5, no. 51 (Dec. 20, 1901): 5–6. Item 29 in *MBB*.

self in the great purity that only life for and in an idea can bestow. Here one must not think of consciousness; the movements of the masses merely express the dark, overflowing feeling of the masses. But just in this feeling lies the source of the deepest and sweetest secret of our existence.

I do not believe that considerations of this nature encouraged some Zionists to bring up and propagate the thought of a Day of World Zionism. But similar thoughts might have cropped up in some form in this context, perhaps only as a quietly passing mood, and we may hope that the realization of this plan will prove this mood right. They will, first of all, have thought of the immediate usefulness of such a day for the movement.

A Day of World Zionism! First one envisions the picture of an enormous demonstration, a demonstration so great that its beauty is not at all impaired by the ordinary nature of everyday life. We forget the adversity of time and space, of the meager stubborn powers. In one and the same moment the Zionists of all countries will rise and witness to their truth. In one and the same moment the whole world will resound in Zionist words. If this hour or this sequence of hours could be dedicated in full purity to the power of our soul and its expression, if the deep, subterranean, banished will power of the people would break forth in a great stream with the force of a nature power and shine through the dark, the most beautiful prophecy, then this sequence of hours would no longer be called demonstration, but revelation.

That which is inadequate will never be an event. Where our dreams end, we must be satisfied with the world as is. Even then there is much that is strong and right in the idea of a Day of World Zionism.

The evening before the Fifth Congress was suggested. On this day, or on one close by, all over the world festive meetings will be held. The program is dictated by the day—from the First to the Fifth [Zionist] Congress or, to say it another way, four years of Zionist activity. Some will say, Why not twenty? Why not forty? I agree with them. In fact, it will be impossible on this day not to speak of *two thousand* years of Zionist activity. All the good and productive things that have happened within Judaism in these two thousand years were, in the deepest sense, Zionist, for these things led to life. If we, with careful earnestness, put the efforts of the last few years next to these, then we will be able to ascertain their meaning. I believe that the sanctity of the deed will shine forth even from their inadequacies.

The Day of World Zionism, therefore, will be a day of introspection, of consciousness raising.

That which has been wrought appears in a harmonious picture. We can grasp it and evaluate it. We will not emphasize that which is purely idealistic and programmatic. We hope it will be within every heart, even without words. We will not discuss the idea, but the deed. What has been done until now? This evaluation will be a blessing. We will be able to look back with proud self-consciousness to that which we wrought. The gaps will show where new, more determined, more strictly organized effort needs to occur. When we see the initial efforts, we will become aware of our energies, and we will learn to collect and exercise them for new and greater tasks.

There are two kinds of criticism. Analytical criticism dissects, frays, destroys, dissolves, negates. Never will this result in creative production and the creative fire of a great life. Synthetic criticism sees and evaluates that which exists in its totality, builds that which evolves. Building is the one thing that is needed [*das Eine das noth tut*] to counter the demons of feeble doubt. And the truth does not rest in the fragment but in the whole living thing. Therefore, synthetic criticism is our maxim. The Day of World Zionism will serve this goal.*

[Signed:] Baruch

24. _____

Buber here blames Emancipation and the Jewish woman for the demise of the Jewish community. Juxtaposing the biblical, Talmudic, and ghetto woman with the emancipated Jewish woman, he squarely places responsibility for Jewish degeneration, and even more, regeneration, on Jewish women, a position that will not endear him with feminists.

---

* "Weltzionistentag," *Die Welt* 5, no. 38 (Sept. 20, 1901): 1–2. Item 30 in *MBB*.

The Jewish Woman's Zion

From a lecture by Martin Buber

The Jewish woman's Zion—Do we mean by that the development of the Jewish woman as Jewess and woman some day in the land of our dreams? Shall I describe how the new life in freedom on our own soil, the new kind of coexistence with others in kindness and beauty, the steady blessed working, how all of this and the other riches that Zion will bestow on the Jewish woman will unfold her dormant capabilities to wonderful strength and simultaneously with the new Jewess how the new woman in all of her sunny splendor will arise on the ancient, eternally young soil? For only in a new land that knows nothing of the old forms and formulas, which does not know the dust and chaos of the old world, only there can the new woman come into being as the new human being in general. Shall I speak only of this Zion of the Jewish woman, of this distant fulfillment and completion of her being? For today, I have chosen a narrower, quieter, and more modest task. I wish to speak of the Zion that has to exist before we can begin work on the great future Zion: I mean the Zion of the soul. Zion has to be born in the soul before it can come into existence in visible reality. When all who call themselves Zionists will live their Zionism with their entire being instead of only with words, when all of them will see their lives as a sacred preparation for that which will be new and wonderful and will live life as such a preparation with faithful seriousness and firm inner activity, when such a Zion of the soul will exist, a great, quiet group of mature people who will be ready to act—then, that you can be sure of—the other, the Palestinian Zion will not be long in coming. For where there is true dedication, there is also strength. Today I would like to speak about the Zion of the Jewish woman in this sense, that is, of the transformation that must occur in the soul of the Jewish woman so that Zion can become a reality.

First, I would like to ask you to look at the history of the Jewish woman. In the period of Jewish national life all of the inner life rested on the organization of the family. The woman was the—equal—lady of the house, and the biblical description of her was truly regal. She was prophetess and poetess, the inspiration of all that is good and strong, and she bestowed the victory prize. First, she developed that wonderful, patient heroism, an inheritance from the tribe of Judah. She initiated the great national efforts; it is meaningful that the tradition credits the noble women with the liberation from bondage in Egypt.

During the period of building a spiritual homeland after the loss of our home [Eretz Israel], in the time of the development of the Talmud, the esteem of the woman grew even stronger. In the writings of this time, she appeared as the naïve mistress, whose free and unspoiled disposition grasped the essence of matters and resolved them resolutely.

Woman reached her greatest importance in the ghetto period. Here all life concentrated within the family. The free life of the state was replaced by the more narrow but joyous life in the family. Here the woman became the creator of a closed family culture. She took much of the everyday toil from her husband, making it possible for him to pursue his intellectual interests. Amidst the most severe persecutions, she provided him with courage and hope. She raised her children to be courageous and committed Jews. She brought a wonderful, natural freshness to the home, which replaced the lost young green of the homeland. She, at one and the same time, maintained the living connection with mother earth and developed life in its totality.

It is the Jewish woman who, in this period of suffering, encouraged the men to hold fast to their faith. The Spanish women encouraged their husbands to commit joint suicide. We can learn of the situation of German Jewesses from that old novella "Maskir," a memoir by Mr. York-Steiner. Here we learn of a long, long list of Jewish martyrs who died in the great struggle of the European nations against the Jews. One example from this book reads as follows:

"Remember the victims in Bamberg: Mrs. Gutta with her four-day-old child; Mrs. Gnenmelin murdered her son Solomon and three children with her own hands; the young girl Matrona and her sister Rahel, who chose death by fire; Hanna, the heroine of Blois,* whose child was born in the fire.

---

* See Jacob R. Marcus, "The Ritual Murder Accusation at Blois," in *The Jew in the Medieval World 315–1791* (Cincinnati, Ohio: Union of American Hebrew Congre-

৩๛

Now put the figures of the majority of today's Jewish women beside the regal figures of the Temple period, beside the motherly and strong figures of the exile. What you see is degeneration. Degeneration of peoplehood, of the home, of the personality.

This phenomenon has two causes, which seem to be mutually exclusive: the persecution of the Jews and so-called Emancipation.

During the ghetto period the sufferings of the Jew were as incredibly great as his joys were deep and intense. For good as well as bad he was part of a great destiny and that affected his development. Suffering released his strength, his passive heroism, his familial happiness, his goodness and willingness; both together caused him to be loyal, loyal to his contemporaries. This changed gradually. With the advancement of so-called civilization, persecution became increasingly more pedantic and more perfidious. It no longer continually threatened the totality; it intruded into every hour of life, into every activity of life. One thrust of the knife turned into a thousand pricks with needles, the great fate that drew out heroism from the human being and "an abundance of passions, virtues, decisions, renunciations, struggles, victories of all kinds" had become a painfully dragging, tormented, and hurried existence. And when the sufferings diminished, the joys also diminished. The beautiful unity of homelife dissolved; the increased struggle for daily life separated spouses and obstructed the education of children; the seemingly smaller danger acted against the strong defense instinct of the people, against the unifying and the outwardly separating (from the outside) ethnic customs.

This situation of dissolution was greatly furthered by the legal Emancipation of the Jews. Their drive for self-preservation adapted itself to the new life conditions in the same extreme manner as their segregation had previously. Women, who adapted themselves most easily to their environment and adapted its ways, participated in a most lively manner in the evolving fanaticism of assimilation. And be-

gations, 1938), 127–30; and Steven T. Katz, *The Holocaust in Historical Context,* vol. 1 (New York: Oxford Univ. Press, 1994), 356. [G. S.]

cause everyone wanted the latest, the internal development of Judaism was paralyzed, all internal drive was stifled, the family destroyed, general solidarity suspended, [and] autonomous culture destroyed.

In this way we can explain the degeneration of so many Jewish women.* The tight family organization in which the life force of our people rested disintegrated in the face of the new; not only Jewish customs were lost, but the Jewish home, loyalty, and love as well. We tried to subdue the feeling of abandonment, endangered by the lack of inner joy, through loud outward affluence. In this way the woman became more and more alienated from her circle of activities. She, who once was mistress in her own house, now became the servant of her Christian servants. The best in her became stunted. She submitted to a boring, nervous idleness. The beautiful, ancient Jewish charitability became pretentiousness in her. The Jewish woman's royal desire for beauty became distorted into tasteless and unhealthy gaudiness, as if one turned a beautiful national dress into a flashy carnival costume. No longer was the Jewess characterized by a heartfelt, self-sacrificing trust, nor was this trust replaced by a new, strong world-view. The exhausting rituals become obsolete; a few simpler ones, which do not really capture the meaning and do not provide a sense of the sacred, are quickly carried out. Under the influence of this pedantic and empty passivity the Jewish male loses more and more of his high-minded zeal and lives primarily in his work, and the youth, the youth which is our life and our future, in whose hands lies the fate of future generations and perhaps even that of our people, grows up without direction and without concern for the future. Is the Jewish woman not partially responsible?

The Jewess will play a greater part in the renewal of the Jewish

---

* Martin Buber had at best a problematic relationship with his mother, Elise, who left his life before he was three. He met her only once more, and in his own mind he coined the term *Vergegnung* (mismeeting) to characterize their missed relationship. These perceptions strongly affected his relationship with his wife, Paula Winkler, in whom he sought a substitute for the missing nurturer, and colored his view of the Jewish woman as such. See Maurice Friedman, *Martin Buber's Life and Work: The Early Years, 1878–1923* (London: Search Press, 1982), 1878–1923, 5. [G. S.]

people than in Jewish degeneration . . . for [Jewish] national renewal can only originate with the Jewish woman. For a people without a country, for a people in the Diaspora, the home is the moving
force of life. In the galut the Jewish home is the Jewish nation. Salvation will come from our hearth, which has always been the source
of the fire of our life.

How can the woman serve her people? In the first place, with the
same things that the man does: by being active in word and deed in
the dissemination of the national idea, by calling for self help, and by
working untiringly. But she can do much more than the man. When
he works for the idea of national unity, she can renew the living
Volkstum [tradition] through her love and her Jewish soulfulness.

The woman possesses the gift of economic intuition and economic
activity to a much greater degree than the man. She can understand
the causes of Jewish suffering and try to alleviate it, not through
charity but through great national deeds. And she can accomplish
this better than the man because she will give it everything she has.
Through the warmth of her nature and her vigor she can help to once
more unite the dispersing members of our people; her love for her
people can create a new fatherland of the soul.

But to do this she has to educate herself. She has to realize that
she can become a whole and living personality only when she honors
the peculiarity of her people, when she nurtures and develops that
which is intrinsically Jewish.

ぐら

(During the lecture the tasks of the Jewish woman are delineated,
especially the raising of her self-esteem, the living study of Jewish
history and literature and Hebrew, the cultivation of a truly Jewish
sociability. These demands are then summarized.)

Growing up in the *heimisch* [homey] atmosphere, the Jewish
woman will once more turn home and family life into what it once
was—a center of life, a place of recovery, a source of ever-new
strength. Imagine this new house—Jewish art on the walls, Jewish
books on the table, the practices of meaningful Jewish customs.
Then the family will once more collect the quiet strength that easily
overcomes everything threatening. Then the woman will once more

be queen and we will say about her what Solomon said, "Strength and beauty are her raiments, she anticipates the new day happily." She will again inspire and lead her husband to self-help when he, despairing from the daily struggle, returns at the end of the day. She will fight and suffer like the ancient heroines. She will once again create culture and transmit culture.

Above all, she will again be a mother. She will not be ashamed of her child's Semitic features; on the contrary, she will be proud of them not only because they are the characteristics of her tribe. She will also be aware that Jewish characteristics served as an ideal of beauty for the great masters of Holland and Italy.* She will try to develop this type as far as this is possible in a foreign land. In her children she will foster, through careful physical care, through the harmonious unfolding of their strength, the necessary personal courage that the Jew needs so badly. She will stifle neurosis, the central illness of the modern Jew, in the core. Under her guidance, body and soul will develop evenly: the spirit will be happy and courageous, the strong body will be willing and ready to carry out the great commands. Growing up in this way in the modern Jewish environment, raised within Judaism and at the same time introduced to the world by the gentle wisdom of his mother, the Jew of the future will be wholly Jew and wholly human being.

But when, in the final instance, I summarize everything I have said and everything that should still be said to the Jewish woman (and there is still a great deal to say) in one word, I know none other than that which only women can know in all its deep beauty, love — true, living love toward the great fate of your people, strong helpful love for its existence, and for every poor and oppressed individual who lives alongside you in dull, breathless yearning; hopeful, productive love for your people's noble future of which you dream brilliant dreams. Such love alone, practiced in quiet dedication, can once

* I am not sure what Buber refers to here. Neither Michelangelo nor Rembrandt used "Jewish characteristics" for their famous representations. Michelangelo's statue of Moses has horns! Rembrandt supposedly used his own father as the model for his "Jeremiah," not a Semitic image. Rembrandt's "Esther" does not fit "Jewish characteristics" either, at least not in the sense of "Semitic" pioneered by bold artists such as Maurycy Gottlieb. [G. S.]

again return the Jewish woman's noble nature to her; only from such a love of the Jewish woman can the Zion of the souls go forth. And when someday the land of Zion becomes reality, as a result of this inner Zion and its power, then our work over there [in Eretz Israel], our language, our festivals, all of our life over there will owe its existence to the Jewish woman. For it is the man who will find and theoretically develop cultural ideas, but only the woman can realize them, only she can create living, continuous culture. But what does that mean—to create culture, Jewish culture? It means this—just as more and more stretches of the once rich, but now decayed soil will be snatched from death and returned to life, so new areas of the once so productive national soul [*Volksseele*], in ruins for thousands of years, will be snatched from death and returned to life, to the works of life. But only that love which is stronger than death can create such culture of life—the love of the new Jewish woman for her people. For the Zion of the Jewish woman is called love.*

25.

It was Buber's belief that a spiritual center would have to be created in the Diaspora to educate and reeducate Diaspora Jewry. He was convinced that emigration first, then education, was a mistake. "I do not believe that we should load people onto a ship like dead freight, send them across to the land, and then expect the soil to perform a miracle." He, Feiwel, and Weizman proposed a Jewish college, but nothing came of it. The Frankfurt Lehrhaus much later would be the first such educational institution. (The Hochschule für die Wissenschaft des Judentums was not acceptable to Buber for the Zionist purpose).

A Spiritual Center

By Martin Buber, Vienna

A few weeks ago, at the Congress of Russian Zionists in Minsk, Ahad Ha-Am, the deepest thinker of Jewish renewal, once more

---

* "Das Zion der jüdischen Frau," *Die Welt* 5, no. 17 (Apr. 26, 1901): 3–5. Item 32 in *MBB*.

voiced in clear and strong words his demands for a spiritual center for our nation.* "A spiritual center, dedicated to the renaissance of our national spirit [*Volksgeist*], a home in which all rays of our souls' energies can come together." This goal he [Ahad Ha-Am] put side by side with a homeland for the people, not as something intrinsically different and apart but as the other necessary side of the same ideal and of equal value, the liberation of the people.

To be sure, he mused, this goal could be criticized as a misunderstanding of the natural development of a people: this [development] usually occurs from below to above, from the beginnings in its economic growth, its physical strengthening through a long evolution, to the development of the spiritual energies. Such a priori correct objections do not take into account the unique and incomparable nature and situation of the Jewish people. We develop from above to below. We are like that strange *bachur* [young man], the philosopher Salomon Maimon [1753–1800], whom [Immanuel] Kant [1724–1804] honored as his greatest adversary, and who learned the German alphabet only *after* quite a bit of philosophizing in German. The clever ones and those knowledgeable in evolution also might have advised him to first finish learning the alphabet and only then to begin with philosophy! "We have to build at one and the same time from below to above *and* from above to below. This may not be the natural order, but it is necessary."

This paradox will be understood as the most direct truth by everyone who is still rooted in that strangest of kingdoms, the Jewish people, whereas those who are estranged will probably not get it. They continuously bring up the history of other nations because they do not recognize their own. That is why it will be a good idea to transplant the discussion from the realm of theory, where analogical proofs are valued more than intuitive recognition of absolutely incomparable individuality, to that of the will and the effort to affect what is going on.

Of course, we can only talk with those who consider making the national identity [*Volksart*] productive and unfolding the national soul [*Volksseele*] as absolutely desirable. We do not consider those here, who are only filled with "social feeling"—in reality nothing

---

* Even though this essay is numbered 1, there is no 2. [G. S.]

more than a kind of pity—and for whom the Jewish question is primarily an issue of the Jewish people and only in the second and third instance, or perhaps not at all, an issue of Judaism. But even those, for whom the rebirth of the Jewish spirit is something intrinsically valuable, do not wish to attribute the same significance to "cultural work" as to the economic and political work. Their objections are of two kinds. One, for instance, argues, "How can you educate the people spiritually and morally without first having raised their economic level so that they are capable of understanding your teaching?" And the other one [says], "The cultural products that you hope to produce will remain 'piece work' unless they are preceded by a territorial unification and unification of the people so that they are able to develop steadily in a normal fashion."

Here I cannot respond in detail to a third general objection, namely, that it is useless, even impossible, to try to affect the course of evolution.* It [the objection] rests in the final analysis on an all-too-exclusive acceptance and use of a materialistic version of history or on that "historical determination" that is an outgrowth of a one-sided generalization of the scientific method and wants to organize human history causally, whereas we can understand it only teleologically.

If we then return to those two particular objections, it will immediately become clear that they are concerned with two different aspects of our cultural work: the first objection wants to awaken and free the dormant or oppressed energies; the second wants to find activity for the existing energies and to facilitate further development, namely, creative productivity and development, among their own people and their own community. These two sides are deeply connected (the second is merely a kind of continuation of the first), and one serves the other. The first prepares a receptive people for the productive spirits, and the second facilitates a freer and richer production of national culture, which, in turn, influences the education and cultural elevation of the people. There is a most lively exchange between both sides on every item and in every moment (just as between them and other moments of cultural work that will not be dis-

---

* This I will deal with in a work, "Evolution and Revolution in Modern Judaism," planned for 1903. [To my knowledge, no such essay was published. G. S.]

cussed here). Yet it is obvious that the first kind of work will occur among the intellectually most highly developed and creatively most talented minority. This is also the case with the two major objections [to cultural work] mentioned above.

The first of these objections is similar to the one quoted by Ahad Ha-Am, but it does not draw for its evidence on the "normal development of the nations," as he does, but on the "real circumstances." The question is raised, how do you intend to educate the lower class of Jews [*Lumpenproletarier*] because they have neither leisure nor the physical opportunity to avail themselves of education through reading or listening. First, you must provide them with time and leisure, satisfy their basic human needs, and provide them with a regular organization; only then may you consider educating their minds.

As emphatically as this objection reflects the actual circumstances, it lacks all knowledge of their specific nature. The argument may be pretty accurate for the Ruthenian farmer; for the Jew it is completely wrong. If the Jewish shopkeeper or worker would be mentally indifferent, only capable of producing thoughts for a more or less narrow physical sphere, it would be a silly, even cruel undertaking in the face of such deep economic misery to carry out educational experiments. But these shopkeepers and workers are precisely the mentally sharpest of all groups.

The life of the Ruthenian farmer is a powerful economic system. He hardly thinks beyond that which he needs to satisfy his various direct and indirect physical needs. Sometimes he experiences a thoughtful curiosity, almost always directed toward the practical, sometimes a clumsy brooding that is void of all substance. That is all. On the other hand, the life of the Jewish intellectual [*Luftmensch*] is everything but materialistic. A large portion of his time and energy is spent in the pursuit of an intellectual activity that has nothing to do with real life. He thinks a lot, but not about his memories and his desires nor about people and things in his life. He reflects on the convoluted, petrified explanations of passages from a few old books—a few books of whose historical significance, intellectual, moral, artistic values, or actual background he knows nothing. His thinking is beyond all relation to anything real. And he is totally devoted to this empty thinking, this spinning of abstractions. It is not only the many who elevate "learning," that is, the ingenious but totally unrealistic and sterile pondering of specific passages, to their life's work, and let their wives support them, committed businessmen are also filled with this specifically Jewish intellectualism. It fills all of their doing, every word, every gesture, with an abundance of hair-splitting reflection. The farmer, too, is not only an instinctual being. He, too, ponders things before he acts in his slow, clumsy way. But his level of thinking corresponds to the particular purpose and does not exceed it. In every case the Jew thinks more briefly but at the same time more broadly and more diversely. And his practical considerations are interspersed with a thousand reminiscences and intellectual flourishes that scarcely ever affect these [practical considerations]. He thinks for the sake of thinking; the opportunity arises everywhere, and even the most miserable, subjugated human being affords himself this luxury. Nowhere else in the world are there human beings who, at one and the same time, suffer such great anguish and live in such intellectual luxury. The intellectual is the true person of luxury.

This Jewish intellectualism is an immense fact, perhaps the most striking of the great illnesses of the Jewish people. Therefore, it is not a matter of awakening intellectual interests but of *transforming* intellectual interests. There is unending mental activity, but it is distorted, rigid, sick, perverse, unrealistic, unproductive, un-European, inhuman. The great challenge is to influence it, to heal it, to transform it. It is not a question of developing the ability to absorb intellectual nourishment; this capability exists and is in use on a daily basis, but we need to provide different nourishment in such a way that it is acceptable. This is necessary so that the nation becomes mentally well, and it is, therefore, the problem of our life. For only when his desire has been awakened can we provide the stubborn Jew with a human basis for existence, and that is a matter of intellectual education. (I do not speak here of the Jewish industrial workers, who naturally assimilate the modern way of life).

Occasionally, such explanations are contrasted with the future homeland in Eretz Israel and the power of one's own soil where these have been recognized as irrefutable. Recently, I was deeply moved when reading about a *chevrat lomde schas* [group of Talmud students] in one of the settlements, I think it was Rishon l'Zion. Maybe that is a prejudice on my part; surely contemporary settlements and the homeland, as we imagine it, are two incommensurable entities. I am also convinced that the territorial unification, renewed interaction between different elements among our people, the possibility of quiet, steady activity of all energies, perhaps even the climatic conditions of the land under whose influence the Jewish national race originated will exert a great healing influence on the life of the people. Yet I believe that all of this can only develop the nation's own seeds of the new; cultural seeds will develop into cultural monuments. I do not know whether we can assert that this life will also clear up all the sick Jewish mentality, that the Orient will heal this degeneration of oriental characteristics. I do not believe that we should consider loading a people onto ships like dead freight, send them across to the land, and then expect the soil to perform a miracle—the restoration of the sickest of all people to true life. With an undertaking of this nature, characterized by uniqueness and unrepeatability, its failure would mean the death of a great cultural possibility. Rather, we must work on transvaluating the Jewish mentality,* not through theories but through deed, to continuously develop new waves of human beings capable of settlement and simultaneously to design a plan on the basis of which it would be possible for the most developed levels to become the core of the settlements, once "large-scale settlement" begins. The development of human beings is intricately tied to national education; in true cultural activity they appear together. Every reform of the *cheder* [Hebrew school for boys] brings us closer to a strong, mature generation capable of settlement, and every agricultural school acts as a fountain of national youth.

The most important issue of national education is, of course, the education of our youth. To be sure, adults can also be influenced, and

---

* This is what Ahad Ha-Am suggested as well. See "The Transvaluation of Values" (1898) and "Slavery in Freedom" (1891) in *Selected Essays by Ahad Ha-Am*, ed. and trans. Leon Simon (Philadelphia: Jewish Publication Society of America, 1912). [G. S.]

once the organization of this segment of cultural work has begun,* we will have quite a bit to say about this. But it is obvious that complete transformation works best with young and open minds not yet set on a direction, and even here only gradually from generation to generation. This work, however, is always dependent on influencing the adults: a thoroughgoing reform of the *cheder* (in the modern national sense) is pointless if the parents are not enlightened about its necessity and are not admonished to send their children to the new schools, and if the home destroys what the school has wrought, nothing much will be achieved. That may be a dilemma, but one that can and must be solved through intensive activity. To facilitate and organize this intensive activity a centralization of national education [and] the creation of a great national educational institution will be necessary. This issue is not yet ready for discussion—particularly in light of the peculiar circumstances especially of the Russian Jews—and can today only be presented as an idea. Until we reach the next stage we can only appeal to those who work for national education, wherever they are, to work even more intensely than [they have] up to now.

If the cause of a spiritual center cannot yet be furthered through national education, things are much different concerning another aspect of cultural activity that is tied to a form of national education that is already now centralized. I characterized the feature of this work as the effort to encourage the expression and development of existing energies.† Before I discuss this set of issues in greater detail, I would like to comment on the existing objection. The following objection has recently been voiced against me and my friends. "You aspire [to create] a Jewish culture," we were told,‡ "that can only be achieved when there is a Jewish community; beginning a Jewish culture here and now is impossible."

---

* Buber, of course, became famous for his work in adult education at the *Lehrhaus* [educational institute] in Frankfurt in the 1920s and 1930s. [G. S.]

† Here we add the efforts to collect all intellectual and artistic products by Jews that are an expression of Jewish particularity or a sign of the rebirth of creativity in our people, and to make them available to the Jewish public. [M. B.]

‡ Once we were even accused of "trying," "already today, to create cultural values!" As if one could try such a thing! [M. B.]

This objection misunderstands three things: our efforts, the nature of culture, and the entire Jewish history including this movement in its historical significance.

This objection assumes that a Jewish culture does not now exist, that we are attempting to create one. That is totally wrong. Jewish culture exists; it never stopped existing. We must not confuse the existence of culture with a fully developed culture. The Jewish people never had a fully developed culture, not even during statehood [First and Second Temple periods]. But it does not make any sense to contrast culture and the development of Jewish mysticism, for example, and to speak of the nonexistence of culture in the Diaspora. This is especially true where such historical phenomena as the resurrection of the Hebrew language* are concerned. If that is not an expression of Jewish culture, then I really do not know what else to call it. The claim cited is nothing more than an example of the very common tyranny of a concept that modern criticisms of philosophy and philology ought to abolish.

We do not have to bother with definitions. But we must emphasize that every psychological expression of national identity belongs to a people's culture. A folk song, a dance, a wedding custom, a metaphor, a legend, a belief, a long-held prejudice, a menorah, tefillin, a philosophical system, social action, all of that is culture.† In the history of a people only that which is not intrinsically ethnic, but "accidental," is not cultural. All other phenomena have cultural aspects that tie them to the national culture. It may be poor, morbid, one-sided, undeveloped, but it does not stop being culture. This is precisely the case with Jewish culture. It is poor, morbid, one-sided, undeveloped. It can only become rich, healthy, well-rounded, and fully developed in our own land. I am sure of that. Of course, it does not *have* to happen there either. This has been shown by several periods during statehood. We are strengthened in our hope, however, through a strange phenomenon.

---

* See "The Hebrew Language," 1909 (sec. 41). [G. S.]

† We can see this especially in the life of East European Jewry, where the sorrowful, dull struggle of the national soul can be discerned in all expressions of life. [M. B.]

Diaspora history is volcanic. Nowhere is there a steady stream of [creative] productivity. We lack the continuity of personality and of creative productivity. The energies of the nation glow for decades, even centuries beneath the earth, to erupt suddenly in a great person, in a great work. Creative productivity itself is absent, as is its most delightful product, art. But in the late nineteenth century, at first quietly and then more strongly, an inner transformation set in, which I once called "Jewish Renaissance." Invisible energies return continuity to our nation and the creative productivity of the living spirit, and they bestow on us what we never possessed, namely, art. How fruitless the debate whether we have Jewish art! To be sure, it does not exist in the same way as does Dutch art. But these are merely categories, and the great historical miracle is the fact that there are Jewish artists at all, and the other fact, that in their vision, in their design quietly and mysteriously Jewish characteristics appear, some of the original character of the pure nature of our nation that plays around the nerves of their sight and the muscles of their hands.

The continuity of creative productivity has been restored to us. Intellectual and artistic energies grow more strongly and steadily from the soil. The aura of a richly seeded, blessed field emerges—the young year of an ancient people. We amazed and euphoric ones are showered with the blossoms of this unexpected spring. But the ancient arch enemy watches, that murderous pair of the eons—decay, those "layers of lost, mixed up, decayed leaves," that "mulch of aged, uprooted oak trees," of whom our poet says, that it suppresses the seeds that seek to unfold with mighty force, and the deadly frost that lies dormant in the earth. Internal and external retardation—these two reigned for twenty centuries [two thousand years] and strangled all young, tender, timidly growing energies. What had not succumbed to suffering and confinement was strangled by the iron hands of the "Law," which became petrified in the harsh ban that outlawed and destroyed everything bright, joyful, thirsting for beauty, and inspired. But they were all-powerful only during the volcanic periods; only a few individuals had to be subdued, and the mass of physical and mental misery of humanity armed against them. It is different today, and if the national rebirth is not [only] a slogan for us, but a challenge and an issue, then we must fight a holy war against the two enemies [internal and external retardation], then we must fight the daily demise of young national energies, we must see that they are preserved, that they unfold, and that we will retain them so that they can develop for us.

The leaders and representatives of no [other] nation on earth would quietly stand by and watch the loss of intellectual talents and of art, capabilities, opportunities, and people—everywhere and at all times. We continue to vegetate. Everybody else would initiate a [rescue] action, open centers of activity. We are silent and act as if we did not know that strong and richly gifted people "die" in great numbers daily—not from death, but from need, which yokes them so they forget all Divine voices; from the constrictures of life that incarcerate them in the dark, dull ghetto and do not allow them to view the wide, bright, world, through the tradition that damns the free fire of the spirit and the creative sanctity of art in the same way. But those who have surmounted all of this and who have managed to wade through all of this to themselves as well as to their vocation, will they not become estranged from the community that has blasphemed and tortured them, will they not grasp the outstretched hand of Europe with fervor? A priori condemnation is a very poor beginning. And those who stayed loyal, the idealists of self-sacrifice, to whom can they speak? Is not the Jewish bourgeoisie too degenerate to listen, and the Jewish masses too dim[witted] to comprehend? And the few whose ears and hearts are open, is there a bridge that leads to them? Are there centers of intellectual and artistic communication?

Here a plethora of tasks for cultural work opens. If people would only understand what is involved, to remove obstacles from their path, to create work and development in living Jewish art for these young energies, our most precious national possession, these whom we have gained miraculously! Only in this way can the rule of that old sick culture be broken and a new one installed on the throne. Only this way can we hope to step in a new way onto the soil of a new Palestine. We have entered into the period of continuity. Zion, too, can only arise as a result of internal national development.

Soon we will have some additional information regarding the creation of communications centers, perhaps in connection with the activities of our Eastern European undertakings.* The centers of education are more important. These must deal with the artistic and the intellectual energies separately. I would first like to consider the latter.

Recently, a pamphlet was published by the Jüdische Verlag that is entitled "A Jewish College." It was written by my friends Berthold Feiwel [1875–1937] and Chaim Weizmann [1874–1952] and myself. In the next issue of *Ost und West* we will discuss it in detail. Today I would merely like to indicate the connection between the college and this article.

The Jewish college, whose economic and intellectual needs we trace in the above-mentioned pamphlet, is not only conceived as an educational institution but as a center of communication where those Jews who learn and those who teach can meet for the former to grow, for the latter to work. It shall become the first modern center of the Jewish spirit, the first center of the Jewish spirit, the first center of the modern Jewish spirit, the reborn.† [It shall become] the first organic beginning of a spiritual center.‡

26.

When one is aware of the intense dislike between traditional Jews and the Zionists, it is not difficult to see why the Zionists considered themselves apostates. Perhaps they were even called by this name. As in many other instances, Buber here also affirms his equally intense dislike of "the Law" that in his view already had a negative effect in Talmudic times.

---

* I provided some general information in my address on Jewish art at the Fifth Zionist Congress. [M. B.]

† The Jewish College was only realized in 1925 with the foundation of Hebrew University on Mt. Scopus in Jerusalem. [G. S.]

‡ "Ein geistiges Zentrum," *Ost und West* 2, no. 10 (Oct. 1902): cols. 663–72. Item 41 in *MBB*.

Two Dances

Dedicated to a Grecian Woman

[From the poem cycle "Elischa ben Abuja, Called Acher"]

Acher * and his students stand by a young field.
Evening has arrived in silent splendor,
And everyone feels blessed.
One of the disciples takes the courage
To speak to the master: "See, isn't it beautiful here?
Do not earth and air intermingle in a glow?
Does life not flow proudly and richly and in yearning freedom
In every stem, in every bird?
And we, who feel it, are supposed to be ugly?
We should not blossom in passionate beauty?

---

* Elischa ben Abuja was a Talmudic figure. *Acher* stands for apostate. The image of the apostate captured the imagination of turn-of-the-twentieth-century Zionists as it had that of earlier writers of the Haskalah.

The Hebrew word *acher* means other, different.

According to the *Encyclopedia Judaica*, "Elisha ben Avuyah [was an] (early second century C.E.) *tanna,* one of the great sages of his day, but later renounced Judaism. As a result his former associates disassociated themselves from him, with the exception of his pupil, R. Meir. He was also known as Aher ('another person'). He was born before 70 in Jerusalem where his father was a prominent citizen. . . . There are various traditions concerning the reason for Elisha's apostasy, the most ancient probably that of Tosefta Hagigah 2:3 . . . 'Four scholars entered paradise . . . Ben Azzai, Ben Zoma, Aher, and R. Akiva.' This aggadah is associated with the Merkavah and forbidden subjects of study. It is therefore likely that he dabbled in mysticism and was seen as a heretic of sorts, although the Babylonian Talmud declares that 'he found a harlot and solicited her. She said, "Are you not Elisha b. Avuyah?" But when he transgressed the Sabbath by plucking a radish and giving it to her, she said, "He has become another ['aher'] person".' " *Encyclopedia Judaica,* vol. 6, 669.

In *Die Welt* no. 4, 1901, is a serialization of a novel by Ignaz Jezower entitled "Acher," which characterizes a serious and pale boy who stands out from the happy crowd of children. "Grandfather said you are an Acher," they tell him after he has taken refuge in a different room, 21–24. [G. S.]

The nation who sees all this is not supposed to exist?
You, you only tell us about them,
Homer, the great, and the artist Phidias,
And of that nation within which they lived,
See here, look closer, are you sure there is nothing here,
No song, no deed, no dream?
Nothing at all?"
    Elischa is silent; he lowers his head.
Distant, ancient images flood over him.
Then he says quietly: "Yes, I can still see it,
Yes . . . beauty . . . God . . . yes, we are full of miracles.
Now I want to tell you about two dances.

The first one I once saw on a journey.
They were Greeks, a young, wild nation;
They gathered up their rose-covered dresses ready to dance.
In a green meadow joy had overcome
Them, and the brown arms of a young man
Embraced the tender neck of a young maiden.
Then, when the blessed hour passed [midnight],
They were no longer able to contain themselves,
And each one tremblingly dissolved the embrace
And each one took the hands of his girl
And out of the harmony of many joys
Evolved quietly and wondrously a round dance.
And the play of the bodies was so delightful
And the melody of the limbs so peacefully sweet
That it seemed to me: Now mother earth breathes
Freely after a depressing dream and freely feels
The beautiful, birdlike happiness of her children.

The other dance I saw—how long ago!
As a boy, but it seems that it is today:
For young Jews danced it.
It was the festival of Simchat Torah.
It was toward evening, like today.
I lay at the edge of the forest, dreaming of far-off lands,

For, already then I hated the Law
Like ropes on the staves of a cage.
There I see a long procession
Of young men in priestly garb.
They stride slowly, torches in their hands,
And they walk slowly, silently, they pass me.
I see new torches burn again and again
And again and again new sparkling pairs of eyes —
And they walk through the forest to the meadow,
Known as "the place of Elijahu."
I follow them. They form a circle
And lift up all the torches
So that a powerful purple circle lights up.
And they lift up their eyes, and
The sacrificial flame of a hundred young souls
Blazes toward heaven in a strong flame.
Then they dissolve the circle, but already
Ten more unite: the dancing begins.
Not two and two — they dance in a group.
And those who move in one circle,
They are brothers for life and of like mind,
That is clear. For when they meet,
Eye meets eye, and soul meets soul:
They love each other with a great love,
Strong as death and eternal.
And each one adds the fire of his own yearning
To that of his friend; for they yearn
And desire to break down all barriers
And to be in Eternity like God.
In this anticipation they raise
Again and again, at first timidly,
Then wildly and energetically the
Slender and shining pale arms, throw
The torches up into the night sky,
Upright, as if fighting — oh, they do
Not rejoice in the Law — they are
Sons of the storm,

And in the fever of their heart lies
A new word that will someday renew the world."

Acher was silent. The disciples stood quietly.
Until one of them spoke: "Well, master?" . . . "Quiet! The dance
Is dead!" . . . But he said: "No . . . it lives in us . . .
Look into our eyes . . . it lives in our souls . . .
It merely waits—Look!" And Acher saw.*

Martin Buber

27.

A comparison with the death of Jesus comes to mind.

The Flame

[From the poem cycle "Acher"]

And when the great apostate [Acher] was buried,
The silent women cloaked in white appeared,
And all they wanted was to see the spot.
For, they hoped to remember

Acher's picture from this last dawn.
Once their gifts had patiently waited
To refresh the dark one on his dark path.
He and God shattered their faith in happiness.

Now they stood, together, quietly:
Then the miracle happened. From the grave arose
A powerful white flame, that grew.

* "Zwei Tänze aus dem Zyklus Elisha ben Abuja, genannt Acher," *Junge Harfen,* Berlin, 1903, 31–33. Item 55 in *MBB*.

And each one was silent, in total bliss.
And as the flame grew larger they sang . . .
Arm in arm that old love song.*

Martin Buber

28. _____

An instance of man taking his fate into his own hand, daring God to forsake him.

The Redemption

[From the poem cycle "Acher"]

And there stepped to the grave from which the flame rose up,
Bathing the blue hue of the moon in white,
Meir, Acher's† friend and student,
A mighty one who wore the crown

Of the pious ones and who was privileged
To gaze into the mystery and to fly
To the other kingdom. He came and said, "enough!"
And he raised his arm with a strangely powerful gesture

---

* "Die Flamme," *Ost und West* 2, no. 8 (June 1902): cols. 369–70. Item 40 in *MBB*.

† For an explanation of "Acher," please see the poem "Two Dances" (sec. 26). According to the *Encyclopedia Judaica*, "R. Meir [Elisha ben Abuja's student] is credited with saving his teacher from punishment in the next world. Finding Elisha's grave burning, R. Meir spread his cloak over it and said: 'If God will not save you, I shall'." *Encyclopedia Judaica*, vol. 6, 669. [G. S.]

Die Welt no. 2, Apr. 22, 1898, carried a lead article entitled, "Elischa," which begins, "And the column of smoke was no longer seen. Rabbi Meir had prostrated himself for days in deepest prayer by the grave of his teacher, Elischa ben Abuja. From then on, a deep sadness could be seen on pious Rabbi Meir's face. With his insistent prayer, he had been able to redeem the sinful soul of his teacher Elischa, who had been shunned by all and who was merely referred to as 'Acher'." [G. S.]

As if he wanted to grasp the flame, lift it,
And take it from good or evil
Demons. And he promised: "If now, in this hour,

He does not free you, I will set you free."
And then God put His hand on Acher's wound.
The flame died down. And Meir saw life.*

Martin Buber

29.

This harsh life philosophy may be seen as an antidote to the veneration many a disciple felt for his spiritual master.

The Disciple

[From the poem cycle "Lord Spirit"]

The gray hand of the storm lay on both of them.
The master's hair glowed black.
The face of the pupil, pale and kind,
Was covered and wrapped in silent sorrow.

The path was rocky. Lightning and mountain fire
Wove a flashing web of branches all around them.
The boy's step was soft and more and more hesitant;
The old man walked upright and firm as always.

The [boy's] blue eyes dreamily looked at his,
And shame shot up into his slim face.
His mouth was pressed together as if he were about to cry,
The great yearning of a child [for protection].

* "Die Erlösung," *Ost und West* 2, no. 8 (Aug. 1902): cols. 541–42. Item 39 in *MBB*.

The master said, "From many years of wandering
I learned the golden power of one truth:
If you can belong to yourself, never belong to another."
And the boy silently went off into the night.*

30.

Again, this poem mocks the thirst for absolute truth that spiritual seekers expect of someone they consider wise.

The Magi

[From the poem cycle "Lord Spirit"]

The group of magicians passed by the Lord,
Who silently sat on the black throne.
From their long, thin hands rose
The scent of the nights and passed by.

One of them said, I have faithfully searched
For the glow in the mountain crevice,
For the hint of the hot circle of ore,
And I found the seed of growth in the mountain shaft.

The other one said, I listened to the blood of
The seed corn and heard it grow and I also grew,
The same pace of the cycle was in both.
I found the power of growth in a seed corn.

Thus they spoke. And the art of riddles
Of others told much about the meaning of obscure symbols.

---

* "Der Jünger," *Jüdischer Almanach* (Berlin: Jüdischer Verlag, 1902), 168. Item 43 in *MBB*.

Without words a crowned man passed by.
The master called to him, Tell us your secret!

He said, and each heart stood still,
"Above all power, the desire had remained
For a human being, whom I could love.
For all power is dead." And he fell silent.*

Martin Buber

31.

The mood of this poem again complains about Jewish apathy. Quiet days are a bad omen. The prince encourages the singer to throw off the protective wreath and to take a chance: better to die with a song than with a whimper.

The Daemon

[From a drama]

The Prince

You look so tired. What goes on inside you?
What makes you lower your eyes?
I know:
The quiet days —
A dead dream —
Sink back into the sea.
Does that make you so sad?
See, I spread out my arms.
In these arms a mute house [of David] sleeps,
[In these arms] sleeps a song about this house,
Which is mute and yet laughs.
Raise up the song and sing it out loud.

* "Der Magier," *Jüdischer Almanach* (Berlin, 1902), 168. Item 44 in *MBB*.

The Singer

The quiet days are a blessing.
The blessing blows everywhere
around my head.

It is not a dead dream [but] a wreath of white blossoms
that protects me.

The Prince

Take the wreath and throw it courageously
Into the light air, into the sun.
Let the white flowers glow as if death approached.
As if death came in a burning hand.
And the flowers glowing in death
Shall sing a song of blood for you,
A song of drunkenness and wild suffering,
And they shall seduce you.

The Singer

What does that mean! I will go quietly,
For the world wants to see through me.
And I have to see many tragedies
And quietly mediate them to the world.
And all things beautiful, approaching me with love,
Have to shatter inside me and die:
I have to sing and say it all.
And all yearning turns to action,
and no yearning turns to deed.

The Prince

Isn't that your greatest strength,
the gold of your crown and your life,

that everything that lives and grows for you
never mistakenly becomes concrete,
that every flash and every urge
creates only voice and song?

The Singer

In the morning I walked though the forest
and thought: soon my Lord will come
and call to me with songs from all the bushes.
In the ivy that winds tenderly and trustfully,
And in the stalk of grain that waves in the wind,
He will awaken for me sounds and chords.
Swallows will fly above my head,
And young deer rub against my knee,
And they will all plead: also sing our song.
I will collect voices that stammer incoherently
and others, which speak clearly,
into a song that rises to the heavens.
Then I walked among the trees. And there lay,
at that sparkling turn near the rose garden,
surrounded by the sunny circle of the shaking bushes,
a bloody twitching thing.
The small body of a bird in the throes of death,
Drenched in life's blood.
And a soul laid itself softly
And with trembling into my hands. And I stood
As one who had been given an invisible empire
And an uncertain bliss.
And my own soul wanted to join
That one
And lie down by it
To die, and wanted to flee with it.
  And within me arose a fervent feeling.
  Then the bird looked at me
  and in its eyes there was a song. And I thought:

Will I be able to sing their song,
The great song?
And a voice laughed. *

Martin Buber

32. _____

Nothing spoke to Buber as strongly and as clearly as the Bible. In "Elijahu" he attempts to clarify for himself 1 Kings 19:11–12. Elijah hides in a cave on Mt. Horeb where God finds him and disapprovingly commands him to " 'Go and stand on the mount before the Lord.' For the Lord was passing by: a great and strong wind came rending mountains and shattering rocks before him, but the Lord was not in the wind; and after the wind there was an earthquake, but the Lord was not in the earthquake; and after the earthquake fire, but the Lord was not in the fire; and after the fire a low murmuring sound."† Here God is speaking to the modern Elijah, Buber, and chastising him for following the wrong lead in his search for self, which, for Buber, is God.

Elijahu

1 Kings 19:11, 12.

You wanted to swoop down like a strong wind
And labor mightily like the warm spring wind.
You wanted to blow being to being
And uplift human souls forcibly.
You wanted to stir up tired hearts
And move the fossil to fluid light.

---

* "Der Daemon," *Jüdischer Almanach* (Berlin, 1902), 162–63. Item 37 in *MBB*.
† *The New English Bible with Apocrypha*, Oxford Study ed., eds. Samuel Sandmel, M. Jack Suggs and Arnold J. Tkacik. (New York: Oxford Univ. Press, 1976).

—You searched for me on your storm wind's path
And did not find me.

You wanted to climb like a fire
And devour what could not withstand you.
You wanted to scorch worlds like the sun
And purify the world in sacred fire.
You wanted to set a young thing on fire with sudden force
Toward the blessed poem of new growth.
—You searched for me in your fiery depths
And did not find me.

Then my messenger found you and put
Your ear to the quiet life of my soil.
There you felt the life in the seed,
And you were enveloped in the aura of growth.
Blood flowed and you were silent,
Eternally full, soft, and motherly.
—Then you had to turn to yourself;
There you found me.*

Martin Buber

33. _____

Buber was forever concerned that life, which is the most important sphere of activity, that is, the most important work of art, was given short shrift in comparison to the intellectual and form-producing spheres, such as art. To him life was the ultimate creative product. Two ingredients are needed to make life into a work of art: rootedness, on one's soil, and form-controlled tragedy—the memory and experience of the Jewish people.

---

* "Eliajahu," *Ost und West* 4, no. 12 (Dec. 1904): cols. 1817–18. Item 58 in *MBB*.

The Productive Ones, the People and the Movement

Some remarks by Martin Buber (Vienna)

The productive ones are not "the intellectuals." The pure intellectuals possess too much logic and too little mystery. They insist on truth, not reality. They do not know that truth is only the process, not the meaning of life. Their path is a straight line. "La Vérité est en marche" [The truth is on the march]. They do not lose sleep over multiple interpretations; they do not dizzily stand at the abyss of 'no'; they do not despair in contradiction; they do not struggle with Elohim until He blesses them; they do not experience the great renewal of the soul. The intellectuals stand up for ideas and act in the service of civilization. The productive ones experience what is unique and — create what is unique.

The productive ones also are not "the artists." The pure artists are much more interested in creating than in becoming. The technical perfection of a creation is no doubt a heart-warmingly beautiful matter, but our time has lost the sense for that which is beyond [from] and does not only provide happiness but redemption — the vocation and the destiny of the one who is called. We also must consider here a broader area of material, for there are productive ones who create their products from the human soul, from peoples and cultures, some from their own being, others from completely separate values and revelations. The artist is limited to media of communication; the productive one can produce things that are completely inward and beyond all language and that affect other people only indirectly.

The productive ones are at the same time the intellectuals and the artists. When they can be compared with the sinews [*Ganglien*] in which the stream of nerves that has been released through impulses multiplies and works, a twofold reaction is effected through this central process: imagination and will power. The productive ones are the strong and diversified ones in whom human activity flows together to grow in spirit and deed.

ᘒᕰ

A people is united through primal elements—the tribe, destiny—as far as destiny rests on the development of the tribe and the culture-creating energy in so far as it arises out of the peculiar nature of the tribe.

A people is not united through secondary elements: useful purpose and religion (such as economic or religious groups).

This has to be stressed again and again: a people is a human community whose basis for existence [*Daseinsgrund*] is beyond all usefulness and before usefulness. The first redemption that the individual may achieve is the liberation from useful purpose. He who comes to the people is freed in this way. He comes from utilitarianism to the original powers, from external to internal life, from sustenance in the moment to sustenance in the alteration of generations. He descends to the mothers. He lives with a dark and powerful sculptor.

And this other one [is] beyond all religion and before all religion. Religion has lost its power to take souls into its arms and to deposit them at the heart of the world. Today it lies to life and violates your boiling senses. He who has lost his God is deeply orphaned. On his new road, the nation can be a first stop. This wonderful line of creation and births in which Judaism unfolds, these broadly intertwined relations can for him become the first solid ground. He is still within a narrow circle; but he already sees that the path leads from believing something to being something.

ᘒᕰ

Good, rich, and simple words should not be wasted. Not the word *movement* either. We should only speak of movement if there is an upward movement of seeds. Energies are inhibited, energies want to become free, want to become fertile: that is how they move; that is how they move the world. The movement of a people is the fertilization of a people. For even when it dies, its strategy is illuminated by a unique great fertility.

In the everyday life of a people its common characteristics—tribe, destiny, culture-creating energy—function in a purely physiological way; they remain below the threshold of consciousness. Only in the movement (or when a people for utilitarian purposes is incited to become a false movement) do they become conscious because the movement requires unity and this comes into being through the coming into consciousness of the common, the becoming and growing of the consciousness of the people.

The individual is at all times enriched and strengthened through peoplehood; through the movement of a people only then when it is truly a movement of the people, that is, when he may participate in the upward movement of thousands and thousands of seed cells and in the overall productivization of his tribe and his kind.

Rootedness and controlled tragedy are two basic powers of creative life.

To be sure, the productive one will receive the solution not from yesterday but from tomorrow, and not from the God of old but from the emerging one. And what used to be will be like clay in his hands. But if all of his will power is only governed by the vegetative spirit, then his works are merely like crystals, not like fruits. Thus he takes root in the depths of his own being and he can spread out not only into the free, changing skies but also into the dark and inflexible everlasting earth.

Today Satan does not lead the productive one onto a high mountain to show him all of the kingdoms of the world and their riches. But he tempts him from Eternity and entices him to lose himself in the infinite and to digress into the vast chaos in which everything humanly clear and finite has ended. But, the domain of the productive one is where form and shaping thrive. Rootedness helps him enormously to remain there.

He who sits on his own piece of land experiences rootedness most blessedly — on the earth from whose elements his tribe and the life of his ancestors, and therewith the origins of his kind, began. This earth may be dry or moist, frozen or parched, overcast or clear, flat or mountainous, poor or rich in plant life, with a rugged or a gentle landscape. For him who is exiled the feeling of an intimate organic connection with past, present, and future peoplehood can create an aura of homeland that is insufficient, like yearning, but also full of fire.

The other basic energy I call controlled tragedy. This, that is, the redemptive affirmation of a struggle, is the essence of all productivity. To the productive one deep despair and alienation become harmony. He does not pass by abysses but he has seen and absorbed everything and dares to desire this miserable world.

How will he, who adds to his own destiny also the destiny of his people and absorbs it, be enriched in tragedy!

To be a Jew is an immeasurably great tragedy. He who passes by Judaism experiences only the coarsest and most obvious that does not belong to the essentially tragic. But he who absorbs it into his life, to live it, expands his own martyrdom by the martyrdom of a hundred generations, he binds the history of his body to the history of countless corpses who once suffered. He expands his struggle and his mystical hope. He becomes the son of eons and their master. He elevates tone, meaning, and value of his existence. He creates new possibilities and forms of life. Magical wells open up before his work, and the elements of the future rest in his hand.

৫৯

The productive ones are the secret kings of the people. They direct the subterranean destiny of the people, the outer fate being only a visible reflection. As I mentioned previously, they can be seen analogically as the sinews by which the life of the people—on the one hand, in speech and meaningful form, on the other hand, in action—affects one's personal destiny. The people is the awkward body that is endowed by the central organ with the opportunity for expression and for choice. Without this the national organism reacts only reflexively to the external stimuli. Where there are no productive ones, or where they are only separated from the organic life of the people, the direct connection is missing between experience and deed, which makes this [deed] the answer to that [experience], and normal integrated cultural activity as well as a great and free fate are impossible.

In the course of a blossoming and self-assured rooted people, this influence of the productive ones may at times fall below the threshold of the people's consciousness, but never with a people whose sails are set for a distant and liberating port. Rather, here the influence has to make itself manifest even more intensely and obviously. For some Slavic peoples their poets are indeed their messiahs and heralds of the words.

Others are only in chains, but we are also gravely ill. The most painful of our illnesses perhaps is the position of the productive ones in the presence of our people. They have distanced themselves from the community from which they came. They speak a completely different language from the masses from which they arose. Their will, too, is quite different. No bridge leads from them to the dark and fertile people. They do not want a bridge either.

Is that the case merely because they would rather be satraps in the spectacular distant lands than the freest princes and loved ones of our yearning and our more beautiful brothers in suffering? Or do they feel with all their soul that they belong to a different community? Or is for them, too, that much praised "melting pot" of peoples the desirable basis for their activity? Or are they merely apathetic towards all of this?

As it may be, their estrangement is not a manifestation of emancipation and assimilation, as some Zionists assert, but the result of the great and horrible 2,000-year-old pathology of our people.

ॐ

But those who desire a bridge, yet do not know how to construct it, have a strong and continuously growing helper in the movement. Once the movement has drawn the attention of the productive ones to the people as a living being full of future, and thus awakened their understanding for the people, it likewise awakens in the people an ever-stronger understanding for the productive ones. The movement frees the energies of the people, it unfolds their abilities, it educates the people; rather, it does not achieve all of this, but rather is precisely that—the fertilization of the people. The movement elicits the soul energies of the people. In the miraculously awakening hands of the movement, the people become more capable of absorbing and of integrating. This is the way the people meet the productive ones.

If we understand the movement as the fertilization of the people, we understand the connection between production and movement in our people's presence. For almost the entire diaspora period these two [production and movement] were repressed and spoiled by the sick, distorted, tyrannical ghetto culture, until those who had been born to production became impotent heretics and the forever resurging flames of the movement became dizzy epidemics. Now, in this renaissance phase of our peoplehood, both have to awaken and to blossom. And they will have to come closer, will have to merge with each other. For, in the final analysis, they are one and the same: the indestructibility of being in the most tragic of all peoples.*

34.

Buber's relationship with Herzl deteriorated after the creation of the Democratic Faction and the Fifth Zionist Congress. As we can discern from this article, written after Herzl's death, Buber considered Herzl to have been a man of paradoxes who did as much harm as he did good.

Theodor Herzl [1860–1904]

(1904)

At the end of 1895 and the beginning of 1896, two books by thirty-five-year-old Theodor Herzl were published in quick succession: *Palais Bourbon* and *The Jews' State,* works that indicate a strange contrast but no contradiction.

Palais Bourbon is a collection of essays on people and issues of Parliamentary France. They were first printed in the *Neue Freie Presse* [Vienna], whose Paris correspondent Herzl was at that time. This origin is scarcely discernible in them. They exhibit a good dose of psychological probing and at times a grandiosizing quality by exclusion of the accidental and presentation of the substantive. This perspective on the substantive is remarkable, a perspective that focuses as enthusiastically and with the same precision on an election cam-

---

* "Die Schaffenden, das Volk und die Bewegung," *Jüdischer Almanach* (Berlin, 1902), 19–24. Item 45 in *MBB.*

paign meeting of thirty farmers in a village as on a parliamentary emergency meeting and which always captures the truly meaningful, the decisive gesture, always creatively superior, always empathetically ironic. For these are ultimately, in a peculiar mixture, Herzl's strengths of which we learn in this book—heartfelt irony and the lyricism of the gesture. His irony, which is almost tender when facing the uneven destinies of individuals, becomes angry accusation against the political machinations as a whole: the Parliament, this sleepy or raging colossus, "full of dark impulses and poor in expression," and then again the Parliamentarians, "[these] masks with coarse features and terrifying immobility"; the great statesman, who "consciously employs only small means," and those hot-headed blabbermouths, the petty statesmen. And the journalist who is obliged to report on their speeches and gestures in awed subjectivity shares his amusement regarding all of them between the lines. It is a fine amusement, full of freedom and synthesis, the amusement of the spirit after the hands have tired of recording all of the superfluous pathos. To be sure, a degree of pathos also is hidden in this irony, but a necessary degree. It is the elevation from the realm of usefulness to a view free from all utilitarianism. But in this view is a positive aesthetic value—the beauty of the gesture. The beautiful gesture is an epiphenomenon, a useless structure which arises from the utilitarian activity. Of course, the gesture has intent, but its beauty is a spontaneous addition that wells from the innermost, often from the most unconscious of the inspired organism. We may distinguish from the gesture the posture, which is at first tension that distorts the line and later, mechanization that smooths out the line. Herzl loved the genuine, truly beautiful gesture more than almost anything else. He devoted to it an intensive, fervent cult in his Paris studies. Once he sat in a social democratic group, listened to the loud phrases of the speaker, and observed the enthusiastic public, filled with pity and irony. Then a worker climbed up on the podium and sang a new song. He stood on the tip of his toes, stretched greatly, seemed to grow beyond human size. He swung his right hand high above his head. This hand was crippled. "The thumb is missing. Some brutal accident at the machines. But he is again working with his poor hand; that is clear. Now it flutters and trembles continuously above

his head as if he wanted to show it to his avenging compatriots."
They have now memorized the refrain; now they all sing along.
"They roar. They passionately lift their hands, but highest of all flutters the mangled hand of the singer. And above the assembled flutters a whiff of revolution."

Herzl wrote *The Jews' State* in the last two months of his stay in
Paris. Here the ironic man is silent, and only rarely does one hear a
hidden lyrical tone as, for instance, when the flag of the proposed
state is described. Otherwise everything is serious and measured,
factually reasoned, and spoken in an obscure, objectivating language.
Yet this book has a strong connection to the other one. This connection is long hidden because of a seeming contradiction. There the
radicalizing ironizing of politics is suggested; here an eminently political undertaking. Yet it is a natural developmental continuum. The
disgust with small-time politics produces a yearning for bit-time politics; the realization of the uselessness of all headline events produces
the will to help prepare a work of world history. But current history
will also become world history—when it has occurred, when meaning develops from the thousandfold meaninglessness. What is missing is the immediate harmony, the flow that gives meaning to the
waves from the start, the pure line. Instead of swimming toward the
ocean with a happy heart and happily flexed muscles, one has to
wade through puddles, unhappily and in disgust. Politics, initiated
by an idea! Politics that would be a harmonius unfolding of this idea!
Politics that would be full of surprises because it would extract from
and use the most profound of participating individuals, yet full of
beautiful harmony because the idea would be taskmaster, all heads,
all hands its tools, all deeds its creation! That was the general impetus to "The Jews' State." The particular came from the feeling of a
[common] Jewish fate.

We have to say already here that this feeling was a narrow one,
born more out of pity and external experience, [a feeling] that did
not mine what sensitive personalities today feel to be the tragic ex-
tent of the Jewish fate. "Those who neglect their Judaism experience only the coarsest and most obvious, which does not belong to
the essential that is tragic. But those who incorporate Judaism into
their lives to live it expand their own martyrdom by a hundred gen-

erations; they bind the history of that body to the history of innumerable bodies who suffered through the ages. This individual becomes the son of the eons and their master." Such [insights] Herzl did not attain in his youth in the most formative time of his life. He witnessed Jewish persecution everywhere, some of it in person. In his youth he was not exposed to Jewish emotional sources, extensive knowledge of a Judaism whose internalized defensive struggle and externalized projected mystical hope were written down in a rich and significant literature, especially not to the full and heroic mood of the new Judaism, which is wholly in the making and a promise. Thus, for him Jewish persecution became the Jewish question and the common enemy became the foundation for Jewish peoplehood. "We are a people—the enemy turns us into one without our will," we read in *The Jews' State*. The realization that the true Jewish question is an internal and individual one, namely, the attitude of each individual Jew to the inherited uniqueness of character that he finds within himself, to his inner Judaism, and that this alone makes a people great, was denied to Herzl. That is the reason why he bypassed one of the most curious cultural problems—the problem of Jewish particularity and its productiveness—in *The Jews' State* and all of his later publications. For him the Jewish question never became a question of Judaism; for him it always remained a question of the Jewish people. This he understood correctly and portrayed masterfully, even if he traced it back much too exclusively to Jewish migration, which will stop when the state, whose plan he outlines in his book, is founded.

In *Palais Bourbon* Herzl spoke of "the Jews who accidentally have to spend their lives in an anti-Semitic period." In *The Jews' State* he looked deeper; he understood the emergence of anti-Semitism from the economic conditions, comprehended their inevitable further development; he no longer saw in Jewish suffering a coincidental phenomenon, but a historically necessary one. And this insight guided his demand for the establishment of a Jewish national sovereignty, a state of Jews—a demand that pre-Herzlian Zionism had already debated frequently. But here it was pronounced. For the first time, in agreement with the practical possibilities, a path to the goal is shown. Thus, only Herzl's book was capable of creating a program from the idea, a party from the movement, and to enthuse the masses. First, the institution of the Zionist Congress emerged, and at the First Congress in Basel, in 1897, Herzl was chosen as the leader of the new party. That was not his intention when he began. "With the publication of this work, I consider my task as completed," he had declared. Now the matter swept him up, lifted him up. And thus began his second life, whose seven years provided documentation of a strange migration of the soul or, rather, revelation of the soul, for now a different and greater individual revealed himself.

Until then, his material had been words, now it became people. He had designed deeds, now he was in a position to carry them out. Now it was no longer a matter of writing soulful feuilletons and clever pieces but to realize an ancient royal dream. An unfortunate people, rich in hope, was approached by him almost the way [a sculptor approaches] marble. And he grew with his material. The journalist became the man of his deed, gifted with that suggestive energy that comes only from vocation. He preserved his irony for communication with opponents, otherwise it submerged in a reflective smile on the basis of which rested his steadfast self-confidence that stood up to all disappointments. His lyrical feeling of the gesture did not dissipate; he appreciated each project, each success not only politically but also aesthetically, according to the mood value that the gesture contained. Sometimes this damaged the cause because he loosely introduced many a project from outside instead of allowing all of them to unfold from a unified plan. He overvalued many an external success, considering it progress in the movement. This behavior was connected with a rigid and, as it were, physiological feeling of self, which gave him the grand yet natural demeanor of a benevolent and somewhat clumsy prince. His pathos (empathy) was strong and deeply emotional; there were moments when it encompassed millions, and it influenced the rhythm of his work, not always favorably. Every pogrom encouraged him to attempt, with the inadequate means of these early years, the immediate realization of that which is thinkable only as a slow and gradual work of national regeneration, developing in spirit and morals, and strengthened in will power and capability. He had a great ability to win people over to his point of view, to dominate people, to control them, to use them. He once said, "If there is one in the center who knows how to give orders, centralization can achieve miracles." He became such a person. And centralization was complete. In spite of all the committees and chairmen, he really had the power of a dictator. Soon he also possessed the soul of a dictator, with wide-ranging decisions and far-ranging mistakes, helpful power and despotic suppression of opinion, but especially with the admirable energy of devotion to action. Fortunately, his obstinacy yielded when a great, impersonal power approached him with a grand gesture. He had designed the economic system of *The Jews' State* according to the "Manchester" system; now he learned the meaning of the commune and glorified the socialist idea. He remained unfamiliar only with the grandiose regeneration of all people powers that had fermented for decades in Eastern Jewry. For him all cultural and artistic production that resulted from this unique rejuvenation of the people remained a means of propaganda but was never seen by him as an independent goal. He made only superficial concessions to the Hebrew language, which in our age brought forth a unique and definitely modern literature. That was the first paradox of Theodor Herzl's seven years: completely a son of the West, he took on the leadership of a movement whose strong roots were altogether in the East.

The second paradox was the contrast between his original spiritual disposition, which deeply detested everything political and only yearned for the conceptual purity of the great deed, and his contemporary activity, which could not always achieve freedom and greatness. To a certain degree, this paradox can be dissolved even if not as completely as the apparent contradiction between *Palais Bourbon* and *The Jews' State*. He had negated parliamentarianism, [but] now he founded a kind of parliament, the Zionist Congress. This Congress gave representation to a people who had so far been in bondage and dependent and through this representation an external and suggestive sign of unity, and [at the same time] a temporary bearer of its liberation. It met only once a year for a few days and embodied, in abbreviated form, the progress of a young movement; thus, he could preserve magnanimity and authenticity. Herzl fought any kind of program even more strongly. From Paris he wrote, "What torture a program is for the free spirits among the professional politicians — and how superfluous all the boundaries of a program for those who are already arrogant." [Yet] now he helped to create a program, the so-called Basel Program, to which he faithfully adhered, with the exception of the 1903 project that, contrary to the program, advocated the settling of Jews in British East Africa. But this program was — at least periodically — the necessary synopsis of the diverse congressional elements, which at times expressed their specific opinion with great rigor. It [this program] limited itself to the weak explanation of the aim — "the creation of a publicly legally [öffentlich-rechtlich] secured home for the Jewish people in Palestine" — and to a brief indication of the means. The worst is that the use of these means was not always great and that we are sometimes reminded of Herzl's words about the great statesman. In some way a poor opportunism is probably part of all politics but here it oftentimes interrupted the clear vision in an especially critical way.

The third paradox, which is insoluble and of decisive meaning, is the fact that Herzl was a statesman without a state, who rather wanted to attend to the matter of creating a state. Under these circumstances he did not aim to first create a strong settlement of Jews in Palestine and then ask the Turks for guarantees for them, but he rather considered the first aim to be the attainment of guarantees for autonomy for the future settlement. Accordingly, he negotiated with princes and governments, but even as the representative of such a large mass of Jewish bourgeoisie and semi-proletarians, without state and financial support and without the foundation of an existing large colony he could not now achieve any results that would clear the way.

In addition one of the postulates for the start of action given by Herzl in *The Jews' State*, one of the most important — the scientific exploration of people and land as basis for a systematic plan of action — was realized only very slowly; only toward the end of 1903 a Commission for the Exploration of Palestine was formed, and the work of Jewish statistics is even today left to the initiative of individuals. Only diplomacy was pushed to the foreground, and the masses lived in eternal tension from one state visit to the next. The best part of

Zionist diplomacy was the tool created for the people, the Jewish Colonial Bank, this memorable bank of the people with its one hundred thousand share holders. But yet another institution of Zionism that must emerge from the willingness of the people to sacrifice—the Jewish National Fund, earmarked for the purchase of national land in Palestine—must be seen as ethically and politically more meaningful.

In spite of all his weaknesses Herzl influenced his entire environment incredibly. There was something captivating about him that was nearly irresistible. Most of all he impressed the masses who had never seen him. The popular imagination wove a loving legend around him, submerged his actions in the shadows of the secretive, embellished his brow with a messianic lustre. Even the East Africa project,* which offended the ideal of the people, could not diminish Herzl's power. Disappointments and successes increased his self-confidence and his certainty of the future. This is how he died. He died, scarcely conscious of all the tragic paradoxes that lived in his soul. His death was illuminated by the noonday rays of his sun. Even his opponents were left with the image of a sunlike, harmoniously united being. No one doubted the purity of his being, the faithfulness of his dedication, the sincerity of his work. He was a poet; fate led him to his people and fashioned him into a hero, but he never stopped being a poet. He was often wrong, but to him his own saying applied, "There are, in the life of a people, unparalleled individuals. Their mistakes and good qualities are the permanent property of the nation that created them. They have to live their personality, damage, contribute, dazzle the people . . . they must spread falsehoods across the land like a fertile Nile flood, for a distant purpose."†

---

* After the Kishinev massacre, the result of a blood-libel accusation before Easter 1903 that claimed several hundred lives and caused much destruction of property, Theodor Herzl, in desperation, suggested that the Sixth Zionist Congress (1903) seriously consider Uganda as a temporary refuge for these poor victims and other Jews in distress. The ensuing storm of emotions nearly brought down the World Zionist Organization. [G. S.]

† "Theodor Herzl," *Freistatt* 6, no. 29, July 23, 1904. Item 61 in *MBB*.

35.

Buber's irreverent attitude toward Herzl even in death was difficult to take for those who had seen Herzl as a secular messiah figure. Yet Buber was far from conciliatory at this time as may be seen from his response to a complaint that resulted from this article (sec. 36).

Herzl and History

By Dr. Martin Buber

For a human being who only speaks when he has something to say [Buber] it is a difficult decision to reveal his innermost thoughts at the graveside of a revered and great man [Theodor Herzl]. The awe of eternity does not allow words to surface, and where the wordless power of death has become known, all human speech seems to be terribly sparse and poor. But when we reflect with all our might on life and the future and make the effort, even in this silent, difficult hour, to voice our opinion, then one feels hallowed and committed by one's very decision to tell the truth and nothing but the truth and the entire truth so that we can comprehend and absorb it with our little bit of common sense and our brain. Let all hymns be silent, and let only the collective wisdom speak. The deceased will not be honored through overly lavish words of praise but solely through the effort to delve into the human personality in its entire tragic nature. *De mortuis nil nisi veritas* [concerning the dead (speak) nothing but the truth].* I have elsewhere† attempted to portray Theodor Herzl's personality in this manner and in this essay would like to say a few words on his significance in the Jewish movement.

In this context it is inevitable to see things historically. The Jewish movement comprises everything consciously Jewish that progresses from dark to light, from imprisonment to freedom, from vegetation to production, and in our time the Zionist party and the national group

---

* I thank my colleague, David Dungan, for the translation of this phrase. [G. S.]

† In the Munich weekly, *Freistatt*, dated July 23, 1904. [M. B.]

of the Jewish workers party, the organized sweatshop workers in Whitechapel and the organized Palestinian settlers, the sighing rhythms of Yiddish literature, and the monumental symbols of Jewish representative art, the thought of Ahad Ha-Am and the deeds of Theodor Herzl. This [Jewish] movement is not a thing of the past nor of individuals but the most original life phenomenon of the Jewish nation, the initially sporadic and confused, and then more and more ordered reactions of an enslaved suffering organism of the people. Its strongest, even central, energy, the yearning for a new national life in Palestine, is the same whether expressed day by day in sometimes dull and sometimes sobbing prayer, whether in the midst of centuries of humiliation in a powerful messianic manifestation, whether after the late entry into European civilization in the first clumsy steps of national politics and in the hesitant attempts of preparatory efforts for people and for land. We can only determine the achievement of one man in the movement—the degree of his success in becoming a messenger of the power that moves the hearts and hands of the new Jews [to action] or, to be a "servant of the light," in his own words—when we have first assigned a place to his predecessors and have appreciated their new and continued contributions to the cause, even if he were elevated to dictator by a large part of the people. It seems to me that we should pose the question in this way: the advancement of the nations, which was marked by the French Revolution, gave the Jews the opportunity not only to strive as individuals to achieve the happiness that other human beings had achieved but also as a national group to achieve the autonomy of other nations. After that—who knew, on the one hand, to renew the ancient idea in the spirit of the newly achieved cultural values and who, on the other, to revive and to activate the consciousness and will power of the Jews. What credit should each one get in the achievement of the generations for the modern form of the Jewish movement?

Let me mention here just three of these men, representatives of three different periods, three different milieus: [Moses] Hess [1812–1875], [Leo] Pinsker [1821–1891], [Nathan] Birnbaum [1864–1937]. Only with considerable limitations may we count Hess as a representative of his age. Apart from periodic and nearly ineffective messages, he is not only the first of those who awakened but also the one who aroused the next generation to whose world belong many of his thoughts and even preceded it. His Hegelian view of history strikes us as alien, his strong, energetic synthesis of the national and social spheres as familiar. His book [*Rome and Jerusalem*] that came out in 1862 is not only confession, not only proclamation, but also and above all prophecy, and in it are contained outlines of ideas that Zionism today has not yet completed. In understanding that the seed of the future rests in the east European masses alone and in seeing the primary task in the regeneration of the hearts, as does Ahad Ha-Am later, in appreciating the significance of Hasidism as a deep manifestation of Jewish peoplehood for the Jewish movement, he anticipates most of the protagonists of the next generation. From the fullness of Jewish historical and Jewish sociological reality that gave him the visionary power of his thinking, he forged the theory of Jewish nationalism. The two basic principles [of this theory] remained the principles of all later programs: the declaration of Jewish nationality, whose rebirth is a part of the great historical movement of modern humanity, and the demands of the restoration of the Jewish state as a foundation for this rebirth.

In a time that was not yet ready for his idea Hess was a solitary figure. He was not blessed with a broad sphere of activity. He could only attract individuals—kindred spirits, sons of the future like himself. Pinsker, who sent his warning, "Autoemancipation!" into the world twenty years after [Hess's] *Rome and Jerusalem,* was already inspired by a rising, if still weak, wave of national consciousness. He, therefore, not so much paved the way as maintained it. Hess revealed the situation of the people, Pinsker described it, putting it into a causal relationship. Hess discovered the soul of the nation, Pinsker analyzed it. Analysis is his basic element. He approaches the problems scalpel in hand. He analyzes Emancipation and shows that it is merely a postulate of legal logic, but never a spontaneous expression of feeling. He analyzes anti-Semitism and proves it to be incurable psychosis. He analyzes above all Jewish degeneration and characterizes in an unforgettable way its severest symptom, anorexia, the lack of a need for national autonomy. The analyst is happily complemented by the political realist; for him the diagnosis never exceeds the premises of the healing deed. He understands the deed to be more positive, more practical, more detailed than Hess: he discusses or at least skims the issues of sovereignty, neutrality, guarantees, land acquisition, national fund (subscription); he now demands a national congress (as did Laharanne previously), which he conceives in a rather undemocratic way. In the choice of his territory he is not as certain as Hess, whose historical sense considered only Palestine; that was because of the terrible pogroms that urged action. But he realizes with noble thoughtfulness that action can only be slow and gradual. "The port that we seek with our soul is far, very far off. . . . But no road must be too long for the thousand-year-old wanderer."

Pinsker was rewarded with seeing the beginning of the deed and partly leading it. Ahad Ha-Am told many a dark and sad tale from this period. But it was a beginning. Even if the founding period of the settlements was not always pure and exemplary, the Biluim* were the first heroes of the new Judaism. Even if many a spirit was half-developed and many a will brittle, a young, liberating storm ran through the hearts. It was a time of misery, it was a time of hope. We held our breath and our soul was feverish. It seemed as if a miracle were about to happen, and quite a few individuals tremblingly felt the call. During this time twenty-year-old Nathan Birnbaum in Vienna began to issue a journal called *Self-emancipation*. Almost ten years later, in 1893, he published a small pamphlet, "The National Rebirth of the Jewish People in Their Land." In those ten years he and the movement had matured, had grown within through work and deliberation. At the same time the movement was also externally strengthened, evolving naturally. The Zionist milieu developed, rough and incomplete, but promising.

It has to be stressed that I can only describe here the Birnbaum of those years, not the later one who was characterized by his since then maintained pseudonym, Mathias Acher. The later Birnbaum grew beyond that one and tried to achieve in Jewish Modernity and in later works what Moses Hess had begun, the synthesis of the national and the social idea in Judaism, and then distanced himself

---

* Bilu stands for Beit Yaakov Lechu v'nelecha (Isaiah 2:5). It was the first organized effort at settlement in Eretz, Israel, in the late nineteenth century. [G. S.]

more and more from political Zionism. Here I am only examining Herzl's predecessor, the author of the pamphlet. What was new in it was first of all a deepening of Jewish nationalism in the direction of cultural issues, then the modern formulation of the postulate of "equality of state and human rights" of the Jewish people. Here the basic national psychological insight was clearly expressed that the Jewish nationality is anchored in the inner particularity of the people; here the possibility of a new Jewish culture in Palestine that was based on Hess's thought was discussed, here the already now existing cultural seeds were credited, especially the renaissance of the Hebrew language. But here also was laid the foundation of national politics supported by the [Jewish] people amid the nations.

Barely three years later Herzl's book, *The Jews' State*, was published. This clever and energetic book, pregnant with expectations, with the convincing matter-of-factness of its explanations, often clarified, even liberated, in a time of gestation and becoming, of conventicles and discussions. When we survey, however, what has been achieved in ideals and programs, we cannot deny that the essential historical meaning of the book lies merely in its exposé of the action. What Hess intimated and Pinsker outlined and Birnbaum detailed was completed in the *Judenstaat;* it provided an outline of the way. The others also correctly recognized the goal and at times determined it with more farsightedness [than did Herzl]. They had described the beginning with a deeper understanding of the national idea, with a deeper probing of the Jewish national identity. For them the human rights postulate was merely a consequence of their nationalism: they demanded the "vast free soil" (Hess), our "own land" (Pinsker), the homeland (Birnbaum) as a precondition for the development of Judaism to new life and new culture. Herzl's premise was merely the dire situation of the Jews that needed to be corrected. The others considered the Jewish question from within, Herzl from without. For them it was a question of the maintenance and regeneration of the singular, incomplete, and irreplaceable values, for Herzl it was "a fossilized piece of the Middle Ages." They saw assimilation as a fateful deviation, Herzl did not see it as "shameful," but on the whole impossible; twice he repeated it in *The Jews' State*, "If they would leave us alone . . . but I think they will not leave us alone." If they would leave us alone . . . if there would be no "emergency situation" of the Jews, would the national ideal still be the flame of our soul and the building of the homeland the task of our life? *The Jew's State* says no, matter-of-factly. The true Jews say, Even more so! for then we could achieve even greater things than now with free minds and stronger arms, aware of the immediate hope of fulfillment. For them the nation is a being sick unto death to which their being is tied with unbreakable, loving bonds, to whose life their life is tied, whose death is their death, a deathly ill being to which we could restore not only its health but with it immortality. Immortality, which would also be their immortality, for in the national home their activity would no longer break off, their labor no longer end in nothing, the stream of their humanity no longer peter out in the desert sand, but the product of their soul would be carried from generation to generation like a never-extinguishing torch in a beautiful torch dance. But for the Herzl of *The Jews' State* we are a people because "the enemy achieves this without our doing." And the same opinion exists concerning all intrinsic values of the nation. "It is impossible for us to speak Hebrew with each other. . . . Even over there we will remain what we are now." Later Herzl moved closer to Judaism in quite a few things, but he retained this basic world-view. Still in *Old New Land* [1902] he describes a Jewish state that does not possess a single institution or cultural treasure in which the national personality of the neo-Hebrews has been formed in its particularity.

Perhaps I should mention here that these differences basically originated in birth and education. Hess was a Western Jew, who, as a descendent of Eastern Jewish rabbis, received the profound impressions that shape the tenor of life in traditional and yet living Judaism that is ultimately more national than religious, the impressions that are the most immediately effective document of Jewish continuity, and when he returned to his people "after a twenty-year period of alienation," he had studied its history with the great free vision that only intrinsic love can engender. Pinsker was an Eastern Jew with a Western education; he grew up amid the Jewish masses surrounded by their misery, surrounded by their sighs, with a dedicated heart. In this way the suffering of his tribe seeped into his blood and nerves; he not only empathized, but it imbued him until it was wholly his suffering, his innermost suffering, which cried from his mortally wounded soul: "Our fatherland, the *galut;* our unity, the dispersion; our solidarity, general hostility; our weapon, humility; our defense, the exodus; our originality, the acculturation; our future, the next day." We cannot a priori apply to Birnbaum the historical perspective that encompasses all of life. About him I would only like to mention the seemingly most fortunate mixture of Eastern and Western Judaism and the strongly instinctive understanding of the working-class psyche, which is the basic problem of the Jewish movement, [that springs] from a life in full national individuality and from our intensive, never interrupted social feeling. Herzl was a Western Jew without Jewish tradition, without Jewish childhood impressions, without Jewish education, without self-earned Jewish childhood knowledge. He grew up in a non-Jewish environment and never interacted with the Jewish masses; no human being was as foreign to him as a working-class Jew. He had remained faithful to passive Judaism not because of Judaism but because of character; he entered active Judaism not because of Judaism but because of a crystallizing manliness. He was a whole man, but he was not a whole Jew. I admired his stature with all my heart during the seven years of Congressional Zionism: his beautiful greatness and superiority, his noble commitment and energy, his straight unbendable loyalty, also in its humanly broad mistakes. As a Jew he always seemed to be half and incomplete. It is fundamentally wrong to celebrate him as a Jewish personality. [Baruch] Spinoza [1632–1677] and Israel Baalshem [1700–1760], [Heinrich] Heine [1797–1856] and [Ferdinand] Lassalle [1825–1864], even [Moses] Hess and [Peretz] Smolenskin [1840–1885] were Jews. There was nothing fundamentally Jewish in Theodor Herzl. He did not represent a revelation of the national daemon. The soul of our people only stammered a few words that revealed her innermost being during the years of the *galut;* Herzl was not one of those.

In comparison, the fact that the mistakes nearly all stemmed from his system appears to be small and insignificant. The most serious was his inability to see the Jewish movement as a totality. He never understood that the Zionist party is only the conscious member of a great organism, that the Zionist activity is only the organized part of a great evolution. He saw Zionism exclusively as something that is produced, not as something that evolved and in which all activity is merely the fulfillment [of ideas], not as an inner development whose expression can only be furthered by the producing human hand. Even in this development he did not consciously participate. He never felt that Jewish renaissance with his heart. To be sure occasionally he read translations of [Haim Nahman] Bialik's [1873–1934] poems* and looked at Ury's Jewish monumental art, but for him all of that was only propaganda. He allowed the appeal of an organization of Jewish mutualists that had formed among Romanian workers—a definitely great idea in spite of all the difficulties—and he received the news of the formation of national labor unions with the demeanor of a party leader, but he did not concern himself with the details. He allowed the Congress to approve one thousand francs for the school in Yaffa, [but] they were not close to his heart. Some free spirits who had left the party were renegades in his eyes, and he saw Ahad Ha-Am as an obscure, shameful journalist. Once he wrote to a representative of the radical party wing, "Make every effort to return to the party." To the movement!

He could not help but identify the movement completely with himself. That was the root of his greatest weakness, but also that of his greatest strength. He did not believe in himself as a person, but as a cause. This faith gave him the steady and unshakable energy that made him the most effective activist of the new Jewish era. His concentration of the masses and many individuals around his own cause [diplomacy] withdrew the best energies from a number of other areas of the movement, but one must acknowledge that he advanced the cause of the one chosen area tremendously.

His book pointed the way; that was its great merit. He walked the way; that was the considerable merit of his activity, which we cannot praise enough. It was a narrow path, but he walked it. He did not look left or right but focused on his goal. On his journey he trampled a number of young shoots, but his step remained firm. He fought

* Most famous of Bialik's poetry is "City of Slaughter" in which the poet gives a heartbreaking account of the Kishinev pogrom in 1903. Reprinted in Mendes-Flohr and Reinharz, *Jew in the Modern World*, 410–11. [G. S.]

against those who disagreed with him as if they were enemies of the cause, for the cause and the deed were one and the same for him, and he felt that only he was up to the deed. His direct and unshakable optimism and his stern, inexhaustible energy were grounded in this feeling. He was proud of his calling; his pride was at times destructive but more often fruitful. Thus, he was able to achieve that which he has achieved with a regal demeanor and against the greatest obstacles.

We can essentially summarize his achievement with one word— *form-giving.* He came at a time of ferment and birth, of ups and downs and activity. A thousand things were in the making, but everything was still unclear; ideas were batted around, plans ripened in the privacy of hearts. The basic writings were completed, thoughts thrived in discussion, but the idea had not found formulation in a joint program. It was a time of intimations and of yearning, of greater flights of the spirit, and of quivering motions of the soul. It was a time of diversity that could lead to anything. Herzl introduced clarity, his kind of singularity. The spiritual mass of Zionism was still unformed with limitless possibilities. Herzl's hand—a sure, yet insensitive hand— gave it form. How many noble possibilities were killed! But it was an artist's hand, nevertheless. The Zionist movement was formed. I almost think it happened too soon. But now it existed. Now the movement had crystallized into a party. For good and for bad. For good, because now a working organ existed that could become a tool of the great double task: the obtaining and preparation of people and land. For bad, because only the first half of the task was valid and because even it was conceived and treated too narrowly: to convince people merely as propaganda to join the party and to contribute to the party institutions, to obtain the land merely as diplomatic activity. Little attention was paid to the fact that this people needed to be trained for settlement, that a nationally organized center for future settlement needed to be created in the land and that the people and the land had to be studied in their origin.* [Herzl] also did not realize that a true

---

* This latter demand was repeatedly stated in *The Jews' State;* the realization has partly been undertaken after the last. Congress (Palestine), partly (statistics) left to personal initiative, which has not been supported by the party. [M. B.]

conversion of the heart can only occur through a regeneration of the heart and a true reclamation of the land only through positive labor in Palestine. That is why we have to say of him whom we lost today—after six Congresses, in the third year of operation of our unique National Bank, after the promising beginning of our most wonderful, most meaningful institution, the National Fund, but especially after seven years full of the most intensive, most devoted, energy-laden activity of him whom we lost—the task is still ahead of us. We still have everything left to do.

It is difficult to discuss the political successes because the material is not accessible. Herzl was the first Jew who conducted politics in exile. This we will never forget. Herzl negotiated with Europe's powerful rulers in the name of our people. This fact may not remain unrecorded in our history. But, besides the financial backing, the negotiations lacked sui generis the backing of a state. Yet he did not wish to embark on the other path, the path of slow, modest and hopeful politics, the useful settling of Palestine with Jewish farmers and artisans, without autonomy, yet with an eye toward autonomy, and also at first the path of an equally modest and relatively simple diplomacy, the negotiations with Turkey concerning the negation of the legal statutes that hinder the settling [of Palestine]. Today there is no more need to pass judgment on this issue.

Seen historically, the personality of Theodor Herzl is also beyond all final judgment. It is not our place to unlock the innermost recesses of his being, to assign a place to his spirit. Although he aroused public interest in Zionism, personally he was really a thoroughly private person. Involved in a number of external disagreements that encompassed world-view and political orientation, thought processes and vocation, he carried deep within his soul—scarcely consciously, yet full of sorrow—an unbalanced contradiction. He was harsh and warm, excessive and measured, noble and petty, a sentimental person and a man of action, a dreamer and a pragmatist. The enigma of his being is undeciphered. He was the hero of a transitional period. He was the master of a sick people. His greatest deed is one he did not will: he gave his people a vision, not the image of a real person, an ideal image, a sincere, encouraging model. This is the way poets in their works create their own wishful ideal; they create whom they would wish to be. Theodor Herzl was not a great poet of the word and of artistic form. He was a great poet in his own unconscious. Living, building, erring, producing good and bad for his people, he created an image, a model for the people to which they gave his name, a model without flaws and mistakes, only with the pure features of the genius, his forehead aglow with the brightness of the messiah. This is a gift of illusion, a gift of grace.*

36.

An Explanation

First I would like to comment on the method used by "Veritas" in his article, "Truth for Truth," which appeared in no. 45 of *Jüdische Rundschau* and came to my attention only recently. This method consists of Mr. Veritas's quotation of some of my sentences, completely outside their context, and the transitional words, "here he means," thereby creating a nonsensical, far-fetched misinterpretation. This method consists of the quotation, "Theodor Herzl was an unimportant poet in word and form. He was a great poet in the subconscious of his own life," with the second half of the sentence simply suppressed, creating nearly the opposite effect of what I said. Sentences that do not belong together are connected and sentences that follow have been dispersed until Mr. Veritas has achieved the effect he desires. But the climax of this method is that he cites whole sections from my essay in quotation marks that I never wrote. The first two sentences from p. 381, column 1, fourth paragraph will not be found in my essay, and the meaning given to them is also a distortion and contortion of my argument. Faced with such literary honesty I have no other choice than to implore the reader of the *Rundschau* to compare [these lines] with my essay.

I would like to call Mr. Veritas to account on another matter; namely, the tone that he enjoys using, which is even lower than his

---

* "Herzl und die Historie," *Ost und West* 4, no. 8 (Aug. 1904); and no. 9 (Sept. 1904): cols. 583–84. Item 60 in *MBB*.

objectionable method and to which I take exception. Where on earth does he get the nerve to doubt the neutrality of my perspective and to see in my basic criticism malicious attacks? Have we come to this in our party, that I, after seven years of writing and organizing in the movement, cannot utter a dissenting view without being accused of the lowest motivation? May this gentleman, who dares to treat an expression of painful conviction like a flood of shameful hate, [may he] declare in public what is the source for his assertion that I attempted to reduce [Herzl] to dwarfdom. Let him show where—in my life, in my writing—he gets this idea.

Regarding this matter, I can point merely to the opening question of my essay, "in which men have been able to, on the one hand, review that ancient idea in the spirit of the newly won cultural values, which, on the other hand, rejuvenate and reactivate Jewish consciousness and willpower?" For the first part of the question I gave the credit to our forebears, for the second to Herzl. I have shown that the development of the idea had occurred essentially before Herzl;* I have shown that the movement owes its development to Herzl: way and form. I wrote, "It was the great credit of his book that it showed the way. It was the greater and never sufficiently appreciated credit of his work that he himself walked the way." To be sure, I also did not ignore the mistakes of his way, according to my knowledge and conscience. I will not debate these mistakes, which Mr. Veritas considers good qualities, with him. There is a subjective ought that one cannot fight. For many Zionists this means to elevate the party above the idea.

As far as my concept of Herzl is concerned, I would like to refer to my essay in the weekly *Freistatt,* dated July 23, where I discuss Herzl in greater detail. This essay concludes with these words from Herzl's book, *Palais Bourbon:* "There are in the life of a people . . . unparalleled individuals. Their mistakes and good qualities are the permanent property of the nation that created them. They have to live their personalit[ies]—damage, contribute, dazzle the people . . . ; they

---

* Mr. Veritas chose to characterize as handymen those men who created and developed an idea that was only later realized on a large scale by others; so, for example Marx and Lasalle. [M. B.]

must spread falsehoods across the land like a fertile Nile flood, for a distant purpose." *

Berlin, November 27, 1904

Dr. Martin Buber

37. _____

The anger toward Herzl and the irreverence have given way to quiet reflection. Eons have passed for Buber, who has spent the past six years studying Hasidism and publishing two seminal works: The Tales of Rabbi Nachman of Brazlav *and* The Legend of the Baal Shem. *He has also collected a volume of ecstatic confessions from different faiths. Perhaps the encounter with others' spirituality has helped him understand Herzl's heroic presence for thousands. Buber's tone in this article is one of contrition and of reconciliation.*

> To show what Herzl was to us, what he was to the Jewish people, that shall be the purpose of this *Gedenkschrift*. Here I wish only to emphasize the most beautiful of the purely human teachings which he gave us: "No office is more fulfilling than that of servant of the light."
> —David Wolffsohn

He and We

1

When peoplehood was for those of us who are today thirty and older that which we had conquered for ourselves and that which we had to defend against the onslaught of "facts," when it [*Volkstum*] was for us only an idea and not yet a way, merely slogan and not yet life, merely

* "Zur Aufklärung," *Jüdische Rundschau* 9, no. 48 (Dec. 2, 1904): 417–18. Item 62 in *MBB*.

program and not yet deed, we did not see humanity in the people whom we encountered in the Jewish movement; we saw only whether they agreed with our idea, our slogan, our program. It appeared as if we were engaged in battle day in and day out, year in and year out, without rest and reflection surrounded by people without seeing a face. We must not forget that we fought on many fronts. But that will not whitewash that we were ideologues, lyrical ideologues: we felt greatness and beauty in the storm of history that roared around us (or seemed to roar around us), in the wave of the deed that carried us (or appeared to carry us?), in the flames of Jewish experience that burst our soul (this surely was no illusion, Do you remember, you who are thirty and older now, do you remember?), but we did not feel them [greatness and beauty], we did not feel them enough in the individual human beings whom we encountered. We did not feel them enough because we were ideologues who inquired above all into the essence of a human being. What is your view of the essence of Judaism? What do you think about the work in Palestine? That was the standard.

The decisive years of life on earth have since passed, and we have changed. Ever so gradually and unnoticeably, peoplehood entered into our humanity, gradually integrating itself in a natural way. There we recognized, in the light of the absolute, the Judaism that lives within us as the reality of all realities, which is eternal like the living soul and untouchable like the soul. Then it was no longer an idea but direction, energy, certainty of our path; no longer slogan but the sound, rhythm, melody of our life; no longer a program but drive, energy, meaning of our work. Only now did we truly see the humanity of human beings whom we had met in the Jewish movement. Only now did we recognize that the decisive thing—the decisive thing for humanity, for Judaism, for Jewish affairs—was not the matter of the human spirit, but the manner. Whether our view of the essence of Judaism, of Jewish culture, the work in Palestine has remained the same or has changed, our standard became untenable in the face of the humanity of which we became cognizant. How pitifully the small wave of battle dashes against the rocky doors of the soul! Pure vision grasped us. Only now could we truly reflect on a human being who is no longer alive.

2

Theodor Herzl thought differently about Jewish matters than we; he saw them differently. We do not wish to speak here of the details, of his views about what was to be done and what was to be rejected, not his agreement and rejection. Six years ago, when I was still involved in the battles, not yet free of the heroic life at the surface, I formulated these issues, wherein he thought differently, which he saw differently. When I was still in the grasp of ideology, of the judgment of the matter, I wrote, accurately, I still think:

> The realization that the true Jewish question is an inner and individual one, namely, the attitude of each Jew to his [or her] innate unique essence that he [or she] finds within, to his [or her] inner Judaism, and [the realization] that this alone characterizes a people, was denied to Herzl. That is why in *The Jews' State* and in all his later addresses he passed by the problem of Jewish uniqueness and its productivization, which is one of the strongest cultural phenomena.*

I shall reiterate: I still agree with this formulation. But beyond it and untouched by it I now perceive the essential.

I call that the essential, his exemplary greatness for us—for us as Jews—which is encapsulated in this weakness. And that it [his greatness] must remain forever inaccessible as displayed in him because it is naïve, primary, elemental, as all greatness arises for us problematic ones from a lack, an elemental lack.

How do we know that the true Jewish question is an internal one? We know because for us our Judaism is problematic, because our inwardness presents itself to us as a problem; existence is for us a problem.

That is the great and tragic Jewish legacy, the problem of the *galut* form of inner dualism.

Internal dualism! All great images of unity within Judaism resulted from the yearning to be free of it. But the *galut* Jew was too weak to produce new images of unity; the yearning became his problem.

* In the weekly, *Freistatt*, July 23, 1904. [M. B.]

The elemental active person perceives his inwardness as a wealth of impulses, which he only recognizes in order to realize them. For the elemental active person existence is a wealth of realities that transforms him and that [in turn] waits impatiently to be transformed by him.

The problematic individual perceives his inwardness as a wealth of questions that demand of him an answer and that will never attain a final answer in the personal, only in the absolute. In the problematic individual existence is a plethora of contradictions that yearn to be resolved by him yet allow a final solution only in the metaphysical, never in the empirical.

The elemental active person's desire to act is so strong that it keeps him from pure knowledge. The desire of the problematic person to know is so strong that it prevents him from acting in full strength.

The elemental active person becomes aware of his Judaism: there arises in him the will to help those Jews to whom he now avows kinship, to get them to a point where they may live in freedom and safety. Now he does what his will tells him; he does not see anything other than that.

The problematic person becomes aware of his Judaism: there he is enveloped in an incredible contradiction, the incredible paradox of our existence as Jews. He sees everything, all degeneration, all guilt, all inner restraint. Before he can act, he must defeat a thousand despairs.

The elemental active one walks in the light, even when he is wrong. The problematic one suffers in the dark, even when he knows.

The error of the one is at times more productive than the knowledge of the other.

3

This is the exemplary greatness of Theodor Herzl, that he was a pure and strong, elemental active individual.

I call his greatness exemplary because it poses a task, one of the greatest tasks that the human soul knows: to achieve unity within.

There is a way for the problematic individual to overcome his problem.

To be sure, he does not have access to the naïve, the primary, the elemental. This he can only possess, not achieve.

He cannot negate his inner duality. But he can propel himself beyond it into that unity of soul powers, which becomes capable of receiving enlightenment, enlightenment that teaches the task and the deed.

The darkness of no problem is so deep that it cannot be penetrated by enlightenment.

But, to receive it, the problematic person must become as unified as the elemental active person is from the beginning.

Thus, the elemental active person becomes his model.

This is the highest form of education—unified existence.

We are being educated by a great, deceased man through his unified being, which is more real to us now than ever.

But there is no liberation of Judaism, no way to a new Jewish people without overcoming problematics. Alone in this way creative instincts are freed. Problematics are the inhibition of everything creative. Spinoza provides the great example of how the Jew must rid himself of problematics to achieve true knowledge, that is, unity and enlightenment.

The soil of Palestine will not transform us if we do not transform ourselves. It will only be able to firm up, secure, complete.

But there is a transformation through will power. All creative Jews know that.

Spinoza is the great example for a life of thought. But what matters above all for us Jews today, who live in crisis, in decision, in transformation, is not the life of thought but the life of deed.

Theodor Herzl is a leader for a life of deed.

4

While I write these words, I suddenly realize that he would now be fifty.

Earlier on I did not understand this, as I do now, this simple harsh [reality], which stops the heart and silences the lips.

And now I feel as I never did before that we are orphaned.

And now I know as I never did before what we are lacking.

Not this or that program.

Not this or that method.

Not this or that work.

Only greatness!

Theodor Herzl's travels to his goal may have been fruitless wanderings.

But when he spoke of his travels, the souls of millions trembled with yearning, with expectation, with happiness.

With happiness because of him!

Because of greatness, greatness through his greatness, the soul trembled, the silent soul of millions awakened, stammered, lived.

Only from such a life will the new people for which we yearn be born.

Pure strength! Unity! Greatness!

Let us beseech fate for this!*

Martin Buber

38.

Here Buber presents a historical development of the Jewish movement, "as old as the Jewish nation's destiny." He wants to stress that the movement is not something new but something that evolved via Yehuda Halevi and Spinoza and the Bilu to his day (1901).

The Jewish Movement

1

We can understand the essence of the Jewish movement only from its history because it is an original life phenomenon of the Jewish nation, as old as its destiny.† The movement encompassed first the de-

---

* "Er und Wir," *Die Welt* 14, no. 20 (May 20, 1910): 445–46. Item 104 in *MBB*.

† Even though this section is numbered 1, there is no 2. [G. S.]

fense of a threatened, enslaved and tortured *Volk* organism and then the sporadic and confused but gradually more even and more ordered efforts of liberation. At first the movement flared up to gigantic heroism in the battle against the Romans, whose tremendous arrogance we can only surmise from Josephus. The movement advanced with undiminished energy from rebellion to rebellion. Then, its first fire was extinguished, suffocated by the power of the enemy. The exile began. For a while the movement was silent, overpowered. But then, turning from earthly battles, the movement raised its arms heavenward wailing, reminding, demanding, fighting. The dream of dreams arose in new splendor; the message of the prophets resounded everywhere as if it were the living word. The waiting for the Messiah began. And then those heartrending pleas for the rebuilding of Zion, born entirely in a human and earthly yearning for community, arose daily from cramped houses of prayer, from dark rooms, in dull or tearful prayer. Then sorrow and hope wept in song, and the greatest of the poets, Yehuda Halevi, wrote his songs of Zion. Then the masters of the Kabbalah announced future redemption in Daniel-like numerology. And those strange men of vision and inspiration appeared who were called the false messiahs. Again and again the Jewish movement flared up. In the days of the Shabbatai Zvi [1626–76], the frenzy erupted, unfettered and ever so powerful, so that the masses left behind their possessions and traveled to the land of redemption [Israel]—until reality checked the frenzy. Even the most apathetic individual was moved by the waves. [Baruch] Spinoza [1632–1677] spoke of the restoration of the Jewish state. In this way violent, almost unconscious release met with the wisdom of the wisest.

But even the messianic form of the movement that experienced its impure final aftershock in the activities of the Frankists* died, partly because of Rabbinism that condemned all exaltation and all activism

---

* The Frankists were a Jewish sect led by Jacob Frank [1726–1791], from Podolia. This sect "comprised the last stage in the development of the shabbatean movement." See Gershom Scholem, "Sabbatianism and Mystical Heresy," in *Major Trends in Jewish Mysticism*, foreword by Robert Alter, New York: (Schocken Books, 1995), 315–20. [G. S.]

as well, partly destroyed by the occasional intrusion of Europeanization. And then began a long hiatus, which lasted until the late nineteenth century. What probably contributed the most [to this
hiatus]—apart from the emancipation process—were the internal
emancipation efforts that became manifest in Hasidism and
Haskalah, in Jewish mysticism and Jewish enlightenment, in the renewal of feelings and ideas. This internal effort at emancipation re-
tarded the external emancipation tendencies until it succeeded; only
then did it begin to support external emancipation. Hasidism, gradually degenerating, itself needed regeneration before it could become
definitive; but the Haskalah was largely incorporated into the national movement. As previously noted, this occurred only a few
decades ago. Until then there were only sporadic manifestations of
this underground stream. If we read the letters of the young [Hein-
rich] Heine and the diaries of the young [Ferdinand] Lasalle, we will
see that even those men who had grown distant from Judaism were
filled by a definitely Zionist feeling in the most personal [*unmittelbar*]
period of their lives. If we leaf through the literature from the time of
Syrian Jewry's persecution (1840),* we find surprisingly realistic
political plans for the foundation of Jewish autonomy in Palestine,
primarily suggested by Jews. But all of this was no movement. The
movement was awakened only by the national idea.

A national idea can result only from a struggle. With few excep-
tions in peaceful times the existence of a nation remains below the
threshold of consciousness; only in the struggle for national existence
and national rights will it become part of consciousness, and only in
the process of battle will it become elevated to an idea. It was the
Jews' fate that the national idea had to evolve from internal struggle.
It was the battle of those rooted in Judaism against those who fell
away in the stupor of assimilation. It was essentially, if not always, a
struggle of the self-assured Jewish East against the self-effacing
Jewish West. The German Jews believed that they became most
worthy of their civil rights by tossing their Jewish nationality over-
board. For this purpose their leaders constructed two unique theses:

* See Mendes-Flohr and Reinharz, "The Damascus Affair (1840)," in *Jew in the
Modern World*, 313–15. [G. S.]

one for the masses, the "religious community," and one for the elect, the "mission of the Jews."* "The Jews are not a people, but a religious community" and "the Jews need to remain dispersed in order to influence the nations": these two theses formed the program that until today has had such a divisive effect. These two theses are, as Salamon Schiller [1879–1925] effectively explained, "one of the strangest, most unnatural metaphysical contradictions which humanity has ever created. Certain peculiarities were to be connected with a theme whose essence was incomprehensible, a world historical mission to be attributed to a something which did not form a living, organic whole." A powerful opponent to this "caricature which consisted of a Jewish idea rooted in the prophets coupled with one derived from German speculative philosophy," to this "shameful, cowardly compromise between the feeling of belonging to Judaism and the material need to be a true son of the people in whose middle we live," arose in the West in the 1860s. [This man was] Moses Hess, the free socialist, the "philosopher of the deed," the coworker of [Karl] Marx [1818–1883] and [Ferdinand] Lasalle, of the critic [Max] Stirner [1806–1856], the creator of theoretical Zionism. In the East in the 1870s and 1880s Peretz Smolenskin [1840–1885], the brilliant representative of the modern *haskalah* [enlightenment] the most unusual Hebrew writer, laid out the national idea historically philosophically. In the 1890s and in our day Asher Ginzberg, known by the nom de plume Ahad Ha-Am (one of the people), completed the structuring of this idea into an organic philosophical system. Ahad Ha-Am is the greatest thinker of the Young-Hebraic literature, and he is one of the most powerful fighters for truth of all time. The center of Ahad Ha-Am's system is the task of regeneration of Judaism through the creation of a spiritual center in Palestine, of an exemplary Jewish social culture that is to be seen as the only true mission of the Jewish people. The development of the national idea, which was a force, created the national movement. Of course, this movement became primarily powerful in the East where it touched all levels of the society and penetrated even into the organized workers movement. Even within it a strong nationalistic group formed de-

---

* Here Buber refers to doctrines of the Reform Movement. [G. S.]

spite all hostilities. Just as all liberation efforts in all historical phases of the exile were accompanied by the tendency to restore the Jewish community to the homeland of Judaism, so now, in the phase of a conscious will the work to settle Palestine began. This activity was fueled and misguided by the poor economic situation of the people. It intensified considerably after the Russian pogroms against Jews.* It depended, however, much too much on philanthropy and much too little on self-help. The true power of the movement expressed itself in those settlement efforts that were initiated by the young students who dedicated themselves entirely to the idea and discarded all bourgeois considerations, who were dreamers, yet wonderful, and provided a noble symbol of renewed peoplehood. Here we shall recall only one group, the Bilu group from Charkow. These young people wanted to go to Palestine, form "socialist settlements there, which they would then turn over to the people when they were well established and well organized, and then go on to build new settlements, and so forth." By its very nature, this program could only be realized on a small scale. But it deserves to become part of history as the document of a young, proud, and courageous people willing to make sacrifices.†

Martin Buber

39.

In the year 1905 Buber withdrew from public life to study Hasidism. With this three-part article Buber continued his response to the critics of cultural Zionism. He first outlined the history of the Jewish renaissance, which began with Hasidism, juxtaposing it to "the Law," Rabbinic Judaism, of which Buber was highly critical. Buber also acknowledges the achievements of the Haskalah, the Jewish enlightenment in the East, which developed at the same time as Hasidism (eighteenth century). Buber is most appreciative of the Haskalah's Europeanization of Judaism, which did not spell denationalization, and its revival

---

* The period 1880–1 in the Pele of Settlement. [G. S.]

† "Die Jüdische Bewegung," *General-Anzeiger für die gesamten Interessen des Judentums* 4, no. 36 (Sept. 3, 1905): 1. Item 68 in *MBB*.

of Hebrew as a literary language. The current phase of the Jewish renaissance required the Jewish people to unify to become a power, a political power. Buber argues, however, that "no [land] charter is of any help if the people are not ready to implement it." Responding to critics that the cultural Zionists wish to provide "the people with culture instead of bread," he argues that culture is bread. The key concept of the third section of the essay, "On Cultural Activity," points out that education must begin now, in "the young year of an ancient people." Somewhat alienating is Buber's comparison of the Jewish bourgeois and the Slavic farmer. The latter is almost racially stereotyped, whereas the Jew is elevated in his search for learning, a learning that Buber denigrates in the context of the Yeshivah.

The Jewish Cultural Problem and Zionism
By Dr. Martin Buber, Berlin

1. On the Renaissance

We are speaking of the Jewish renaissance. By this we understand the peculiar and basically inexplicable phenomenon of the progressive rejuvenation of the Jewish people in language, customs, and art. We justifiably call it renaissance because it resembles—in the transfer of human fate to national fate—the great period that we call Renaissance above all others, because it is a rebirth, a renewal of the entire human being like this Renaissance, not a return to old ideas and life forms, [it is] the path from semi-being to being, from vegetation to productivity, from the dialectical petrification of Scholasticism to a broad and soulful perception of nature, from medieval asceticism to a warm, flowing feeling of life, from the constraints of narrow-minded communities to the freedom of the personality, the way from a volcanic, formless cultural potential to a harmonious, beautifully formed cultural product.

To understand this beautiful and joyous phenomenon we must comprehend it as of one piece, trace it back to its origin, into the period during the late eighteenth century when two powerful influences penetrated the petrified existence of Judaism from within and from without—Hasidism and Haskalah—creating a new, incredible, and unimagined life.

Until the mid-eighteenth century the energy of Judaism was restrained not only from outside but also from within by fear and suffering, by life constraints and [physical] threat to life, not only from the suppression of the "host nations" but also from within, from the forcible enslavement of the "Law," that is, a misunderstood, ornate, distorted religious tradition, by the ban of a hard, petrified imperative that was removed from reality, which falsified and destroyed everything that was intuitively bright and joyous, everything that thirsted for beauty and all flights of fancy. And the Law achieved a power as no law in any other people or period. The education of the generations occurred exclusively in the service of the Law. There was no personal action born of feeling; only action based on the Law could survive. There was no personal creative thought, only the message that resulted from the exegesis of books regarding the Law and the hundreds of books of commentary on the Law and the thousands of books of commentary on the commentary. To be sure, heretics emerged again and again, but what could the heretic achieve vis-à-vis the Law? Dogma, which one is to believe may be shaken by heretics who appeal to reason rather than faith. But a law for life that governs action can only be repealed through the development of human beings to self-determination or be overcome through the development of human beings to a higher law. Here finally, both happened. For centuries it surely struggled beneath the surface, and those heresies that appeared daily anew and were stifled were surely manifestations of this struggle that undermined the Law. Then it announced itself in a double rush against the philosophy and the doctrine of the Law. First, the progression to a higher law for life found expression in Jewish mysticism, namely Hasidism, the liberation of feeling; then the progression to self determination, in the Haskalah, or Jewish enlightenment, the liberation of thought. Both led to spiritual and physical struggles filled by the most moving tragedy and the most grandiose comedy. Both brought about the Jewish renaissance without wanting it and without knowing it.

To be a Hasid means to be pious, and one could almost interpret Hasidism to mean pietism. If we take this word in its usual sense, however, that would be wrong. The Hasidic world-view lacks all sentimentality; it is mysticism full of power and emotion, which definitely brings the Beyond to the here and now and allows this [life] to be formed by the Beyond as the body [is formed] by the soul—an absolutely original, popular, and living renewal of Neoplatonism, a simultaneously most divine and most realistic direction to ecstasy. It is the teaching of the active feeling as a bond between the human being and God. Creation is everlasting; creation continues today and always, and the human being participates in the creation process through energy and love. Everything that is done with a pure heart is worship. It is the goal of the Law that the human being becomes a law unto himself [or herself]. This shatters the forced rule. But the founders of Hasidism were no naysayers. They did not abrogate the old forms, they infused them with new meaning and thereby liberated them. Hasidism, or rather the deep spiritual stream that created and sustained it, created the emotionally regenerated Jew.

The Haskalah followed another path; it fought Hasidism and Rabbinics as well because both were based on "faith" and not on "knowledge." The Haskalah emerged in the name of knowledge, civilization, and Europe. It wanted to enlighten and was as superficial as all enlightenment given its premise of knowledge as a sure and unproblematic thing; it wanted to popularize, and it was just as dull and useless as all so-called popular philosophy that lives off the blood of others as do all true parasites. The Haskalah is ahead of the parasite in several things; first, in its enemy, the most rigid and most established of all orthodoxies, [then in] its fresh youthful aggression and the fact that it was at all times involved with the feeling of a holy war for self-determination, for the determination of action through our own thinking, not through the traditions. But it also contained positively Jewish, futuristic elements, as much as it believed that it was negating the tradition. The Haskalah wanted to Europeanize the Jews, but it did not consider their denationalization. It treated the language of the Bible with cultic reverence. It turned a dead and unrealistic language, Hebrew, into the tool of a living struggle and thereby enriched and strengthened it. And what has been done for the language has also been done for the ideas. In this way the Haskalah also indirectly served the regeneration of Jewish thought.

From these inner transformations, expressed and used simultaneously by Hasidism and the Haskalah, the Jewish renaissance was
born. It is noteworthy that here the same elements interacted as in
the great time of the 1300s and 1400s—the mystical-emotional [ele-
ments] that then appeared partly as Divine wisdom and partly as poetics and the linguistically ideal that was then called humanism. And
just as that time—I would like to emphasize this again—the Jewish
renaissance does not mean a return, but a rebirth of the whole human
being—a rebirth that evolved very slowly, very gradually, from the
days of the Haskalah and of Hasidim to our time and will continue to
evolve. Slowly and gradually a new type of Jew will develop.

The Talmudic Jew was a passive hero. He suffered all stages of
martyrdom without complaint and without pride, with silent lips and
a silent heart, motionless. His refusal of the world was his only resis-
tance, and nothing could break it down. This passivity, however, was
not only greatness but also misery and pity. The Jew did not only
struggle passively, he also acted and thought passively. One individual, Spinoza, possessed enough *natura naturans* to step from the
ghetto into the cosmos actively and peacefully and to take hold in the
Infinite as no one else before him. But how much of the most deli-
cious temporality did he have to sacrifice? How much of the most irreplaceable emotional connection with past and future generations of
his tribe? Which new and unspeakable martyrdom did he have to
take upon himself and with him into his great peace? what barely intimated mystery of an incredible separateness did this liberated Talmudic Jew leave for posterity! The new Jew, the Jew of the
Emancipation era strolls in the paths of Spinoza, without genius but
with a daemonic daring. He was no longer passive, but acting freely;
he no longer acted according to the Law, but according to his own
thought and feeling; and the abnormal strove for the creative. But
creativity was denied to him for a long time and even to this day has
not revealed itself to him in its ultimate secrets: self-unburdening,
self-purification, self-redemption. At first he was not granted quiet
activity. The emancipated spirit rushed into the unlimited instead of
acting within the existing or by creating something new. The irreplaceable connection was sacrificed without the gain of something
more. The rebirth of the Jew begins with a tragic episode, which still

today has not ended and which did not even mean an emancipation of the people from ignoble elements. Even some of the best could not stand up against it; in fact, it was precisely those who were most aglow by the daring who drifted the furthest apart. Actually, some original individuals at the beginning of the nineteenth century achieved a peculiar cosmopolitanism, a being-at-home in the universe, but it could only prevail in all its beauty as long as the spirit of these Jews had to conquer their freedom, thereby gaining a fascinating greatness. When spiritual freedom [*Geistesfreiheit*] had become an accomplished fact also for Jews, even this cosmopolitanism turned into assimilation. European civilization had descended on the Jews too quickly and too directly for the *maskilim* [Jews of the Haskalah] to digest it in peace. This way a portion of the people were misled to fall from their unspoken ideals of autonomy and to accept, at the expense of their own souls, the new ready-made from the hands of the cultivated nations instead of acquiring it and incorporating it gradually. This pathological manifestation was encouraged by two factors: the geographical dispersion and the abnormal acceleration of the emancipation process as a result of the great revolution.

The fact that assimilation did not manage to negate the renaissance, in spite of all this, but became merely a slowing factor is based on a major reality of the Jewish problem—the fundamental difference in essence and destiny of Eastern and Western Jewry. Eastern Jewry had always been less dispersed than Western Jewry; its character resembled more a great and self-contained community and, thus, also possessed more Jewish cultural components. To this we can add that civilization crept east ever so slowly and that the emancipation process had almost no validity here. Therefore, the Haskalah, which had a place here like all other factors of the renaissance, was able to incorporate the elements of civilization gradually and naturally. A more large-scale assimilation also was not thinkable because the host nation was not stronger culturally, but weaker. Additionally, the Jews of the East were socially healthier because they were less affected by the evil of an unproductive money economy. If western Jews had to succumb to their environment because they had no language [of their own] and adopted not only foreign words but also foreign ideas and thoughts, Eastern Jews achieved stabilization in a strange, absolutely abnormal and yet thoroughly healing linguistic development. On the one hand, a rich Hebrew literature and commentary developed, and the language of the Bible became more and more a perfect instrument of modern science and of modern ideas, and simultaneously it became the coarse yet full-sounding tool of an original type of literature; next to it and simultaneously the idiom of the people — Yiddish, which was wrongfully called "jargon" — developed. Yiddish is by no means a dialect (as is usually assumed), but a *res sui generis* [unique matter], a completely equal language, less abstract but warmer than Hebrew amended with Yiddish, without the purely spiritual pathos [of Hebrew] but full of incomparably gentle and coarse, tender and malicious nuances. In Yiddish the popular itself became language, and this much-despised language has created the beginnings of charming poetry, melancholically dreamy lyrics, and strong novellas based on sound observation. This dualism is the strongest symptom of the Jewish renaissance in its rich attempts, yet pathological forms, at expression.

Now we can understand why piece after piece broke off in the West while the renaissance was able to take hold and create positive values in the East. The Jewish movement is its strongest expression. Sometimes we also mistakenly call the Jewish movement the national Jewish movement. It [the Jewish movement] is conceived more broadly and more deeply than national movements generally; it is more original and more tragic. Its content is national, the striving for national freedom and autonomy, but its form is supranational. The complex of ideas that it brings forth belongs to the thought process of all humanity. And the liberation for which it stands approximates the great symbol of redemption.

In the final analysis the Jewish movement is a striving for free and total activity of the newly awakened energies of the nation. If we wish to conceive the renaissance people in the form of an organism (without consideration for all contrary or undeveloped elements), the national idea is its self-consciousness, the national movement its will power. And just as will power occurs initially reflex like and spontaneously then becomes more and more differentiated and intellectual because of the influence of the developing consciousness, so the Jewish movement under the influence of the renaissance idea develops from a drive for survival to an ideal.

If the Jewish movement sees the most favorable conditions or the necessary precondition for the accomplishment of its goal in the creation of a new Jewish community in Eretz Israel, and if it endeavors to create such, we call that Zionism; whether it is pursued with greater or lesser exclusivity, whether we think in terms of the creation of a Jewish state or a public enterprise that will achieve greater autonomy over generations, whether we consider diplomatic negotiation with European governments or positive cultural and settlement work as a means to an end, all these and some other observations we group under the name Zionism insofar as they grow from the soil of renaissance, that is, insofar as they set as their essential goal the free and complete employment of people power. On the other hand, we will have to consider all views and actions that reject the regeneration of Judaism and wish to find a home for Jews merely to alleviate their plight, not as Zionists, but as a humanitarian undertaking guided by more or less high-minded ideals and which may well meet the Jewish movement here and there but has nothing in common with it.

But also within Zionism we can discern two basic concepts: a logical and an illogical one. For the latter, the notion of territory displaces all other thoughts and allows it to negate, fully or partly, openly or covertly, all cultural work, that is, the current and direct promotion of the people's energies. The logical person includes cultural activity in his agenda because he feels himself to be the renaissance that has become will power and sees in it his natural circle of activities. To this perception we juxtapose the assertion that this creates the diffusion of energy. This assertion is false, for true cultural activity is simultaneously one of the most significant means to reach territorial goals—to win the land. I show how in the next section.

2. On Politics

Zionist politics comprise of necessity three elements that are interconnected—propaganda, negotiations, settlement work—three elements that do not follow temporally but by simultaneous collaboration. It is clear from the history of the settlements that settlement work is not necessarily a consequence of negotiations but often a precondition. In our movement, too, this will become clearer and clearer from the facts. According to my thinking—which is contrary to the existing perception—it is necessary to show that all three elements have to be founded on cultural considerations and work in order to lead to great and permanent successes. Positive national cultural works are the only ones that can affect our innermost life; in the absence of political power, national cultural power is the only one that can influence our negotiations; education is the premise of a well-planned settlement policy. In short, Zionist politics must become cultural politics if it hopes to achieve results despite its exceptional character—the absence of a polis, rather, merely striving for a polis—results that are usually only granted to activities of a recognized power.

First, we must be aware that culture does not mean something purely spiritual to us. The culture of a people is nothing but the synthetic productivity of this people, that is, [the productivity] understood in its totality. Cultural politics is the most logical and best-organized effort of productivity for freedom.

Zionist propaganda is of a dual nature; it comprises outward publicity that attempts to win the achievement-oriented empathy of the nations and Europe's leading spirits for its cause and the internal publicity whose purpose is to spread Zionism among the Jews. Let us look at the former.

With all the meetings and negotiations we, in the Zionist camp, completely forgot the great truth that governments come and go but peoples persist. When we speak of nations, we mean the most advanced, spiritually freest, and most educated faction, the one that represents and vouches for the future—the leading spirits of today are the bourgeoisie of tomorrow. The philhellenic movement proved how valuable the empathy of the nations is. At the same time it is instructive for understanding which sources produce such powerful empathy. This source is of cultural interest, even if it is the interest of pietism versus a long dead culture from whose representatives a chain of hereditary traits led to the people who are the object of that empathy. We could say that this pietism ought to exist also in our case. To be sure, eons of the unhappiest coexistence with the nations have counteracted such sentiments; besides, our undeniable degeneration, that seed of the exile, which has only begun to root out the renaissance, is not hidden, as that of the Greeks, but plainly visible. If we wish to secure modern, living Europe as our brother, we have to put something else on the scales, and that something else can only be living culture. It is not enough to say that we strive for the creation of a homeland for the Jewish people. For we may receive the answer, "What is the Jewish people? Why should we arise and create a home for it? Does it have any strength left to live? What will it still accomplish?" Let us show them what the Jewish people is. Let us set its energy free, as far as this is possible in the *galut*. Let us shape and promote it that it may produce as much as a banned and disenfranchised person can produce, and then let the deed speak, let it awaken the sense of what there might be. Let us show that there is Jewish peoplehood with particular creative possibilities all its own and that it may have to create on its own soil a new land [*Neuland*] of the spirit and new forms of human coexistence. Let us give it everything — action, attitude, and accomplishment — let us try to be and shape others to be as much as we can be to prove our point.

But not only to show the outside world, but even more for ourselves. May our own existence and every other one accessible to our work be infused with the living productive spirit of the people so that we are in truth Zionists, not in the sense of lip service but in essence, the carriers of a becoming Zion.

The yearning for an increase in numbers of party members has become the driving force of Zionist propaganda. We preached the view that it is the most sacred task of the Zionist to add money and people to the party until this view became a destructive dogma, rather than to influence the life of the people in all of its elements. May we point out, in contrast, that all this work in its present form is nothing yet compared to what we have to do, not complete an intense inner activity but form the activity of the Zionist. Zionist propaganda must become a transvaluation of all activities, transformation of national life in its depths and foundations as well. It has to touch the soul and demand the soul. Until now, publicity touched merely the surface and only asked for shekels and signatures. That is not the way to engage a people. That is not the way the international workers of young Italy became conscious. We must tease out the living energies of the nation to free the bound instincts. To be sure, this can be achieved only by a true liberation movement, a lavalike, uncompromising, unconditional liberation movement; no compromises, no opportunities. A movement of struggle and of sacrifice. Parties make diplomacy, movements struggle. Our young movement became a party all too soon. It began to negotiate with powers before it was a power itself. It frightened away the largest part of the freedom-loving elements through a series of opportunistic practices and superficialities. A number of personalities who had felt the ideal of their own nature in the ideal of regeneration fell away when anti-Semitism was decreed the premise of the movement, liberation from anti-Semitism its essence, and diplomacy the only way. The movement increased in numbers, won some intellectuals, some shekels, and some [Fund] shares. But we did not win the living energies of the nation and not the people who are capable of awakening these energies. For Zion today is not what it should be—the paragon of pure, sacred, total freedom. The [Jewish] national movement has not yet created a Masada of the spirit. The [Jewish] national movement has not yet revolutionalized the Jewish spirit. Yes, a revolutionizing of the national spirit is important; those prophets who wanted to educate the nation in exile for a new Palestine also were revolutionaries.

Zionist propaganda will become an education of the people, a revolutionary education to freedom, stirring to the very depths, beginning with ourselves and ending with the lowliest worker [*Lumpenproletarier*]. Ending? It will be called a never-ending task. But when we raise ourselves up, we will realize that in an even deeper way Zionism itself is an unending task or, what will mean the same, an ideal, and it is the purpose of life to get closer to the ideal with all of one's power and in every moment.

National education does not only mean publicity, not only the one thinkable total winning over of the people, but it is at the same time a necessary foundation for negotiations and settlement efforts, and the more developed it is, the stronger and more secure a foundation it will be.

[National education is a] foundation for negotiations first in the sense of the external publicity already mentioned. But we must also grasp the problem in a broader and deeper sense. Politics and justice [*Recht*] are the expression of real power relations. Only a real power can successfully negotiate with another power. Diplomacy, which is the art of using power, may be able to create the illusion of slight shifts but cannot create illusions about something substantial. But even if it could, it would still not be able to bestow on the Zionist party the aura of real power. Our movement completely lacks the support of statehood and almost entirely financial backing; it also lacks the very important foundation that a large, well-organized settlement that is capable of production would grant. It is, therefore, at best potential power, so to say, the seed of a power from which might arise [real] power only after the negotiations have led to a favorable result. And so far, even for this case no positive guarantee could be provided, we could not prove in a concrete way that the Jewish settlement that will be founded will be a power, that is, will be in a position to honor an obligation of reciprocity. The unproductive nature of previous efforts can easily be explained in terms of this abnormal, unhealthy state of affairs. The situation appears to be a dilemma without an escape. Yet there is one. It consists of our effort, as paradoxical as it may sound, to become a power. To internalize this goal, however, we must learn to count in generations instead of in years. But if we cannot muster the courage to such active resignation, if we cannot get up the strength to sacrifice ourselves for future generations, this would be our end and we would have no hope left.

To become a power, a power factor, we must become a strong, self-conscious, unified, and organized people. In our people lie energies. They will wake up when the people will recognize themselves and will begin to work on themselves and for themselves. The degenerate and demoralized masses will only be the tool, not the power. Recently, at a party meeting of Austrian Zionists, someone dared to say they could only be the object, not the subject of Zionism. Masses that had become conscious—not yet healed but already combating the illness, not yet moral but afire and charmed by pure yearning—will be a phenomenon for Europe, a revelation. Masses with a mature will, a political sense, economic organization—that will be a nation, that will be a power. These will no longer be unorganized, chaotic, taciturn masses but people who know what they want and who they are.

But this is still not enough. To demand autonomy for their settlements the people must be able to point to an already created center in Palestine. Every settlement develops in this way; people settle, organize, establish values, and receive autonomy as the population, organizational stability, and production grow. Our settlement is rather abnormal because it has no homeland, merely a nation, and second, wishes to settle Turkish land, not unoccupied land, and the relations of Turkey are definitely not well disposed toward the normal development of our settlement to autonomy as previously described. Someday we may well be in a position where we will wish to carry out negotiations with European powers, but successfully only when the people, who have become a real power in Europe, and the settlement, which has become a real power in Turkey, will work together. In any case, the settlement has to exist. To achieve this there will have to be negotiations, but only regarding unhindered settlement work. Already now, these negotiations may be carried out with promise of success because it would be possible to provide guarantees or reciprocal services* in contrast to those who aim at the guarantee of a prior autonomy. A scientifically grounded settlement and agricultural plan would be of great significance. This question, which does not belong to our topic, will be dealt with separately. Here I would only like to point out that this scientific work, if done properly, would mean exploration of people and land and therewith great Jewish cultural activity.

All of this, however, is not enough to begin a settlement in the sense of which we speak, not small-scale settlement but settlement on the largest scale and within the framework of the people's political purpose and means.

In this most peculiar of all national problems, everything is so closely tied to everything else that national education provides the

---

* Of course, we also intend, beyond any negotiations, to make the land into a de facto more and more Jewish land through inner settlement (settlement of the municipal Jewish population in Palestine) and through agricultural and cultural work in Palestine. [M. B.]

necessary basis even for settlement work. We have to stress again and again that no charter is any help if the people are not ready to implement it. For a peculiar settlement plan such as ours, which is almost without parallel, we need a physically, spiritually, morally strong people; a people that is strong enough to carry out the hardest and most taxing work, to stand up to the most severe dangers, to survive the most desperate disappointments. It is absolutely wrong to charge that we wish to provide "the people with culture instead of bread." We want to enable and prepare the people to fight for bread, which is, in reality, the struggle for national existence. We want to awaken in the people that moral strength which provides the courage and endurance for work; we want to lead their thinking from relativism to a sense of reality and their will power from haste and greed to a powerful steadiness. We want to attract first small, then ever greater groups for settlement in Eretz Israel. We may expect the utmost from future generations, if we invest everything to influence the next generation. He who works to lead the education of our youth in a new direction will have contributed the most to Zionism. There is only one way to a great Jewish culture, namely, culture.

3. On Cultural Activity

To justify this from yet another angle and to focus a little more closely on the issue of education as well as some other areas of cultural activity,* I would like to first comment on two objections that are generally raised in addition to the one we already discussed — fragmentation of energies. One of them says, "How can you educate the people culturally and morally without first enabling them economically to absorb your education?" And the other is, "All cultural products that you endeavor to produce have to remain piecemeal if the people are not first given the opportunity of steady and normal development through territorial unity and unification."

It is clear that these two objections concern two different aspects of our cultural activity: the first concerns actual national education,

---

* Many parts of this section are similar to "A Spiritual Center" (sec. 25) but are sufficiently different so that I provide the entire text here. [G. S.]

the effort to awaken or to free the slumbering or enslaved energies; the second concerns the attempts to provide activity for the existing awakened and free energies and thereby to make further development, that is, activity and development within our people and our community, possible. These two sides are intimately connected—the second [development] is merely a continuation of the first—and each serves the other, for the first prepares a receptive people for the creative spirits and the second makes possible a freer and richer production of national cultural goods, which again affect the education and elevation of our people. At every point and in every moment exists the most lively reciprocity between the two sides. Yet it is obvious that the first pattern of work has to do first and in a most direct way with the masses, the second with an intellectually elite, creatively gifted minority. This is the relationship between the two objections mentioned.

The question the first objection asks is, How do you intend to educate the Jewish worker [*Lumpenproletarier*] because he has neither leisure nor the physical opportunity to avail himself of education through reading or listening. First, you must provide him with time and leisure, satisfy his basic human needs, and provide him with a regular organization; only then can you consider educating his mind.

As emphatically as this objection reflects the actual circumstances, it lacks all knowledge of their specific nature. The argument may be pretty accurate for the Slavic farmer; for the Jew it is completely wrong. If the Jewish shopkeeper or worker would be mentally indifferent, only capable of producing thoughts for a more or less narrow physical sphere, it would be a silly, even cruel undertaking to carry out educational experiments in the face of such deep economic misery. But these shopkeepers and workers are precisely the mentally sharpest of all groups.

The life of the Slavic farmer is a powerful economic system. He scarcely thinks beyond that which he needs to satisfy his various direct and indirect physical needs. Sometimes he experiences a thoughtful curiosity, almost always directed toward the practical, sometimes a clumsy brooding that is void of all substance. That is all. On the other hand, the life of the Jewish intellectual [*Luftmensch*] is everything but materialistic. A large portion of his time and energy is spent in the pursuit of an intellectual activity that has nothing to do with real life. He thinks a lot, but not about his memories and his desires nor about people and things in his life. He reflects on the convoluted, petrified explanations of passages from a few old books, a few books of whose historical significance, intellectual, moral, artistic values, or actual background he knows nothing. His thinking is beyond all relation to anything real. And he is totally devoted to this empty thinking, this spinning of abstractions. It is not only the many who elevate "learning," that is, the ingenious, but totally unrealistic and sterile pondering of specific passages, to their life's work, and let their wives support them, committed businessmen are also filled with this specifically Jewish intellectualism; it fills all of their doing, every word, every gesture, with an abundance of hair-splitting reflection. The farmer, too, is not only an instinctual being. He, too, ponders things before he acts in his slow, clumsy way. But his level of thinking corresponds to the particular purpose and does not exceed it. In every case, the Jew thinks more briefly, but at the same time more broadly and more diversely. And his practical considerations are interspersed with a thousand reminiscences and intellectual flourishes that scarcely ever affect these [practical considerations]. He thinks for the sake of thinking; everywhere the opportunity arises; and even the most miserable, subjugated human being affords himself this luxury. Nowhere else in the world are there human beings who, at one and the same time, suffer such great anguish and live in such intellectual luxury. The intellectual is the true person of luxury.

This Jewish intellectualism is an immense fact, perhaps the most striking of the great illnesses of the Jewish people. Therefore, it is not a matter of awakening intellectual interests but of *transforming* intellectual interests. There is unending mental activity, but it is distorted, rigid, sick, perverse, unrealistic, unproductive, un-European, inhuman. The great challenge is to influence it, to heal it, to transform it. It is not a question of developing the ability to absorb intellectual nourishment; this ability exists and is in use daily, but we need to provide different nourishment in such a way that it is acceptable. This is necessary so that the nation becomes mentally well, and it is, therefore, the problem of our life. For only when his desire has been awakened can we provide the stubborn Jew with a human basis for existence, and that is a matter of intellectual education. (I do not speak here of the Jewish industrial workers, who naturally assimilate the modern way of life).

Sometimes, in contrast to such expositions, there is a hint of the future home in Eretz Israel and of the power of the maternal earth where they have been irrefutably recognized. I am absolutely convinced that territorial unification will have a great and healing influence on all of national life, the renewed reciprocity between the different popular elements, the possibility of quiet activity of all powers, perhaps also the climatic relations of the land under whose influence our people once came into being. But I believe that all of this cannot achieve anything other than an unfolding of the inherent buds of the new, cultural seeds that will grow into cultural deeds. I do not know whether we can expect that it will also eliminate this entire sick Jewish intellectualism.

I do not believe that we should consider loading a people onto ships like dead freight, send them across to the land and then expect the soil to perform a miracle—the restoration of the sickest of all people to true life. With an undertaking of this nature characterized by uniqueness and unrepeatability, its failure would mean the death of a great cultural possibility. Rather, we must work on transvaluating the Jewish mentality, not through theories but through deeds, to develop continuously new waves of human beings capable of settlement and to design simultaneously a plan on the basis of which it would be possible for the most developed levels to become the core of the settlements, once "large-scale settlement" begins. The development of human beings is intricately tied to national education; in true cultural activity they appear together. Every reform of the cheder brings us closer to a strong, mature generation capable of settlement, and every agricultural school acts as a fountain of national youth.

As already noted, the most essential question of national education is, of course, youth education. To be sure, adults can also be influenced with word and deed. But it is obvious that complete transformation works best with young and open minds, not yet set on a direction, and even here only gradually from generation to generation. This work, however, is always dependent on a reeducation of the adults: a thoroughgoing reform of the cheder (in the modern national sense) is pointless if the parents are not enlightened as to its [the reform's] necessity, and when the home destroys what school has wrought, nothing much will be achieved. That may be a dilemma, but one which can and must be solved through intensive activity. To facilitate and organize this intensive activity a centralization of national education [and] the creation of a great national educational institution will be necessary. This issue is not yet ready for implementation—particularly in light of the peculiar circumstances especially of the Russian Jews—and can today only be presented as an idea. Until we reach the next stage we can only appeal to those who work for national education, wherever they are, to work even more intensely than [they have] until now.

If the initial objection rested on ignorance regarding specifically Jewish relations, we may accuse the representatives of the second objection of an even more far-reaching ignorance. They tell us, "You endeavor to create a Jewish culture, but this can succeed only in a Jewish state; here and now the beginnings of a Jewish culture are impossible."

This objection misunderstands three things: our efforts, the nature of culture, and the entire Jewish history including this movement in its historical significance. This objection assumes that a Jewish culture does not now exist, that we are attempting to create one. That is totally wrong. Jewish culture exists; it never stopped existing. We must not confuse the existence of culture with a fully developed culture. The Jewish people never had a fully developed culture, not even during statehood [First and Second Temple periods]. But it does not make any sense to contrast culture and the development of Jewish mysticism, for example, and to speak of the nonexistence of culture in the Diaspora. This is especially useless where such historical phenomena as the resurrection of the Hebrew language are concerned. If that is not an expression of Jewish culture, then I really do not know what else to call it.

I already pointed out that the culture of a people can be nothing other than its productivity, the work of the nation. We call every conscious or subconscious representation of a spiritual experience production, and a piece of art is at the same time the embodiment of spiritual particularity. All products that express the psychophysical particularity of a people belong to its culture. A folksong, a dance, a wedding custom, a poetic phrase, a legend, a belief, a traditional prejudice, a menorah, tefillin, a philosophical system, a social deed—all of this is culture. We can see this especially in the life of East European Jewry, where the suffering, struggling national soul is evident in all expressions of life. To be sure, a culture may be poor, pathological, one-sided, undeveloped, but it does not stop being culture. Precisely this we can say of Jewish culture. It is poor, pathological, onesided, undeveloped. Only in its own land can it develop richly, healthily, comprehensively, and fully; of that I am convinced. It, however, does not *have to* turn out that way even in our own land. That can be seen by the various periods of statehood. But we are strengthened in our hope by the example of the renaissance, to which I would like to return.

The history of the Diaspora is volcanolike. Nowhere is there a steady stream of productivity. We lack the continuity of personality and of productivity. The energies of the people glow for decades or centuries underground to break forth suddenly in one great human being, in one great work. And then begins, gradually, at first quietly, then more strongly and more strongly, the inner transformation, which I will call Jewish renaissance. Invisible powers return to our people the continuity and the steady productivity of the living spirit. That we cannot doubt. How idle and unproductive is the debate over the existence of Jewish art! Surely there is no Jewish art in the sense of Dutch art. But these are merely categories, and the fact that there even are Jewish artists is the great historical miracle, and the other [miracle] is that their vision, their form conception contains seeds of Jewish essence, something of the characteristics of our heritage, which envelop the nerves of their vision and the muscles of their hands.

The continuity of production has been restored to us. Intellectual and artistic energies arise more strongly and more steadily than before from the soil. The mood of a richly seeded, blessed field emerges. It is the young year of an ancient people. Already we are showered with the blossoms of this unexpected spring. But the ancient enemy lies in wait, the murderous pair of the eons—the narrowness of life and of the spirit, the outer and the inner ghetto, the powers that have not yet been subdued. They, however, were powerful only in the volcanic period; only a few individuals had to be subdued, and they faced the greatest physical and spiritual misery of human history. It is different today; and if the rebirth of our people means for us not only a slogan but a serious matter and issue, then we are commanded to fight a holy war against these two opponent powers, then we must not allow young energies of our people to be destroyed every day, then we have to labor to preserve them, that they unfold, and that they are preserved for us, that they unfold for us.

The leaders and representatives of no nation on earth would quietly stand by and watch the loss—everywhere and always—of talents of the spirit and of art, capabilities, opportunities, human beings. But we continue to vegetate. Everybody else would initiate a great [rescue] operation, establish activity centers. But we are silent and pretend that we do not know that strongly and richly gifted human beings are lost daily, not through death but through the yoke of daily life so that they forget all heavenly voices, through the narrowness of life that imprisons them in dark alleys and does not allow them a glance into the wide, sparkling world, through the tradition, which damns the fire of the spirit and the representative sacrality of art equally. But those who have overcome and who have broken through to their own selves and to their productivity, will they not become alienated from the community that defamed and tormented them? To damn [anything] a priori is a very poor beginning. But the faithful ones, do they have at least their own public for a dialogue? Is not the Jewish bourgeoisie too degenerate to want to hear them, and the Jewish masses too dull to be able to understand them? How can they educate, attract a Jewish public? And the few who already today understand them and agree with them, do we have a bridge to them? Are there centers of communication, of intellectual communication and of artistic communication?

Here a plethora of tasks for cultural work abounds. These sketchy comments are not the place to go into more detail. They merely attempted to outline broadly the relationship of Zionism to the Jewish renaissance and to the Jewish cultural problem. They were meant to remind the Zionist that Zionism can be realized only on the soil of positive cultural activity.

We have entered a period of continuity. Zionism, too, can only arise as a result of inner national development. It is our task to guard and to further this development.

We have entered a period of continuity. Now we must endeavor to produce continuity also in ourselves, one above all—the continuity between the idea and the deed. These are sketches of ideas. May they become deeds!*

40.

At a time when actual travel to Palestine is still fraught with hardship, Buber suggests that we might be inspired by the next best thing—Palestine in art. The artist he recommends is Hermann Struck, an Orthodox Zionist, who helped found Mizrachi in 1902. Struck's etchings at that time were already world-renowned. He was a student of Josef Israels and a teacher to Marc Chagall.

The Discovery of Palestine

By Martin Buber

For how many Jews is Palestine alive in their souls?

To note: not "the [Jewish] homeland," but Palestine; and not in the mind, but in the soul. Or, to be even more clear: How many Jews can visualize Palestine?

Whose eyes are so filled with the land that they transcend reality

---

* Das jüdische Kultur-Problem und der Zionismus," *Die Stimme der Wahrheit: Jahrbuch für wissenschaftlichen Zionismus,* ed. Lazar Schön, volume 1 (Würzburg: Verlag N. Philippi, 1905), 205–17. Item 70 in *MBB.*

as if it did not exist and see only the land? Who is so entranced with the vision that he is surrounded by it no matter where he goes so that the vision becomes the true, actual, eternal reality?

Some see, but is it our land that they see? All these fabulous and colorful things, the blessed possessions of which they dream, is that our land? Our land in a twofold sense, our land, as it is, and our land, according to our mood? For it has rightly been said that the landscape is a state of the soul. And in the final analysis that is all that matters. For, "How is it?" How is anything? The way we see it, only therein lies our reality.

Our question, whether our land is a reality for us, means Do we really see it, and then again, do we see it according to our mood?

Eleven years ago, in a forgotten, small aphorism, Theodor Herzl called mood the most powerful element of life. He might have added, for the Jews. We live completely in mood. To be sure, some of us live more in moods than in mood, but the existence of all Jews, who really are Jews in their consciousness and deeds, is supported by the strong wave of *one* great mood. And, therefore, I ask one more time, Do we see Palestine from our one great mood?

If we answer this question in the negative—and we must—we feel poorer. But there is a way beyond this feeling.

A friend once told me, "We have to discover Palestine." That's just it; we must discover Palestine for our eye, for our soul's eye, and for our mood.

We should travel there, not only to get to know "land and people" but to create our own Palestine in our soul.

That is something only a few can do. The friend whom I mentioned earlier wanted to get to Palestine to absorb it and to let it become his vision and to tell others about this vision in words so that it would become their vision as well. So far it has not happened. He had enough mood; I cannot say whether he has enough energy to transform his mood into an image, an image that would grasp and mesmerize others.

Into an image. There is a still straighter, more direct path of inspiration than the word. This path is the picture in the narrower sense: the painting, the drawing, the sketch.

So far, artists have painted Palestine in the so-called oriental manner with a blazing wealth of colors and incredible poverty in mood. We are still waiting for the artist who will paint for us a Jewishly perceived Palestine.

Yet just recently we received a fragment, an attempt, a first step. I am speaking of the sketches and drawings by Hermann Struck, which accompany the text of Adolf Friedemann's book, *Travelogue from Palestine* (Berlin: Bruno Cassirer, 1904). This is not the place to discuss the text, which is well written and informative, filled with concrete facts and strong convictions, but I would like to say a few words about Struck's drawings.

We knew the works of Hermann Struck. Above all, his Jewish heads, simultaneously artistic and full of character, stylistically generous and modest, without sharp ethnic features, not accentuated, yet, or perhaps because of it, incredibly Jewish in their effect, reveal quiet Jewish life in the innermost soul and direct it to the people's soul.

And now about his Palestinian landscapes. For the first time they bring to us the true land of our feeling, an absolutely vast mood full of yearning. Technique plays a role here as well, but to see in a truly Jewish way is the decisive factor. In truth, Struck presents us with Jewish soil seen through the medium of a Jewish temperament.

Look at his works, page by page. There we see a lonely palm tree near Jaffa, reaching upward in a hot, hazy landscape, clear and firm before a cloudless sky. And there we see the well near Jaffa, somber beneath dark cyprus trees. There is the legendary tomb of Absalom, strange and fantastic. There is Rachel's tomb, frozen in structure and dome, a petrified accusation.

There we also see the young blossoming of the settlements. What a warm, budding strength we see in them! There we see the palm-lined street in Rishon l'Zion, Ekron, and Wad el Chanin; there are a few houses from Petach Tikvah, expressive like human beings; and then there is Sejerah, barely visible.

We leaf through the book and are enriched by this new way to see our land.

But one etching of Struck's is not in the book—Jerusalem. I saw it in his studio. It has the effect of a symbol, a broad plateau with a tender veiled view of the city, nothing else. How awesome and holy it is rendered! It is not poetry but direct feeling; this is a Jerusalem that waits. This is the place from which to see our land.*

41.

To have lost the connection to Hebrew was an enormous concern of the Zionists. Of course, today it is difficult for us to understand that the connection to the language was perhaps Israel's weakest link to the past. Yet the very fact that there was a conference on Hebrew language and culture in Berlin in 1909 shows that the turning point had already occurred. Although Buber feels out of his element he read Hebrew quite capably although, perhaps, did not speak it as proficiently.

The Hebrew Language

From a lecture delivered at the conference on Hebrew Language
and Culture in Berlin, December 19, 1909

I followed the invitation of the committee to open the discussion of the Congress with some trepidation. The most serious reservation I had was the fact that I have to speak about the Hebrew language in another language because I am not able to think in Hebrew and I cannot bring myself to translate thoughts that I think in a foreign language [German] into my own, but less-familiar language.

The tragedy of this situation reaches far beyond the individual case. We can only then clearly recognize our mission, which we have to decide on today, when we have grasped this tragedy in all of its dimensions and only when we can imagine the role of language in the life of the people.

We can best orient ourselves regarding the different manifestations of a national life if we divide them into form and content; where phenomena of direct life or phenomena of consciousness are concerned, we can discern life forms and consciousness forms, life con-

* "Die Entdeckung von Palaestina," *Ost und West* 5, no. 2 (Feb. 1905): cols. 127–30. Item 67 in *MBB*.

tent and consciousness content of the nation. Life content of the nation encompasses the entire circle of purposes and interests, of economic and social impetuses unique to this community; life forms represent the form in which the pursuance and achievement of these purposes occurs. To them belong customs and traditions, specific forms of socialization and organization. The consciousness contents of the people encompass their spiritual and emotional lives, in as far as they can be seen as belonging to the sphere of national communality. The form of consciousness of a people is its language: it has other consciousness elements but no other consciousness form.

First, it is quite obvious that the durability of the forms is incomparably greater than their contents; that we could even say, with some exaggeration the contents change but the forms prevail. What needs to be particularly emphasized is that the consciousness forms are more durable than the life forms. This reality is already established in the basic fact that consciousness, in the individual and in the people, represents the personality, the ego, vis-à-vis all other life functions. Consciousness also presents the temporal unity of the personality vis-à-vis its different phases of development.

Another point. What really makes a group of like-minded individuals into a national community is the unity of their relations characterized by specific basic forms, which leads to that complex of concrete, normed relationships that we call the life of the people. This unity of relations prevails, on the one hand, toward the outside, vis-à-vis all other peoples from whom this people clearly keeps their distance; on the other hand, from within, vis-à-vis all individual groups within this people—economic, social, religious—that are part of this unity. The specific basic form of the relations that gives it national unity is, again, the language.

Thus, the language at the same time represents the unity of the people in relation to its individual growth phases and the unity of the people in relation to individual parts. We may, therefore, simply call it the shared unifying form of national life.

From these simple premises, which can be checked by anyone, we learn that of all the illnesses of our national life this is the most difficult and most dangerous: our language has lost its living continuity and has stopped connecting all elements of the people. This illness does not only threaten a single organ but the unity and the connectedness of the entire organism. And if we cannot enjoy a normal national life because we do not have a land of our own, the loss of our language threatens the continuation of the nation, the life of the people as such. This is especially true because the unity of life forms has been shattered. Let us no longer believe the illusion that a renewal of the national will, of that which we call "national movement," replaces the lack in national unity, that lack in national life and consciousness forms. An elevation of pure will power can only unify a people for the struggle, the struggle for national freedom and independence as we see in the example of all national movements. The reason for this is that the will only has the capability to fuse human beings into a group that acts unified at its highest, most elevated level of intensity. This highest level of intensity can be achieved only through that stimulation which is particular to moments of the struggle. Furthermore, the great struggle, the struggle of the greatest stimulation of the will, this struggle against the outer enemy never was within the domain and mission of the Jewish movement.

It is this realization of the uniqueness of national movements on the whole and the Jewish movement in particular that has recently occurred within this movement: the turn to the positive, the striving to connect to the natural functions of national life, to reach from the changing areas back to eternal forms that represent precisely these functions, and to do this in such a way that the personal life of each is saturated by these forms and functions and made fertile through them. Here I cannot possibly trace all of the paths in which this transformation occurs, not even the most important of all which consists of the fact that more and more Jews build their personal life in Palestine and thereby solve the big question only for themselves, but in an exemplary fashion. We are here interested only in one way, the effort to return the unifying form of consciousness—the language—to as large a part of the people as possible.

We arrive at the same results when we consider the meaning of Hebrew for the individual Jew.

Of all the functions in national life language is that which enters the life of the individuum first. Before children begin to speak, they belong merely to the great mass of humanity; in truth, they become a member of their people, participate in national life only with the first words that their lips form. And once more we see the suffering and illness of our national life in no other manifestation as clearly as in the fact that the language in which our children utter their first words almost always is not the language in which the unity of our people once, in space and time, came into being and in which it was a living reality. It is of the greatest significance in what language the individual begins to speak; it is not inconsequential. In the language of a people its original energies have been stored, ready to become active in everyone who experiences their language as the necessary, even unique expression of their original stirrings; in the language of a people continue the deep sources of its kind and its greatness, ready to nourish all who receive this language in the first, most impressionable time of their lives, and who do not receive it as a language, but as *the* language, as the wonderful word of being itself. Everything that one's genes have planted into the individual in national species, in national being, all of that grows only as the result of the spoken language to a pure, full life. Their genes give them their disposition, the language their activity; only then can life and teaching develop the consciousness as well.

We lack or nearly lack the middle stage; it is easy to assess what this means for the people, what it means for the individual among the people. One considers that especially for us, especially for the Jews of our time, Hebrew could have a meaning that the language did not have for another people and for no other time. When we inquire into the deepest meaning of the epoch of Jewish history in which we live, when we inquire into the deepest meaning of the Jewish movement, which arose from this period, when we inquire where we got the right to classify this movement as renaissance, it comes from this, that we connect to our antiquity, to the great classical time of our people, as the Italians of the thirteenth century connected to the classical time of their people and that we do this not only in the field of culture, as they did, but in all the fields of Jewish life. We wish to save Judaism from decay and we see only one way, we have only one great helper on earth to whom we can appeal, the *Urzeit* [founding period] of our people. We connect to this period. The reawakening of Palestine means exactly that, we connect to the *Urzeit* of the land.

The rejuvenation of Hebrew means exactly that, the rejuvenation of the language of our *Urzeit*. It is not only that the great creations of the *Urzeit* were written in this language but this language is itself one of the greatest creations: from its words, from its forms and images the spirit of that tremendous time speaks to us; from it we learn in our innermost being the meaning of Judaism, from it we receive the revelation of our pure unique *Ur*-being [original being]. The persons who truly make Hebrew a part of their lives, incorporate the moving strength of Judaism into their lives, they know henceforth how to serve the genius of our people. They who make Hebrew part of their lives, incorporate the creative function of the national spirit into their beings; they are no longer only Jews in contents of thought and will power but in the innermost form of their beings. Let there be a group of such Jews and may they have space to act; only then will we have a truly Jewish movement.

People are seldom as fortunate as we are to become aware of their historic movement and their historical task. We know that the movement in which we live is great and weighty; that it is one of those movements in which death and birth, decline and elevation, end and beginning, despair and hope live side by side, even intermingle, are meshed together so that everything and every event has one side that faces death and one that faces birth, and ultimately it depends only on the deed, the deed that shall decide which side will determine the future. We know the deed we have to fulfill—to regain unity for our people. For the portion of our people who do not live in their own land unity exists most clearly in the *Urform* [original form] of their consciousness, namely, in its original language. But can we really achieve this? Is language something that can be influenced from without? Can we "make" a language? they ask. Does it not develop according to its own inner laws?

These questions, which have developed from a doctrine that I do not want to discuss here, are misleading. To be sure, a language develops according to its own inner laws, but only in its kind and substance not in the scope of its development. A language may spread through human will power; conquerors did it often with strange peoples, we should be able to do it with our own. This is the objection, however, only in so far as our activity does not hinder the external circumstances, the "living conditions." This belief in living conditions, which springs from the same doctrine, is correct when it serves the complete realization of a cause; it is wrong and damaging when it develops into a dogma that paralyzes our will and halts our action. It is merely an aide for the knowing person not instruction for the acting one. It is valid only for the past, for the future only when it has become the past. Our deeds are the result of our wills and of living conditions; the greater the participation of the will, that is, the stronger the possibilities provided by the inner development of the people towards both sides, the closer together live death and birth, end and beginning.

Let us not brood whether there is something we can do, let us try to do something! Let us try, not contrary to living conditions but by considering living conditions, but also our wills and our strengths.

But what to do? How to do what we believe?

Here I wish to say only the most general, with which you are all familiar, and I, therefore, merely wish to formulate it clearly.

Life of the Hebrew language in our time can naturally be perceived from two sides: the productive and the receptive sides. Thus, there are essentially two areas for our activity: promotion of Hebraic productivity, that is, Hebrew literature, and the promotion of Hebraic receptivity, that is, Hebraic-linguistic education in the broadest sense. To be sure, the two areas are not strictly delineated; the promotion of literature serves not only the productive ones but also the public. On the other hand, the promotion of education can influence the development of the productive ones. One hopes, in a later stage of our activities a third, joint area, as it were, will develop in addition to these two areas: the work in the complementary expansion of the language itself through the development of an institution specifically for this purpose. At present, however, we will confine our activities to the two areas mentioned.

The promotion of Hebrew literature is a twofold task: the promotion of the productive ones and the mediation between them and the public. Both tasks, which are connected, have been underway for some time. What we have achieved so far can be considered only as a

beginning despite our appreciation of all the energies and achievements, as a beginning that has, in recent years, suffered a most
regrettable interruption in a number of areas as a result of
circumstances, perhaps also in view of a specific very dangerous fa-
talism connected with the circumstances. This conference will discuss the details thoroughly; I would like to point out only one thing.
There is no people on earth which does so little for the young, shy,
and helpless talents as in ours, who calls itself the people of the spirit.
The other nations know that these shy and helpless young people,
who at times precisely because of their shyness and helplessness are
careless and directionless, have ideas beneath their shyness and helplessness, works of art beneath their irresponsibility and directionless-
ness, which will awaken tomorrow and elevate the soul of the people,
perhaps even transform their lives, if they are guarded and nurtured.
But we overlook the shy ones, condemn the irresponsible ones, and
even those who loudly complain that there is no new growth in our
literature do not consider nurturing the talented ones. In addition we
do not have an actual literary public, and the contact between the
small existing public and the productive ones is made more difficult.
Thus, many a valuable piece is not published, much more is unwritten, and many of the young people who could be our future perish
miserably; many others disappear in the daily mire and sacrifice their
souls to be able to live.

If Hebrew productivity is presented as a relative unit, receptivity,
according to the living conditions that we want to consider, is to be
seen as three specially separated levels and to be treated differently
depending on their difference.

The first level is formed by Palestinian Jewry. Here the tendency
of our living conditions parallels our will, and it is only a matter of
whether the natural development is furthered by support and expansion of the school system.

The second level is formed by East European Jewry, if we exempt
the intermediary level of the great Jewish emigration centers. Here
the living conditions are already quite unfavorable, yet, intensive and
centralized activity will make it possible to use the existing unified
communications avenues of the Jews, on the one hand by forming

small Hebrew-speaking communities, linguistic pioneer groups, as it were, on the other hand, to educate a great, Hebrew-reading public. Here it will also be possible to influence education on a large-scale.

The third level forms Western Jewry. Here we can influence only individuals (at least according to my personal opinion), who may congregate into several small groups, groups that in any case will scarcely achieve the character of strong, unified communities the way they exist in the East. But individuals are also important; I believe that the Jewish movement in the West will win substance and souls only in this way—the way of substitution—of the lost life forms through the consciousness form. That is why this extensive [but] lesser activity will not be carried out less intensively. Yes, especially here, where the outer and inner living conditions oppose our intentions, the exerted will power will have to be greatest.

෧෨

Basically, that which we call experiment when we look into the future will become development when it has become past. Revolution and evolution are merely points of view. The day after tomorrow every revolution of today will be seen as a piece of evolution; the day before yesterday everything that we today recognize as evolution, was revolutionary. In reality we know nothing about the future, but we know that the movement in which we live is great and weighty and that death and life are intertwined in its tension and that our deed may be decisive. Today this deed seems to be a possibility, which we can realize or destroy; one day this deed or its omission will receive a specific place in the chain of causality and necessity. Let us fulfill what we can; let us put our deed onto the great scale of fate! We do not know whether we achieve a lot or a little with it; we do not have to know it. But we may hope that, when we invest all of our energy, our energy will not remain isolated. We cannot recognize the hidden energies of the people except through our active balancing, calling and activating. Let us reveal the totality of our activity, and the activity of the people will reveal itself. The people need active ideas; active ideas are the light that will illuminate the external *Urkraft* [original power] of the people and make it visible again. In this sense we may remind ourselves with the words of our poet, [Hebrew: *Chashfu haor! galu haor!*] Unveil the light! Reveal the light!*

42.

Here Buber argues that although Jewish regeneration must begin in the galut, *it can only be completed on Jewish soil, and not just any soil, but the soil of the ancient homeland.*

The Land of the Jews

From an address (1910)

The renewal of Judaism, which must begin in the *galut*, will not be able to complete itself in the *galut*. Even the recapture of the relationship to the soil with the natural life that is regulated by the rhythm of the seasons will not be able to effect this completion. It can emanate only from a very specific soil, the soil of the homeland. It [this soil] created our specific kind, our particular energies, our personalities; it alone will be able to renew them, to create them anew. The creative greatness of our *Urzeit* once awoke from this soil; its sap nourished our greatness. It grew in the shadow of the land's mountains, and when its greatness tired, it rested at its bosom and regenerated itself. It was not any old land but this particular land with its hills and valleys, with its lakes and rivers, with the salt deposits in its interior, with its dew and rain, with its flora and fauna, with the clouds and stars peculiar to this land. It was these energies of our land that created these energies of our soul; where else could we go to rejuvenate our soul? A child that has been frightened can only be truly calmed by his [or her] mother; a thousand times thousand frights disturbed our innermost lives. A broken statue can be fixed by innumerable

---

* Die hebräische Sprache und der Kongress für hebräische Kultur," *Jüdische Rundschau* 15, no. 2 (Jan. 14, 1910): 13–14; and no. 3 (Jan. 21, 1910): 25–26. Item 105 in *MBB*.

amateurs, but it can only be truly restored by the artists who created it. We are a statue that broke. We became ill, but our land stayed well; we became lame, but our land remained strong; we wander, but our land stretches over there and waits, still waits—for us.

When the Italians of the early Renaissance wanted to renew their peoplehood, they connected to the great *Urzeit* of their people; they connected to the culture of this *Urzeit*, to its works and values, to its thought forms and life forms; from this they won the rebirth of their peoplehood and their humanity. We, too, have to connect to the great *Urzeit* of our people; we, too, have to grasp the hands of our forefathers across the eons. But we have a greater, deeper responsibility than they had. They wanted to make their lives greater, richer, more beautiful; we want to achieve life again. They wanted to become stronger; we want to heal our wounds. They wanted to become freer; we want to free ourselves from the bonds of the *galut*. That is why it is not enough for us to connect to the culture of our *Urzeit*, its works and values, to its thoughtfulness and life forms; we must descend to the mothers,* we must descend to the powers who created all of the works and values and [Platonic] forms. We must go to our land so that it will bless us and that it will bless itself.

Let us not make that which is difficult easy and that which is great small so that it will not cast us out! Let us not think that it is enough to escape from the external *galut!* What we need more than anything else is to cleanse ourselves from the inner *galut:* we need to shake from ourselves all of the dust and dirt of wandering, all of that which is dull and glaring, all of that which is crooked and without form, all of that which is lascivious and profane, which the generations of despair have strewn into our soul. But even if this inner liberation from the *galut* must be desired wholeheartedly by the individual so that it can lead to renewal, for the people it must remain a piecemeal effort. For the people as a whole it can succeed only in one place on earth, in the spot where that which later became

---

* In *Faust*, Mephisto speaks of descending to the mothers as a last resort. *Faust II*, act 1, Emperor's Palace scene, Dark Corridor, lines 6210–20, ed. Erich Trunz (Munich: Verlag C. H. Beck, 1982), 191. Buber was very fond of and used this phrase liberally as a metaphor for returning to the source. [G. S.]

dulled and hidden and profane had been born in purity and direct-ness and holiness.

Only there can we truly become who we are. Here we are a wedge, which Asia placed in Europe's clockwork, a thing of fermen-tation and disturbance. If we return to Asia's womb, to the great cra-dle of the nations, which was also the great cradle of the gods, we return to the meaning of our existence—to serve the Divine, to expe-rience the Divine, to be in the Divine.*

Martin Buber

* "Das Land der Juden," Die Welt 16, no. 13 (Mar. 29, 1912): 395–96. Item 120 in MBB.

Index

Index

211